"Writing is a field that favors the self-starter. That said, we all get lonely and need the graceful companionship and humorous rigor found in *DIY MFA*. Pereira's book is designed for both the creative and the business sides of writing, for both the person and the pen that he or she holds. If, on the other hand, you are a practicing writer and have chosen to stop learning at some point ... well, that's on you." —Stuart Horwitz, author of *Finish Your Book in Three Drafts*

"Think you need an MFA to become a writer? Not so! With infectious energy and enthusiasm, Gabriela Pereira shows you how to follow a DIY path to writing, reading as a writer, and building a writers' community. Full of practical advice, *DIY MFA* is a guide to your learning journey, from coming up with story ideas to crafting your author brand." —Barbara Baig, author of *Spellbinding Sentences: A Writer's Guide to Achieving Excellence and Captivating Readers*

"A real writer's classroom in a single book. No puffballs and promises here, only the practical tools and mind-set every writer needs to make success a reality." —James Scott Bell, best-selling author of *Plot & Structure*

"The world is changing, but the fundamentals of good writing don't change. The challenge for the twenty-first-century writer is to be single-minded in the pursuit of her art, while remaining open-minded about new routes to market, new publishing opportunities, and new ways to connect with her readers.

"In *DIY MFA* Gabriela Pereira will help you strike a delicate yet necessary balance between writing, reading, and connecting with the wider world. She will challenge you to be bolder and more rigorous in your writing, and more enterprising in how you bring your work to market. She will also support you with solid practical advice about each facet of your career.

"If you want to pursue your writing career on your own terms, *DIY MFA* is a must-read. Even if you already have an MFA, the chapters on community building are the perfect complement to what you already know, helping your finely crafted words reach more readers." —Mark McGuinness, poet, creative coach, and author of *Motivation for Creative People* and *Resilience: Facing Down Rejection and Criticism on the Road to Success*

For more resources for writers, visit www.writersdigest.com.

20 19   5

Distributed in the U.K. and Europe by F+W Media International
Brunel House, Newton Abbot, Devon, TQ12 4PU, England
Tel: (+44) 1626-323200, Fax: (+44) 1626-323319
E-mail: postmaster@davidandcharles.co.uk

ISBN-13: 978-1-59963-934-5

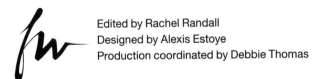

Edited by Rachel Randall
Designed by Alexis Estoye
Production coordinated by Debbie Thomas

diy MFA

WRITER'S DIGEST
BOOKS

WritersDigest.com
Cincinnati, Ohio

dedication

In memory of Lenira Cruz Dias,
who gave me the writing genes

This book is for my word nerds,
because you are awesome.

note

The examples in this book include spoilers that may kill a surprise ending but, on the upside, will increase your knowledge of great literature. These examples include the Harry Potter series, The Hunger Games trilogy, and *Pride and Prejudice*. (Seriously, if you haven't read these books by now, were you really planning on reading them anyway?)

acknowledgments

Writing acknowledgements is like delivering an awards speech. At any second, the band will strike up and I'll be ushered offstage—or, in this case, offpage. I have so many more people to thank than I can fit here, but know that you are all dear to my heart.

To my agent, Jeff Kleinman, who saw what I could do before I had any idea myself. Thank you for believing in me and in DIY MFA.

To my editor, Rachel Randall, who helped me tame "The Beast" and corral my ideas into something amazing. To Phil Sexton, for sharing my vision of what this book could be. To the Writer's Digest team—especially Chelsea Henshey, Alexis Estoye, Kim Catanzarite, and Debbie Thomas—thank you for making this book impeccable and gorgeous.

To my powerhouse team—Elisabeth Kauffman, Bess Cozby, and Emily Wenstrom—without you, DIY MFA would grind to a halt. Elisabeth, you are my counterpoint, balancing my frenzied creativity with calm and good sense. Bess, you curate the website with grace and flair. And Emily, the DIY MFA social media presence couldn't be in better hands.

To the DIY MFA columnists and contributors—Sara Letourneau, Leanne Sowul, Constance Renfrow, S.A. Lovett, Melinda VanLone, Wendy Lu, Becca Jordan, Meghan Drummond, Amy Bearce, Kent Bridgeman, Alicia Audrey, and all our guest writers—thank you for lending your voices to the website and enriching our community.

To designer/developers KJ Parish, Ben Heller, and Nate Thompson for creating an elegant brand and beautiful website. To Jay Donovan and TechSurgeons for keeping that site speedy and secure. To Christina Gressianu for my behind-the-book headshot, now iconic to DIY MFA.

So many friends have supported me on my writing journey. First and foremost, thank you to my beloved Quill & Coffee, especially Jo LoCicero, Debra Rosenberg, Corey Brown, Tracy Anumolu, Julie Randolph, and David Symonds.

To Julie Duffy: We started big writing projects at the same time and have grown up side by side. I am grateful for your calm, measured presence in my life. To Barbara Baig, my "big sister" in the WD family, Thien-Kim Lam for smart business advice, and Jessica Greenfield for challenging me to do great work: You ladies rock!

To the writers who trusted me with their words, especially Al Mongillo, Linda Burgess, Diane Johnson, Anne DiCarlo, Joel Knopf, and Stacey Woodson, and to the original word nerd, Laura Highcove, for always being in my corner. To Ghenet Myrthil, Elizabeth Dunn-Ruiz, Kathryn Holmes, and Michael Ann Dobbs: I can't think of anyone else I'd want with me in the MFA trenches. Shout-out to Gina Carey, Jodi Kendall, Kim Liggett, and the other Write Nite ladies! And a *huge* thank-you to my amazing street team.

To Jane Friedman, for giving sensible advice, always grounded in compassion. To the English teachers who taught me to paint words: Abbey Newlin, Frances Taliaferro, Cassandra Cleghorn, Peter Grudin, Susan Breen, Hettie Jones, and Susan Van Metre. To my violin teacher, the late Louise Behrend, who showed me the value of practice; jazz professor Andy Jaffe for teaching me to improvise; and Dan Blank for setting me on the entrepreneurial path. To all my teachers who, regardless of subject, taught me the same important life lesson: *If you keep getting answers you don't like, ask another question.*

Tomoe Kanaya, you are more than a dear friend; you are family. Thank you for sticking by me through those less-than-glamorous moments. Melissa Paris, thanks for the awesome workouts and even better girl talk. Jerry Finkel, you helped keep me balanced, and Tia Odeves, you always believed in me.

Shout-out to my barista buddies: Tarsha, Chelley, Blair, Andrea, Jasmine, Ralph, Alex, Nene, and the whole crew! Thanks for the smiles and caffeine.

To my parents, Sergio and Maria Pereira, thank you for everything. Seriously, everything. Dad, you're my hero and the ultimate role model for running a business. Mom, you're a shining example that it's never too late to follow your passion. To Steve and Karen Maskel, my in-laws, thank you for supporting my love of books and teaching, and to my sister-in-law, Kaitlin, you've proven what it means to take a leap of faith. To my brother, Paulo, and his wife, Sarah, thank you for the unconditional love and support. And to the brilliant, talented Juli: I feel so lucky you are my sister.

Nicholas and Mariana (a.k.a. Little Man and Lady Bug), you amaze me. Every moment with you is an adventure. And thank you to Elizabeth Andeza for taking care of my precious little humans so I could steal away and write this book.

Finally, to my husband, best friend, and partner in crime these thirteen-plus years: Greg, you made this possible. You make *everything* possible. DIY MFA is as much yours as it is mine. Thank you for helping me make this dream a reality.

about the author

GABRIELA PEREIRA is a writer, teacher, and self-proclaimed word nerd who wants to challenge the status quo of higher education. As the founder and instigator of DIY MFA, her mission is to empower writers to take an entrepreneurial approach to their education and professional growth. Gabriela earned her MFA in creative writing from The New School and teaches at national conferences, at local workshops, and online. She is also the host of DIY MFA Radio, a popular podcast where she interviews best-selling authors and offers short audio master classes. To join the word nerd community, go to DIYMFA.com/join.

table OF contents

Foreword 1

orientation

CHAPTER 1: Discover the DIY MFA Mind-Set 5

CHAPTER 2: Customize Your Learning 15

CHAPTER 3: Set Goals and Start Strong 23

write with focus

CHAPTER 4: Motivate Yourself 31

CHAPTER 5: Fail Better 37

CHAPTER 6: Generate Ideas on Demand 41

CHAPTER 7: Outline Your Book Like a Boss 55

CHAPTER 8: Create Compelling Characters 66

CHAPTER 9: Bring Those Characters to Life 78

CHAPTER 10: Begin at the Beginning 89

CHAPTER 11: Muddle Through the Middle 99

CHAPTER 12: Arrive at the End 110

CHAPTER 13: Give Your Story a Voice 120

CHAPTER 14: Choose Your Point of View 126

CHAPTER 15: Weave Your Story's World 143

CHAPTER 16: Deliver Dazzling Dialogue 151

CHAPTER 17: Revise in Layers 158

read with purpose

CHAPTER 18: Be a Reader First 171

CHAPTER 19: Read Like a Writer 182

CHAPTER 20: Build Your Expertise 196

build your community

CHAPTER 21: Establish Your Circle of Trust 208

CHAPTER 22: Work That Workshop 219

CHAPTER 23: Craft Your Author Identity 233

CHAPTER 24: Develop Your Home Base 244

CHAPTER 25: Know Your Reader 254

CHAPTER 26: Network Like a Pro 263

CHAPTER 27: Submit Your Work 273

Commencement 286

Index 289

Foreword

Jacquelyn Mitchard

When I went to graduate school nearly ten years ago to earn my Masters of Fine Arts in Creative Writing, it was just a couple of years before I turned fifty, and I had already published fifteen books, including three novels that were *New York Times* bestsellers.

Why did I do go back to school?

I had good reasons.

I wanted to earn the credential. The importance of the MFA was just coming to the fore, and "the equivalent" in published works didn't have quite the same impact in the academic world. I had long wanted to teach at the college level, to help others learn some of what I had learned (mostly on my own, it must be said), but then, quite suddenly, I also needed a regular, reliable job. A crooked financial advisor my husband trusted took every single cent of our savings—most of it comprised of what I had earned over more than twenty years as a writer. Though the crook would go to prison, and I would eventually forgive my husband (the rupture in our relationship was as painful as the rupture in our lives) we would never see a dime of our money again. We lost our home, and I had to transition from being a full-time writer to a writer-and-something-else. But that wasn't the only impetus.

I also wanted to bring other minds to bear on my writing, writers and professors whose skills I admired. This turned out to be the most extraordinary gift of the low-residency MFA program where I went for two years, on a full scholarship as a teaching fellow. At the time, I didn't think that there was another way to seek out that critical component: I thought that I was much too shy and awkward, too busy as a mother, and, frankly, too well-published, to join a writers' group of hopefuls. I also must confess that I didn't realize just how high the level of accomplishment and ability could be in a writers' group—until I experienced the ones some of my friends attended or organized!

If my primary goal had been to write and publish a book, would I have considered it necessary to attend an MFA program? I might not have.

Would I today? I don't know that I would.

The diversity of paths to a creative life is practically infinite. Indeed, for most of my writing life, I have been self-taught. While I grew up in a family in which storytelling took the place of entertainments that cost money, I was not a born writer, nor part of a scholarly culture: I was, in fact, the first person in my family ever to graduate high school. As a sixteen-year-old college freshman, I had taken a semester of creative writing from a fellow (the great Mark Costello) who turned out to be a legendary instructor. But that was the extent of my formal training. Mostly, I read every good book I could find, and I read as a writer, careful to see how they did what they did. And that was it. Especially when I started writing, I had a dream; I had determination, and I had the university of good books to guide me. The dream was the most urgent. Life had dealt me a crippling blow when I was widowed before I turned forty: I had three little boys and no money (yes, things can happen twice in a lifetime).

I worked sixteen-hour days writing speeches at the university, writing ad copy, even writing warning labels for paint sprayers (yes, someone does write those!). When none of those things, or the demands of being a single mom, claimed my attention (that is, in the middle of the night), I wrote a story about a woman whose son returned to her nine years after he was abducted. I knew that it was as good a book as I could write, and I wasn't surprised when it was published. I was surprised when Oprah Winfrey decided to start the world's largest book club with my novel *The Deep End of the Ocean*. It would go on to sell nearly three million copies and be translated into thirty-one languages.

What I think now, as I finish my twelfth novel for adults, is that not all the things that are important to me as a writer were part of any curriculum, except the curriculum of the human heart and mind. Among those are the reasons I write. I write because I want to understand what happens to people, to characters and their relationships, when they are pushed outside their comfort zones. I want to see how these ordinary people change in extraordinary circumstances. I don't write for me, although writing saves me. I write for the reader I imagine out there, and the dance isn't complete until the reader takes my hand: Still, publishing is the public recognition of something that began in a very personal place.

Now, I do teach in an MFA program, but I never used my MFA to be a full-time college professor. I am a full-time book editor. As editor in chief of a realistic Young Adult imprint, Merit Press, I encounter many new writers with high hopes, imagining that day when they see their name on the cover. About half have completed their novels as part of the MFA thesis (as I did, writing a YA novel called *What We Saw at Night*); the other half, equally accomplished, did not. It remains true that intensive study and academic achievement can help a writer into the portal of publishing, but study cannot replace that personal drive and determination.

When I was approached to write this foreword for Gabriela Pereira's *DIY MFA*, I wondered: Do writers really need another book about writing? But this is not your typical how-to book, nor is it a memoir of one writer's journey. Instead, Pereira distills the traditional MFA into three core elements—writing, reading, and community—and sets out to show writers how to re-create the graduate experience without going to school. The graduate school experience can be invaluable, but, in a given moment, is not for everyone. However, all writers may need some of what the MFA experience offers.

To that end, Pereira offers tools and techniques in *DIY MFA* that writers can adapt to their own goals. Pereira wants writers to have the freedom to braid together learning and personal experience, and I agree with her that the surest way to grow as a writer is to grow as a human being. To know yourself as a writer, and perhaps, first, as a person ... well, that's not always something you can learn in school.

Jacquelyn Mitchard is the number one *New York Times* best-selling author of twelve novels for adults, including *The Deep End of the Ocean*, which was the inaugural selection of the Oprah Winfrey Book Club and also made into a major feature film. The editor of a realistic young adult imprint, Merit Press, Mitchard also is the author of seven novels for young adults. Her work has won the Bram Stoker and Shirley Jackson awards, as well as the U.K.'s Walkabout Prize, and was short-listed for the Orange Broadband Prize for Fiction. She is a professor of creative writing at Vermont College of Fine Arts and a contributing editor for *More* magazine. Mitchard grew up in Chicago and now lives on Cape Cod with her family.

orientation

Discover the DIY MFA Mind-Set

Welcome to DIY MFA! I am thrilled to share these tools and techniques that will help you get the "knowledge without the college." Before we begin, let's go over some core aspects of the DIY MFA philosophy. While you can skip around with the later chapters, I recommend reading this chapter first, as it will give you a strong foundation for everything that follows.

What Is DIY MFA?

DIY MFA is the do-it-yourself alternative to a master's degree in writing. *DIY* stands for "do-it-yourself" and *MFA* is short for "Master of Fine Arts," the graduate degree for creative writing. The goal of this book is to give you structure and techniques so you can re-create that MFA experience in your own writing life without attending a university.

I developed the DIY MFA curriculum to help writers improve their craft and get published, but many of the techniques presented in this book will apply to other facets of your life as well. I've been told by many of my students that DIY MFA is not so much a writing curriculum as it is a way of life, an approach to learning and problem-solving that will change the way you write, read, and look at the world. This book isn't just about writing; it's about balancing your writing life and your real life in a manageable way. When you finish reading this book, you'll not only be a better writer but also a better thinker and *learner* as well. The DIY MFA approach isn't about spoon-feeding you knowledge and information. I want to empower you to figure out answers for yourself so you may continue to grow as a writer long after you have finished reading this book.

"In a time of drastic change, it is the learners who inherit the future." —ERIC HOFFER

While the MFA-style curriculum is central to DIY MFA, so is the do-it-yourself mind-set. It's not enough to read this book; you must put the techniques into action and adapt the tools to fit your writing and your life. By adopting this mind-set, the techniques you learn will be sustainable for the long-term. This book includes exercises and step-by-step instructions so you can implement what you learn. You'll find these exercises in the sidebars, or you can go to DIYMFA.com/thebook and sign up with your e-mail address to receive them as downloads.

The DIY MFA Mind-Set

All MFA programs include three core components: writing, reading, and community. Similarly, the foundation of DIY MFA is built from three pillars: "Write with Focus," "Read with Purpose," and "Build Your Community." In addition to these core concepts, the DIY MFA mind-set is based on a few fundamental principles that are essential for do-it-yourself learning. It is comprised of mindfulness and meditation principles, combined with an iterative, entrepreneurial approach. I call this the *DIY MFA Mindfulness Manifesto*.

THE DIY MFA MINDFULNESS MANIFESTO

- Writer's block does not exist.
- Resistance is your compass.
- Do not compound failure with guilt.
- There is no such thing as a "best practice."
- Iterate, iterate, iterate.

Writer's Block Does Not Exist

Many writers believe that writer's block is an external obstacle that prevents them from doing their work. Here's the truth no one wants to hear: Writer's block is a scapegoat. We blame writer's block because we can't bring ourselves to sit down and do the hard work of being a writer. If we're not writing, it's not because we're "blocked" or we've lost our creative mojo. The problem is inside of us—but that's actually a good thing.

When we blame writer's block for our failure to do the work, it takes the power away from us and instead puts our writing at the mercy of external circumstances. We tell ourselves that it's okay that we're not writing because we've got a busy day job, or our kid came down with the flu, or we've run out of good ideas. But whatever excuses we dream up, that's all they are: excuses. The only reason writers don't write is because *they just don't want it badly enough*.

Imagine a friend had an extra ticket to an amazing sold-out concert you've been dying to see. Wouldn't you drop everything and jump through whatever hoops necessary to make it to that show? Sure, you might still have that annoying day job, or your kid might have the flu, but if you want to go see this concert badly enough, you will find a way. The same is true for writing. If you want it badly enough, you will make it happen.

Resistance Is Your Compass

Sometimes you desperately *want* to write but you just … can't. Maybe you have great ideas, maybe you even carve out the time, but when you sit down to write, you freeze. This isn't writer's block; it's resistance, and there is an easy fix. Don't waste precious writing time trying to understand your resistance. It doesn't matter *why* you're not writing, just that you're not writing. Stop whining and making excuses, and then put on your big-kid pants and write.

Understand that resistance is not the enemy. It is your compass and can guide you precisely where you need to go with your writing. Resistance always points to the juiciest material and most interesting ideas. Think of it this way: A high-stakes project that excites or challenges you is often more difficult to write than a throwaway project, because you don't stand to lose anything if the throwaway project fails. It's only when the subject is meaningful and significant that resistance rears its ugly head. The next time you feel resistance to a project, I challenge you to dig into it instead of running away. You might just uncover writer's gold.

Do Not Compound Failure with Guilt

Part of the DIY MFA approach involves setting goals for yourself and tracking your progress accordingly. At some point you will probably fail to meet one of your goals. This is inevitable, and you must accept failure as part of your creative process. (In fact, chapter four is all about using failure as a springboard for success.) But when you fail, you must not compound it by layering it with guilt.

Failure is an objective fact. You meant to write 500 words, and you wrote only 497. You meant to finish your draft by August 10, and instead you finished on August 15. These are not feelings or opinions—they are facts. Guilt is a feeling that we pile on top of failure. While the failure might be an objective fact, the guilt that compounds it is a subjective emotion. The former is indisputable; the latter is optional. Flogging yourself for not writing will not make words magically appear on the page.

There Is No Such Thing as a "Best Practice"

When I first started writing seriously, I decided to follow in the footsteps of other writers by studying their processes. I read every writing memoir I could find: Stephen King's *On Writing*, Anne Lamott's *Bird by Bird*, Natalie Goldberg's *Writing Down the Bones*, and many others. These books did, in fact, teach me a valuable lesson, but it was not the one I expected to learn.

In his memoir, *On Writing*, Stephen King reveals his secret formula to being a writer: produce 2,000 words per day, and read upwards of eighty books per year. These numbers might terrify most writers—I probably would have frozen in fear if I hadn't been such a newbie—but I was so innocent, so green, that my initial reaction was relief. I had in my hand the proven formula that had produced Stephen King—*Stephen King!*—and if I prescribed to his methods I, too, could be a "real" writer.

This plan lasted less than a week.

After a few days of struggling to produce my allotted word count, my enthusiasm waned. By the end of that week, I had stopped writing altogether. Worse yet, I now felt *guilty* that I wasn't producing enough words. Before trying the Stephen King method, I would have been thrilled with a few hundred words per day. Now that amount felt like a letdown.

This was when I learned a valuable lesson about best practices. Writing 2,000 words per day might work *for Stephen King*, but my process is not nearly as linear and I can best sum it up as "feast or famine." By trying to superimpose Stephen King's schedule on myself, I had squelched my writing process altogether. The lesson learned is this: Don't blindly follow someone else's best practice. You need to test different approaches and only adopt the ones that give you the results you want. Remember, another writer's best practice might be your personal nightmare. The only best practice is the one that works for you.

Iterate, Iterate, Iterate

If I could sum up all the concepts in this book with one word, it would be *iteration*. Everything you learn from DIY MFA—each technique, each tool—will be useless if you don't make adjustments to fit your life and writing style. That said, you can test the techniques in one of two ways: the "spin your wheels" approach or iteration. The latter is smarter, faster, and more effective.

With the "spin your wheels" approach, you try different techniques at random, you don't track the outcomes, and then you make decisions based on a gut feeling. This method is fine if you have plenty of time on your hands and don't care about getting results. For writers operating in the real world, I recommend iteration.

This approach to writing was inspired by the entrepreneurial model used in Silicon Valley and described by Eric Ries in his book *The Lean Startup*. In a lean start-up environment, developers create a minimal viable product (MVP) and then test and tweak it in cycles to produce the best version possible. As a writer, you can operate in the same way, testing and improving your process over time to become more productive and better at your craft. The key is to build that meta-component into your writing so that you don't just scrutinize the words you put on the page but also take time to step back and examine your process overall.

Iteration is a critical component of the writing process, which is why I like to use the acronym VITAL to remember its five essential steps. This system might seem overly technical at first, almost like I'm telling you to put your creative process under a microscope. As with everything in DIY MFA, you need to adjust this iterative approach to fit your writing and your personality. Use the VITAL acronym as a rule of thumb, but don't let the steps constrain your process.

V = Choose your input and your output **variables**.

I = Collect **information**.

T = Set a **trip wire**.

A = Evaluate and **analyze**.

L = **Learn** from the results and decide what's next.

Choose Your Input and Your Output Variables

Think of input and output variables as what you put into your writing session and the outcome you measure at the end. The input is the "independent variable," the condition or situation you superimpose on a writing session. You'll tweak and adjust the input as you iterate your writing process. Input variables can include the following:

- writing at home versus in some other environment
- music versus silence versus ambient noise
- a writing ritual (lighting a candle or meditation)
- props and paraphernalia (like a special notebook or pen)

The output is the "dependent variable," or the outcome you measure afterwards, and it should be a concrete, specific, and measurable goal or product. In the case of writing, output usually comes in two flavors: time or word count. Depending on the situation, you might want to measure one or the other, or even both. Word count is a measure of progress when you're cranking out a first draft, whereas measuring time can be more useful during a less linear stage of the writing process, like revision or outlining.

Collect Information

This step is the fun part. You've chosen your input and output variables, so now it's time to get some "data points" under your belt. Start writing, then use the Writing Tracker worksheet to note your input variable and track your output: how many words you wrote, for how long, and how it felt. The latter is especially important because while you might have written 4,000 words in one sitting, or for five hours straight, it's meaningless if you hated every minute. Remember: This is a marathon, not a sprint. Your goal is to develop a sustainable process, not one that you'll abandon after a few weeks.

Be honest with yourself about how each writing session feels, but resist the urge to judge the data. Don a scientist's impartial attitude. There's no such thing as a "good writing day" or a "bad writing day." You're writing. That's what matters. Collect the data and move on.

You will need to track approximately twelve writing sessions, or data points; this number will give you enough information to evaluate your results and look for patterns.

This step of the iteration process is easier to implement with the Writing Tracker worksheet. This worksheet helps you keep track of your word count, writing time, and any other aspect of your writing process that you'd like to examine.

Date	Variable	Words	Time	How It Felt

Writing Tracker

Set a Trip Wire

One of the best lessons I learned about writing came from playing the violin. My teacher used to say, "Practice doesn't make perfect, it makes things *permanent*." This is why you need a trip wire, in writing and in life, so you don't practice bad habits into permanence.

A trip wire is a signal that tells you to double-check something. It's the writing equivalent of an alarm or signal flare. It says: "Hey, Writer! Pay attention."

Here's a classic example of a trip wire: According to legend, the band Van Halen required every venue to supply a bowl of M&M's backstage with all the brown candies removed. This clause was written into every contract. While this might be interpreted as a diva move, it wasn't. The bowl of M&M's was a trip wire. If the bowl was missing, or if it contained brown M&M's, it signaled that the venue had not read the contract closely and that the band should pay closer attention. After all, if the venue had made a mistake with the M&M's, they very well may have overlooked more significant details.

A bowl without brown M&M's (while rather tasty) is not a useful trip wire for writers. Instead, I encourage writers to set a deadline for the data collection stage. Research shows that it takes people about three weeks to establish a new habit. While you need at least a dozen writing sessions to see a pattern, you should avoid collecting data for more than three weeks or risk making that particular habit permanent. Set a trip wire that signals you to stop collecting data, and move on to the next step when you reach it.

Evaluate and Analyze

Now it's time to analyze what worked and what didn't. Again, we're not making value judgments; we're focusing on effectiveness. Ask yourself: What's working? What's not working? What has been effective for my writing? What can I improve?

It's easy to get bogged down with details here. I'm a numbers nerd, and nothing gets me more excited than color-coding spreadsheets and testing hypotheses in search of a statistically significant result. If you're like me, rein in your inner geek. Your goal isn't to publish these results in a scientific journal, so keep your analysis in perspective. Focus on looking at overall trends and finding a general pattern, and don't get too down in the weeds with the numbers.

Learn from the Results and Decide What's Next

The entire iteration process culminates in this step. This is where you make a decision about what to do next based on the information you have collected thus far. While this step is crucial, it's not complicated. If something works, great. Keep doing it. If something doesn't work, stop and pivot.

You're not developing a new writing process just for kicks. If something about your process is working, leave it alone. Don't fix what isn't broken.

But what if something *is* broken? What if some aspect of your writing process isn't working for you? This is where the *pivot* comes in. *Pivot* is a lean entrepreneurship term for making a small tweak to a product or process instead of overhauling it. The pivot concept applies to aspects of your writing process as well. It's possible that you may need to go back to square one and try a new approach, but before you do, try tweaking the input variable and noting how it affects your writing process.

If you find that an input variable is not helping you, start by making a small change to that variable and trying again. For instance, if writing at a coffee shop is too distracting, write at a local library instead and collect some data on this new setting. Test a few permutations of the "writing on the go" variable so you can determine what's most effective for your process. You want to tease apart the variables and get to the heart of what truly works for you. Are you someone who just needs to get out of the house to write, or does the *type* of writing environment also make a difference? The point is not to abandon the iteration process altogether just because you got one less-than-optimal result. Instead, adjust your input variable and keep testing, or choose a new one and start the iteration loop all over again.

Also, make sure that you don't test multiple input variables at the same time. Don't change the time of day when you write *and* change the location *and* switch between typing on your computer and writing longhand. Remember the scientific method you learned about in grade school? The same applies here. Test one input at a time so you can determine what's harming your process and what's helping it.

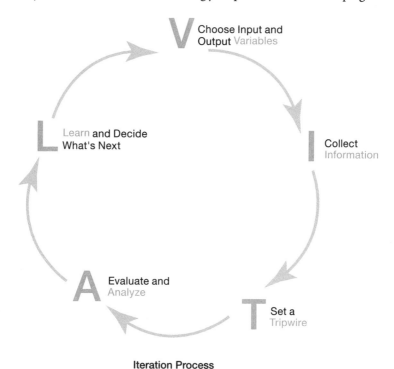

Iteration Process

While the concepts in this introduction may be simple, they are not *easy*. In fact, these ideas are probably the most challenging ones to implement in the whole book. If you're feeling a little overwhelmed, that's okay. I want you to know that it's *normal* to feel that way and that I've intentionally designed DIY MFA with the toughest, most important material front and center because it gives you the tools you need to navigate the rest. Once you get over this hump, everything will feel much easier.

I also recognize that the DIY MFA mind-set is not for everyone. As you've already seen in this introduction, my approach is not about shortcuts and magic-bullet solutions. Put simply, this book is for serious writers. This doesn't mean you have to be "advanced" or "experienced"; in fact you can be a beginner who has never put a pen to the page before. The only requirement is that you must be serious about doing the work. And if you're still reading this, I know that you are.

Welcome to the tribe, Word Nerd. Get ready for an exciting ride!

— 02 —

Customize Your Learning

I started DIY MFA because I wasn't satisfied with how the traditional MFA system worked. I spent two years getting my MFA in writing only to discover that an MFA is completely unnecessary to write and publish a book. Degrees are important in some fields, but writing is not one of them. Yet there are more MFA programs today than ever before, and more writers graduating with each passing year. If you don't need this degree to be a writer, why do so many people pursue it?

Most writers want an MFA for one of three reasons: They want to teach writing, they want to get published, or they want to make room in their life for writing. It turns out these reasons for doing an MFA are actually based on *myths*.

Myth 1: You Need an MFA to Teach Writing

Many writers get the MFA because they think it will allow them to teach writing at the college or graduate level. Once upon a time this might have been the case, but these days so many MFA graduates are looking for jobs and so few teaching positions exist, that it's a challenge to get a teaching job with a PhD, much less with a terminal master's degree. The writers who do manage to snag a coveted teaching position are often so overwhelmed with their responsibilities that they have to put their own writing on the back burner. While in the past an MFA may have served as a steppingstone to becoming a professor, it's not the case anymore.

More important, many teachers in MFA programs do not have that degree themselves. Some professors are successful authors with prominent careers, while others are publishing professionals who bring the industry perspective to the courses they teach. This goes to show that the MFA has little impact on a writer's ability to teach writing. Being a successful author or publishing professional is much more important.

Myth 2: The MFA Is a Shortcut to Getting Published

No agent will sign you and no editor will publish your book based on a credential alone. You have to write something beautiful. If you attend an MFA program and work hard, you *will* become a better writer. And if you become a better writer, you will eventually write a beautiful book. An MFA might help you on your quest for publication, but it's certainly not required. After all, many writers perfect their craft and produce great books without ever getting a degree.

As a writer, you already know how to work independently. This means you probably don't *need* an MFA to help you hone your craft—you can do that work on your own. Ultimately getting published is a matter of putting your backside in the chair and writing the best book possible. For that, you don't need an MFA.

Myth 3: An MFA Program Will Force You to Make Writing a Priority

If you can find time to write only by putting your life on hold and plunging into a graduate program, then your writing career isn't going to last very long. Only a small percentage of writers can support themselves and their loved ones through writing alone. This means you must find a balance between your writing and the rest of your life.

Even within your writing career, you must become a master juggler. Forget that glamorous image of the secluded writer working at his typewriter. These days, writing is only a small piece of the writer's job. Your writing career is *a business*, and you are the CEO. In addition to writing, you must promote your books, manage your online presence, update your social media … and likely schedule these tasks around a day job, a family, and other responsibilities.

The danger with MFA programs is that they train you to write in isolation but don't always teach you how to fit writing *into* your real life, or even how to juggle writing with all the other aspects of your writing career. Not only that, but external motivators like class assignments or thesis deadlines don't teach you to pace yourself and build up the internal motivation you need to succeed in the long-term.

Genre Writing in MFA Programs

Perhaps the biggest problem with most MFA programs is that they focus solely on literary fiction, creative nonfiction, and poetry. While these are noble areas of literature, they cover only a tiny slice of the wide and diverse world of writing. Heaven forbid a writer in a traditional MFA program produces something *commercial*—or worse, *genre fiction*. While a handful of MFA programs allow writers to study genre fiction or children's literature, the majority still focus on literary work alone. This means that if you want to write genre fiction, commercial nonfiction, or children's books, you likely will not learn much about them in your MFA courses.

And yet, writers of genre and commercial fiction are among the most dedicated, driven writers I know. They take their craft seriously and work hard to understand the business side of the publishing industry. In addition, a vast number of associations, conferences, and guilds are dedicated to specific genres or commercial writing. This shows that literary writers are not the only ones who crave knowledge and community. Commercial and genre writers want it, too.

This is why I created DIY MFA: to offer an alternative for writers who do not fit the strict literary mold of the traditional MFA system.

Should You Pursue an MFA?

Let me make one thing clear: MFA programs are not a bad thing. In fact, they are exceptional at serving a small and very specific group of writers. If you write literary fiction, creative nonfiction, or poetry, and if you thrive in a formal academic environment, then the traditional MFA is a great option. If you can afford the tuition without taking out loans, and if you have the time to make the most of the experience, then you are one of those rare ideal candidates for graduate school.

One reason I am extremely grateful for my own MFA is that it gave me the opportunity to work with several phenomenal teachers. I studied YA and middle-grade literature with the brilliant David Levithan. The legendary Hettie Jones was my first workshop teacher. I worked closely with Abrams publisher Susan Van Metre, who served as my thesis advisor and mentor. These experiences were invaluable, and at the time I didn't think I could make connections with such literary luminaries any other way. Now I know, however, that you *can* make connections and find great mentors without attending an MFA program, and later in this book I share the exact networking techniques I use.

How DIY MFA Works

While undercover as an MFA student, I discovered the magic equation that sums up just about every traditional MFA. The Master in Fine Arts degree in Creative Writing is nothing more than a lot of writing, reading, and building community. In the workshops, you exchange critiques with other writers and work toward a manuscript that becomes your thesis project. Most programs also require you to take literature courses both in and outside your chosen area of literature. Finally, you are asked to attend readings or talks by other writers—to build your personal writing community.

To create a personalized, do-it-yourself MFA, all you have to do is combine these three elements.

write **+** *read* **+** *build*
WITH FOCUS   WITH PURPOSE   YOUR COMMUNITY

DIY MFA Formula

Write with Focus

Writing with focus means writing with your eye on the endgame. Many writers start by writing whatever pops into their heads. They jump from project to project, following the stories that feel most inspiring or fun. This is a great place to start, and it's important to explore new projects and take risks at different points in your career.

Eventually, though, you have to commit to a project and finish it. In traditional MFA terms, this project is your thesis, and it's a crucial part of your development as a writer. But you don't need to complete a thesis to get this experience; you just need to finish and polish a manuscript. In DIY MFA terms, I call this "writing with focus." While you can feel free to play and explore early on, you must eventually choose a project and see it through from beginning to end. When you write with focus, you write with a goal in mind.

Read with Purpose

Reading with purpose means reading with a writer's eye. If you're like me, you were a bookworm long before you could hold a pencil in your hand. Writers love books. In fact, many of us *become* writers so we can create the very books we love to read.

While books may be our passion, we often need to retrain ourselves to read like writers. Reading for pleasure is wonderful, and it certainly has its place. Reading with *purpose* is different: It is reading in a way that serves our writing. It's not just about finding out what happens in the story; it's about learning how the author pulls it off. Reading this way isn't just an intellectual exercise. When we read with purpose, we examine *how* an author crafts a story so we can emulate those techniques in our own work.

Build Your Community

In the traditional MFA, building a community happens organically. You meet fellow writers in your workshops and literature courses. You go to readings and conferences to connect with big-name authors. You attend a publishing panel and learn about the industry. The community element is baked into the MFA experience.

In DIY MFA, you create that community for yourself. It takes a little more effort, but you will learn how to find critique partners and fellow writers to support you on your journey. You'll discover conferences and associations that will help you navigate the publishing industry and the business side of writing. Finally—and perhaps most important—you will also learn ways to find and connect with your readers.

Putting It All Together

I like to think of DIY MFA as a pie chart, with each of the three elements representing a different slice. These slices indicate how much time you dedicate to each of these areas. The size of these slices is up to you, and they can change depending on what your life looks like at the moment. As a general rule, my own pie is usually 50 percent writing and 25 percent each for reading and community, but I change these proportions depending on where I am with my writing and other projects.

DIY MFA Pie

For example, while I was writing this book, the writing slice took up about two-thirds of my pie, and the other slices shrunk accordingly. When I'm in writing mode I tend to read less, so during that phase my reading slice was tiny. On the other hand, when I'm speaking at a lot of conferences and attending events to promote DIY MFA, the community slice gets more space and the two other slices shrink.

My DIY MFA Pie While Writing This Book

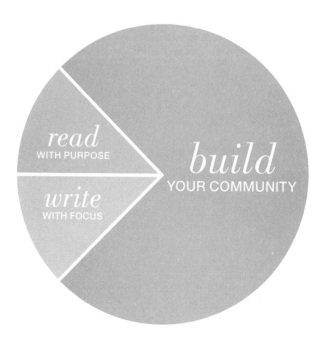

My DIY MFA Pie When I'm in "Conference Mode"

In a traditional MFA the sizes of these slices are decided for you, but in DIY MFA you're the one who determines how much time to dedicate to writing with focus, reading with purpose, and building community. There are only two rules: No slice can ever disappear altogether, and you must evaluate your pie every one to two weeks to make sure that it's still relevant.

It's important to keep each slice of the pie in play at all times. Even if your writing is taking up the majority of your pie, spend five minutes reading a short poem, or send out one tweet per day to build community. If you drop one of the slices altogether, it will kill your momentum in that area, and as you'll learn later in this book, it's much easier to ramp up if you're already in motion than it is to start your motor from a standstill. Avoid letting your momentum drop to zero in any of these three crucial areas.

As for re-evaluating your pie every few weeks, this is part of that iterative process I talked about in chapter one. How frequent you make these check-ins is up to you. Determine a trip wire or end date so you know when to re-view your progress. Then collect data until you hit that deadline. (Remember: Don't judge the data.) When you hit the trip wire, analyze your results and decide if you'll keep doing what you're doing or pivot to something new.

In the next chapter we identify your big writing goals and create a plan so you can make those dreams a reality. If DIY MFA is the journey, the next chapter is your road map.

— 03 —

Set Goals and Start Strong

It's easy to get overwhelmed when setting goals. You might worry so much about making your plans *just right* that you never get around to implementing them. Stop obsessing about the nitty-gritty details. Instead, think of your writing career as a road trip and your goals as the map: You may know where you're going, but there are many possible routes to get you there. Maybe you barrel down the interstate to reach your destination as quickly as possible. Maybe you take the scenic route and enjoy the sights. And maybe you hit a roadblock and have to take a detour. At the end of the journey, you'll still end up in the same place.

Road Trip!

Before you take off on your trip, you need a plan. Of course, you can start writing and see where the muse leads you, but you may end up wandering aimlessly and without purpose. To determine the best route, figure out where you are right now, and where you want to go.

Where Are You Now?

Many gurus and coaches will tell you to visualize success, to have a clear picture of the goals you want to achieve. This is reasonable advice, but it skips a crucial first step. You can't set goals with integrity unless you know where you are at the beginning of your journey. You also need to know what resources you have and what supplies you might bring with you on the road to success. Before you set any goals, take an inventory and assess where you are *right now* as a writer. This inventory is like a big red dot on your road map with the words "YOU ARE HERE" in capital letters. Until you know your starting point, you can't figure out the best route to your destination.

Take a few moments to answer the following questions.

WRITING

- How long have you been writing regularly?
- How much do you write each week?
- Is your schedule structured or sporadic?
- Are you focusing on one project or experimenting with various ideas?

READING

- Do you read regularly? How many books per year?
- What are your three favorite topics or genres?
- What are the last five books you've read?

COMMUNITY

- Do you have writer friends or colleagues?
- Do you have a critique group where you can exchange feedback?
- Have you gone to any events or conferences?
- Do you read any writing blogs, magazines, or websites?
- Do you connect with writers on social media? If so, where?

Don't worry if you left any of these questions blank. This exercise is not about getting the right answers but simply about taking stock of where you are. Before we continue, I want you to answer two more questions:

- What is the biggest "win" you've experienced in your writing, reading, or community building this past year? If you haven't celebrated this win, do something in the next week to honor your accomplishment.
- If you could improve *one thing* in your writing life, what would that be?

Supplies

Now that you've figured out where you are, it's time to pack some basic must-have supplies for your journey. Think of this as your writing emergency kit.

First, you'll need books of all kinds. If you don't have a library card, get one. In addition, you'll want to invest in a couple of key reference books. Strunk and White's *The Elements of Style* is essential for any writer's home library. You'll also want at least one reference book of writing techniques (this book totally counts, by the way), and you'll need an anthology of short-form literature (e.g., short stories, poems, or essays) for inspiration. I call these books The Essentials, and I go into more detail about them in chapter eighteen. For the time being, just make sure you have access to books. Lots and lots of books.

You will also need to set aside some time for this wild and crazy creative journey. A "feast or famine" schedule is better than not writing at all, but I recommend putting your DIY MFA time into your calendar so you'll be more likely to stick to it. Schedule an hour or two each week to study and implement the techniques in this book. Make sure they are hours when you are alert and focused, and protect that precious time from interlopers.

Your Destination

At this point you've established where you are and what resources you have. Now it's time to figure out where you're going. What big vision is spurring you on this writing journey? What motivated you to pick up this book in the first place? You're not just writing for intellectual exercise. You must have a vision for where you want to be, a goal or destination you want to reach.

For me, my big vision changes from year to year. In fact, every January, I jot down my big goal of the year on a slip of paper and put it in a ceramic chalice that sits next to my desk. Whenever I start to lose momentum or focus, I reach into the chalice and look at my goal.

Using just a few words jot down the writing goal you want to pursue. Go ahead, dream big.

Did you write it? Awesome. Now you know where you're going.

One Mile at a Time

Every journey begins with the first small step. You might travel for months or years, but if you don't take that first step, you'll never go anywhere. The quest toward any goal depends on two things: knowing exactly where you're going (so you know when you get there) and clocking the miles.

The best way to know if you've reached your destination and made your big vision a reality is to translate it into a concrete outcome. Think of this outcome as the exact address of your destination, the X that marks the spot on the map. It's fine to say, "I want to be a writer," but how you will you know when you've made it? Does "being a writer" mean you've published something? Or that you write every day? Or that you've finished the first draft of your novel? "Being a writer" means something different to everybody. What does it mean to you?

Once you have established this concrete outcome, the next step is to make the journey, one mile at a time. When you break a project into smaller increments, a goal that may have seemed overwhelming and terrifying can become manageable and even fun. It's like taking a cross-country road trip. When you break it down into smaller segments, celebrate the milestones, and enjoy the sights along the way, a draining journey can turn into a great vacation.

Taking small steps toward your goal will also make it easier to measure your progress. Just like tracking the miles on a trip, logging your progress as you write can be encouraging, especially when you see how far you've come. It might take a year to write a novel, but if you break it into a few hundred words each day, suddenly it doesn't feel quite so daunting and you'll have a good record of all the work you've done.

WRITING PLANNER

Use these questions to help you set your destination and plan your journey toward that goal.

- What's your destination, the big vision or long-term goal you have for your writing?
- What's the concrete outcome that will tell you that you've reached your goal? Now reverse engineer the milestones leading up to that concrete event. Work backwards from the goal and try to make each milestone as small as possible.
- What first small step can you take toward your goal right this moment? Do it today.

Hit the Road

In the next sections of this book, you'll learn how to write with focus, read with purpose, and build your community. But before we dive in, here are some more tips and tools to help you on this journey.

Travel Log

As you embark on this trip, you'll want to keep a record of everything that happens along the way. Some writers keep a detailed journal, while others just log the essential data. I use a goal sheet to help me stay organized and to keep my writing life and my real life in balance. You can download a copy of this goal sheet at DIYMFA.com/thebook by signing up with your e-mail address. Here's how to use it.

Goal Sheet

diy**MFA**

Date

ACTION STEPS

TOP PRIORITY

☐ _____
☐ _____
☐ _____
☐ _____
☐ _____

ON THE RADAR

☐ _____
☐ _____   _write_
☐ _____   WITH FOCUS
☐ _____
☐ _____
☐ _____
☐ _____   _read_
☐ _____   WITH PURPOSE
☐ _____
☐ _____
☐ _____
☐ _____   _build_
☐ _____   YOUR COMMUNITY
☐ _____
☐ _____

Goal Sheet

This goal sheet helps me balance my big yearly vision against the smaller action steps or milestones. It also helps me keep a record of everything I've accomplished so that I can see how far I've come.

Put the start date at the top, and before you move on to a new goal sheet, add the end date as well. Save your completed sheets in a folder or file. Not only does this help you honor your achievements and celebrate your progress, it also gives you insight into your writing habits and process.

The "Top Priority" section is where I write down the big vision that drives me. I limit myself to no more than three big goals—the number I can reasonably complete in one year. I also include big nonwriting-related events in this section because they can significantly affect my writing life. Buying a house, starting a new job, having a baby … you need to account for all of these major life events in your top-priority goals.

Also, keep in mind that your top-priority goals probably won't change from one goal sheet to the next, but it's still important to write them down every time. You must keep your big vision front and center so that you can set milestones and action steps with integrity. This keeps you from spinning your wheels on activities that aren't furthering your most important goals.

In the Action Steps section of the goal sheet, list the incremental next steps that will help you reach one of those top-priority goals. Every time you put something on your to-do list, check it against your big vision. If an action step doesn't further at least one of your top-priority goals, consider whether to do that step at all. This is where you reverse engineer your steps from your long-term goals to where you are now. Focus on keeping these incremental steps as small as possible to avoid missing any steps along the way. Doing so will also help you build a sense of mastery—that "Yes! I did it!" feeling is vital to staying motivated.

The last part of the goal sheet is what I call "On the Radar." This is where you list projects, ideas, and action steps not yet ready for implementation. If something is on the radar, you may not be ready to act on it, but you want to keep it salient so you don't forget about it. As you complete action steps, you can bump some of the radar items into the open spots on your action list and start implementing them. I like to sort my radar items according to the three pillars of DIY MFA—writing, reading, and community—so I have a sense of whether I am keeping these three areas in balance.

The next three sections of this book are where the rubber meets the road. These chapters are filled with practical techniques you can put into action right away, but they also challenge you to look at your writing in new ways. This may not always be smooth sailing, so be prepared to stretch your limits and move outside your comfort zone.

Before we dive into these core chapters, I want to help you avoid two major pitfalls. First, at some point while reading this book, you might find yourself thinking, *This technique could work for other writers, but it could* never *work for me.* All writers feel this way from time to time, so know that you are not alone. But while this feeling is normal, don't let it overtake you. Recognize such thoughts for what they are: resistance. Remember that resistance is your compass, and it points precisely at what you need to do. Shift your mind-set from "This will never work" to "How can I make this work for me?" and then put the concepts from this book into action.

The second pitfall is trying to follow *all* the advice in this book to the letter. Remember what I said about best practices? In this book I'll share *my* best techniques, the ones I've tried and tested myself. That doesn't mean all of them will work for you—in fact, *I* don't even use all these techniques at the same time. There is an ebb and flow to the creative process, and you must pick and choose what works for you. This is why iteration is so crucial. My job is to show you a smorgasbord of options, but you need to test the concepts for yourself and adjust them to suit your own writing life.

Don't worry. You can do this, and I'll be with you every step of the way. Plus, when you sign up for e-mail updates at DIYMFA.com/thebook, you'll gain access to a ton of supplementary material and worksheets to aid you on your journey.

Now let's dig in and get to work!

write with focus

── 04 ──

Motivate Yourself

By far, the question writers most often ask me is "How can I find more time to write?"

This question is deceiving because it assumes that the problem writers have with productivity is related to not having enough time. In fact, many people think that time management and productivity are one and the same. It's almost as if they think they would gain more time if only they could be more productive.

Time is the great equalizer. Whether you are a world leader or a regular Joe, one thing is universally true: We must all operate within a twenty-four-hour day. You might want to stretch or bend that time, but you can't. The only thing you can do is choose how to use it.

This means that productivity has nothing to do with time and everything to do with *choices*. If you learn to manage your choices, you can take control of your productivity. The techniques in this chapter might seem simple, but this is the most important—and most challenging—part of the book.

No matter how much you study the craft of writing, none of that knowledge will matter if you don't put words on the page. Before you can hone your story's theme or voice or character arc, you need to write something. Anything. You can fix just about any problem in your writing, but you cannot revise a blank page.

Reality Check

A writer once asked me how to be more productive without being disciplined. I told him that I was not a particularly disciplined person. If left to my own devices, I would spend the day eating chocolate and watching *Law & Order* reruns. I don't write out of discipline. I write because I'm ridiculously stubborn. I told him that I love my creative work, and because of that I protect it with my life. Heaven help anyone who tries to get between me and my writing.

That writer shifted nervously on his feet. "But that sounds so *hard*," he whined. "Did you expect it to be easy?" I answered.

Let's be real. Writing is too much work to be considered a hobby. You're either going to be serious about it or you shouldn't do it at all. That's not to say that you must have immense talent or innate skill. I don't care if you're destined to win a Pulitzer or if you can't string two sentences together. I've learned that talent is often irrelevant, and what matters is how serious you are about doing the work.

You can't magically add extra hours to your day. You will have to make choices, sometimes difficult ones. These choices are what differentiate writers from other people. Writers choose writing over things that are less important to them. They make writing a priority. Other people might say they "want to write a book someday." Writers actually do it.

Are you willing to make that choice? Are you ready to do whatever it takes?

I thought so. Let's get started.

Effective Writing Habits

Habits are settled, regular ways of practice. Although we may obtain some habits by accident, we can also create new habits on purpose. When we choose which habits to develop and which ones to abandon, we can change our writing lives for the better. In DIY MFA lingo, the word *habits* takes on yet another meaning.

> H = Honor Your Reality
> A = Add Constraints
> B = Block Time and Batch Tasks
> I = Iterate
> T = Ten Percent Rule
> S = Set the Mood

Honor Your Reality

We are human, and we live in reality. We have obligations, limitations, and constraints that affect what we can accomplish. These factors shape our lives and impact how we write. It's important to honor your reality, to respect these obligations and understand the individual challenges you face. Your day job, your family, and your health are all essential parts of your reality. Ignore these factors at your peril.

Just as your real-life responsibilities are important, so are your writing and creative fulfillment. Writing is an essential part of who you are, and you can't ignore that any more than you can ignore your day job or your family. The key to honoring reality is in remembering that this is not an "either ... or ..." choice. Your writing life and your real life can coexist. Sometimes one will tug at you more than the other, but your goal should be to create a peaceful balance between the two.

Honoring your reality is not permission to be *lazy*. You're a grown-up. You know the difference between honoring reality and making excuses. Real writers don't write only when it's easy—they find ways to fit writing into their full and busy lives.

Add Constraints

You can set constraints for your writing in two ways: through word count and time. A word count goal is a useful parameter when you're flying through a first draft, while a time limit is more useful when you're planning or revising your story. Set a trip wire when you write so that you don't work past the point of fatigue. Keep in mind that writing a book is a marathon, not a sprint. You need to pace yourself and build stamina. Start at a level that's just challenging enough to keep you motivated but not so strenuous that you give up or wear yourself out.

When you hit your word count or time goal, stop. That's right: You have permission to *stop writing* when you're done for the day—even if you're in the middle of a sentence. In fact, stopping midthought or midsentence is a great way to dive back into your story the next time you sit down to write, because that incomplete sentence will snap your mind to attention and help you return to your writing zone faster than if you had to rev up your motor from a cold stop. Writing is a lot like Newton's first law of motion: "Objects in motion tend to stay in motion. Objects at rest tend to stay at rest."

To keep your momentum, you must write something every day. It doesn't need to be a masterpiece. Scribble a sentence in a notebook, or jot down a fragment of an idea. You don't have to make it pretty; you just need to keep your hand in the game.

Don't fret if you've taken a break and haven't written anything in a while. Everyone starts from a standstill at some point in their writing careers. Sometimes things come up in our lives that prevent us from writing, and in order to honor our reality we must set aside our writing for a short time.

In this case, you need to ease yourself back into motion in a gentle but firm manner. Focus on the smallest possible step, and work your way up from there.

Block Time and Batch Tasks

Is your schedule out of control? Is your to-do list longer than this book? Don't panic. Blocking time and batching tasks will help you tame your schedule and free up more time for your writing.

Blocking time means that you do specific activities during specific blocks in your schedule. This means *no* multitasking. Believe it or not, multitasking is harmful to your productivity. Research has found that when people try to juggle multiple tasks, they are not only slower but also less accurate. When you switch between tasks, it takes your brain a few moments to reset and shift focus. These "reset" moments add up and make you less efficient over time.

When you block time, you shift from multitasking to focusing on one task at a time. For instance, instead of answering e-mail every time your in-box pings, check your messages at specific times throughout the day. When you're checking e-mail, give it your full attention. Otherwise, stay focused on the task at hand.

It is also useful to batch similar tasks into the same block of time. When checking your e-mail, instead of responding to each message as it comes in, write all your replies in the same block of time. When you work on similar tasks back to back, your brain doesn't need as much time to reboot, so you'll be more efficient.

Iterate

I've covered iteration already, but this is where you must put it into action. Try different techniques, and experiment with your process until you create a writing habit that works. How long should you make one of your time blocks? Test it and iterate. Which tasks should you batch together? Again, you won't know until you iterate. Reading about something and liking the idea is only the first step. You must put those concepts into action. Even the elements of craft you will learn later in this book will only sink in when you actually apply them to your writing. Brainstorming is all well and good, but those ideas are nothing but vapor until you put them on the page. And iterate.

The Ten Percent Rule

Your writing goal needs to be reasonable, attainable. If you set your goal too high, you might fail on the first try and give up. If your goal is too easy, you may become bored or, worse, get lazy. The Ten Percent Rule helps you set a goal that's just challenging enough to keep you motivated but not so difficult that you set yourself up for failure.

Choose a goal that feels comfortable, and then add 10 percent. If you plan to write for thirty minutes, set the clock for thirty-three. If you're shooting for 500 words, try for 550. That extra 10 percent gives you a boost: It makes your goal interesting and just a little bit challenging. When your goal starts to feel comfortable (and it will, in time), you'll know you're ready to scale up again.

The Ten Percent Rule gets you in the habit of setting goals and reaching them. This is called *building mastery*, and it's crucial for success. Every time you reach an attainable goal, you will feel confident that you can reach the next goal. Each small win further boosts your confidence so that over the long-term you will reach your big, top-priority goals.

Set the Mood

While most motivation comes from within, you can also create an environment to help you get in your writing zone. Setting the mood includes sensory cues, like music or a cup of coffee, as well as logistical details such as the place and time you write. Choose something that will signal to your brain "Okay, it's time to write now."

Over time, you can train your brain to respond to these cues on command, like Pavlov did with his dogs. Ivan Pavlov, a Russian physiologist, performed an experiment in which he rang a bell every time he fed his dogs. Not long after, the dogs began salivating at the sound of the bell alone, even when no food was served. This is called "classical conditioning," and it doesn't work on dogs alone. It works with writers, too.

You can use classical conditioning by pairing a sensory cue with the behavior you want to elicit—in this case, writing. This sensory cue can be just about anything. Some writers wear a special hat or light a scented candle before they begin. I listen to a specific playlist I design to match the writing project. One writer I know starts every writing session by meditating for three minutes. The key is to be patient and consistent. It can take up to two weeks for the association between writing and the sensory cue to sink in.

One caveat with sensory cues: While you can use them to jump-start a writing session, be careful not to depend on them as a crutch. If you find that you can only write in a specific environment, that is a sign of trouble. Sensory cues should help you write more, not prevent you from writing when the situation is less than perfect.

If you are serious about writing—which I know you are—then your goal shouldn't be just to write one great book. You need to discover a process so that you can create dozens or even hundreds of wonderful books. While you might have a specific project in mind right now, remember that the process is far more important. By improving not just *what* you write but *how* you write it, you will hone that process and learn to produce great writing again and again.

Until now you've learned tools for helping you jump-start your writing and maintaining your forward momentum. Sooner or later, though, you're bound to hit a bump in the road. In those moments it's important to build your resilience so you can bounce back. Failure and rejection are part of the writer's life. In fact, as you'll learn in the next chapter, they are essential for your success.

05

Fail Better

Rejection is part of a writer's life. No matter how hard you try to do everything right, sometimes a project just misses the mark. In some cases these so-called failures are a result of things you can control, like the quality of your work or simple mistakes you can fix. Other times the fate of your project may be out of your hands and at the mercy of a fickle marketplace or a particular agent's or editor's taste. Writing is subjective, and sooner or later someone will dislike something you write. In this sense, failure is inevitable.

Some writers use these roadblocks as reasons to give up. They throw their hands in the air and moan about the injustices of "the industry." This is a cop-out. Wimps do the work when it's easy but quit as soon as it gets hard. You are not a wimp.

The Secret About Failure

Our culture embraces the mystique of "overnight success." Often we are so focused on the end result that we overlook all the crucial steps that came before. Almost every day a new story surfaces about a wildly successful writer who "comes out of nowhere" and takes the world by storm. We hear about the big book deals and movie options, but what we don't see are the years of rejection and the series of incremental failures that led to that big success.

Failure and rejection are not just part of being a writer; they are *essential* ingredients to your success. Yet knowing this doesn't make it hurt any less when you fall short of your goals. No one likes to fail, and rejection is downright painful. This is why you need a system to cope with failure and bounce back from rejection. I call it "failing better."

> F = Face Your Fears
> A = Assemble Your Allies
> I = Initiate and Iterate
> L = Let It Go

> *"Ever tried. Ever failed. No matter. Try again. Fail again. Fail better."* —SAMUEL BECKETT

The sooner you know something isn't working, the sooner you can eliminate that option and find another that works. Fail fast and fail often so you can establish a creative process that moves you closer to success.

Face Your Fears

Resistance and fear are closely tied. After all, we often resist what frightens us, so fear can be a good indicator of where you should concentrate your actions and attention.

But fear is more than just a signal for resistance. Fear stimulates our fight-or-flight response and pushes us to take action. We might be tempted to ignore our fears, to keep a stiff upper lip and push forward despite our instincts, but remember that fear exists for a reason, and part of honoring your reality is admitting when you are afraid. Fear makes you pay attention. It makes you sit up and take note. It is not a sign of weakness but an essential component of courage. Courage is not the absence of fear; rather, it allows you to take action—a leap of faith—despite all the things that might terrify you. Without fear, you can't have courage. This is why facing your fears is the first and most important step toward learning how to fail better.

> *"I learned that courage was not the absence of fear, but the triumph over it. The brave man is not he who does not feel afraid, but he who conquers that fear."* —NELSON MANDELA

Assemble Your Allies

On the journey from idea to finished book, the writer meets many colleagues and trusted readers. Aside from the obvious allies like an agent and editor, many other people can be involved in a writer's success. You might find allies among your writer friends. These colleagues will read your work and give you honest feedback, flag problems, and offer suggestions to solve them. Bookish nonwriter friends can also give you feedback but from a reader's point of view.

You don't need to wait until the revision stage to enlist the help of your allies. They can also help you beta-test a story or brainstorm project ideas with you. This early feedback can help you course-correct before you've invested so much time and energy in a project that you've passed the point of no return.

Remember, too, that allies can be people in your life who don't contribute to the writing itself but allow you the creative space and freedom you need to work. A supportive spouse who helps fix dinner, kids who let Mommy work on her book for an hour or two, or even a roommate who knows that a closed door means "Shut up, I'm writing," are all valuable allies.

Initiate and Iterate

Now you must cross the threshold and start writing. Don't worry about getting it right on the first try. Embrace the probability that you will mess up, and that these imperfections are simply part of the process. This will free you to take the first leap and start on a project, even if you don't feel ready. Some writers waste months—even years—planning and preparing to write. If you do that, you'll never start. Remember, there will never be a perfect time to write your book, and you will never be completely ready. Stop waiting for the right time and just write. Now.

Remember that mistakes and failure are part of the iterative process, and while they are inevitable, you cannot take setbacks personally. When something goes wrong, don't say, "I failed." Say, "This failed," and then try something else.

Writers often ask, "What if I pour my heart and soul into a project and no one wants to publish it? What if I waste my energy on something that never goes anywhere?" My answer: Have patience, grasshopper. Not every writer's first (or second or tenth) book is meant to grace the bookstore shelves, but that doesn't mean you've wasted time and energy writing it.

Many writers have manuscripts squirreled away in the depths of their desks. I know I do. And even if those books never get published, they are still a core part of my growth as a writer. There is no such thing as wasted writing because those failed attempts were part of my journey to writing something much better. When a project doesn't turn out as you would like, don't let it prevent you from trying again. Instead, think of failure as progress. You tried something, and it didn't work. Now you can cross that option off your list and move forward.

Let It Go

The best way to deal with failure is to let it go. This doesn't mean living in denial and ignoring your mistakes. Letting go means you must first honor that failure and then set it aside where it can do no further harm. Acknowledge your mistakes and learn from them, but don't carry that experience with you as excess baggage.

We writers are perfectionists, and we often make our failures worse by agonizing over them. We pick apart rejection letters looking for hidden clues. We relive the drama of mistakes we made both on and off the page. Just like compounding failure with guilt, when we agonize over our mistakes, we make an already-painful experience worse.

Letting go of failure allows us to recognize and accept our mistakes without wasting additional energy on them. When we obsess over our failures, we use up precious mental real estate that could be better spent on creative endeavors. The more angst and worry we carry with us, the less space we have in our brains for creativity and writing.

Failing better takes practice, but it's easier to do if you have a system to help you manage your negative thoughts. Mine is called the "Angst Jar."

The Angst Jar is a place where I deposit all the negative thoughts and feelings that weigh me down and prevent me from writing. Whenever I feel hurt, angry, guilty, or negative about my work, I write down this feeling on a slip of paper and put it in the jar. This system is effective because it doesn't let me hide or suppress the negative emotions, and it forces me to face the guilt, anger, or hurt that I'm feeling. It lets me honor those emotions but also contains them so they won't impede my creative work. Like Dumbledore's Pensieve in the Harry Potter series, the Angst Jar gives me a place to deposit my negative thoughts and clear my mind so that I can be nimble and creative.

The Angst Jar also plays an essential role when I encounter failure. When I fail, I jot it down and put it in the jar. Then, each time that failure creeps back into my mind (and it does … it always does), I remind myself that it's safe in the Angst Jar, and I let it go. Sometimes I have to let the same failure go a dozen times in a single morning, but after a while the sting wears off. Before I know it, it's gone altogether.

06

Generate Ideas on Demand

One of the biggest mistakes writers make is to hoard their ideas. They come up with an amazing idea, but instead of getting it down on paper, they hover over it like Gollum with his ring, hissing, "My precioussss." But ideas alone are not all that special. They're more like subways in New York City: There's always another on the way. You just have to be patient.

We're not born with amazing ideas, so we must train ourselves to generate them on demand. Honing this skill takes persistence, patience, and (surprise!) iteration. If you've been following the steps in this book, you already have habits and systems for iteration in place. Now you just need to apply these same strategies and techniques to your creativity.

But first, let's debunk a few myths.

Creative Myths

Some people treat creativity like it's a magical, mysterious force, as if only the "true creatives" can wield its power. The sad truth is that these purported wizards are not particularly creative at all, and to protect their tentative position atop the artistic hierarchy they perpetuate ridiculous myths about what creativity really is. Don't be fooled. These so-called creative people are not the real deal. You are.

Myth 1: Creativity Is an Exclusive Club, and You Can't Be a Part of It

Some people act like creativity is a scarce resource, an insiders' club open only to an elite few. They want you to believe that creativity is exclusive and elusive, that they have it and you don't. These creative snobs perpetuate this myth to hide their own lack of creative mojo. They hope and pray that if they keep working their flashy wizard magic center stage you won't notice the man behind the curtain.

Truly creative people know that creativity is an abundant—even infinite—resource. To them, ideas are a dime a dozen, and the real secret to success is hard work and practice. Unlike the wannabes, real creatives know that anyone can be creative, and they're cool with that. In fact, they welcome newbies into the fold. As long as you're dedicated to your art, you're a member of this creative family.

> **CREATIVE TRUTH:** Anyone can be creative, but they have to work for it.

Myth 2: Creativity Is Innate—You Either Have It or You Don't

Wannabe creatives want you to believe that creativity is a talent: You're either born with it or without it. The truth is, creativity is a talent in the same way that getting up in the morning and going to work is a talent. You don't question whether you have to do your job; you just do it. If you make creativity a part of your everyday life, it will become a natural skill you can easily tap.

When I was four years old, I began playing the violin. My siblings also played, and together we won concerto competitions, toured South America, and even played in Carnegie Hall a few times. While I often resented my fiddle (you could say we had a love-hate relationship), it taught me the importance of practice. Other kids might come home from school and switch on the television or play video games, but my siblings and I pulled out our instruments and practiced for several hours. This might not have been "normal" compared to the activities of the average kid our age, but it was our version of normal, and we didn't question it.

If you practice creativity and make it a part of your daily routine, you can train yourself to generate ideas on command. Creativity is like a muscle, and the more you exercise it, the stronger it becomes. It's not a talent; it's a skill.

> **CREATIVE TRUTH:** No one is born creative. You become creative through small, simple steps.

Myth 3: Creativity Is Driven by Chaos, so There's No Way to Control It

Many of us have a romanticized notion of the creative person. We imagine a whacky, eccentric inventor mucking about in a basement laboratory or a tortured artist flinging paint at a canvas. It almost seems that insanity is a prerequisite for creativity.

Certainly the creative process can be serendipitous, and at times it can appear spontaneous—even disorganized—to a casual observer. Don't be fooled: Truly creative people apply a method to their madness. Creativity is a process with logical, repeatable steps. Unless you want your brilliance to be a one-time fluke, you need to be able to re-create that process. This means you have no choice but to be methodical. And just because creativity is methodical doesn't mean it must be compulsively organized. Playfulness is a key ingredient, and you can give that process your own unique flair.

> **CREATIVE TRUTH:** There is a method to the madness of creativity. Embrace the chaos, and trust the process.

Myth 4: Creativity Is All About Getting That One "Big Idea"

Many people think creativity is about luck. They think if you're in the right place at the right time lightning will strike. If your timing is a little bit off, game over. They believe that J.K. Rowling was "lucky" when she imagined the Harry Potter series and that Stephen King just happened to unearth gold when he wrote *Carrie.* According to them, all you need is a fantastic idea and the story practically writes itself.

This is the most insidious creative myth because it puts all the emphasis on the idea and fails to consider the energy and effort required to execute it. It treats writers as though their success hinges on luck, when the truth is that a writing career is fostered from years of hard work and persistence. An idea is nothing until you turn it into something meaningful and tangible—a book, a story, a poem—and share it with other people. Creativity is about putting ideas into action and bringing them to life so they can have a profound impact on the world.

> **CREATIVE TRUTH:** Great ideas are worthless. They're vapor. They're air. They mean nothing until you put them into action.

Myth 5: Creativity Means Polishing an Idea Until It's Perfect

Creativity is not about tinkering and polishing an idea to perfection before you execute it. Doing so can squelch the life out of it before you ever get a chance to put it into action. Truly creative people iterate on their ideas and learn from small failures before they reach success. This is how a creative idea is developed: by persevering through failure after failure until it finally works.

A wannabe creative believes that if a project doesn't work it's because the original idea was faulty. Real creatives know the truth: On the road to success, they will encounter false starts and dead ends. At times, it will feel like nothing works, that the project is a complete failure and that they've already tried all the good solutions. Real creatives know that these small failures are essential to their process. The secret is to keep trying.

> **CREATIVE TRUTH:** Setbacks are part of the creative process. You can choose to give into them, or you can stop whining and write.

Generate Ideas

I believe in systems and processes. The last thing I want is to entrust my creativity to a fickle, unresponsive muse. To me, creativity is logical and straightforward, like turning on a water faucet. You just need to know which spigot to twist so you can start the flow of ideas. My approach to creativity has four stages: inspiration, development, evaluation, and action. To remember these steps, just think of the word *IDEA*.

> I = Inspiration
> D = Development
> E = Evaluation
> A = Action

This IDEA method is cyclical and doesn't stop at the fourth step. The action stage feeds back into any of the three earlier stages, from which you can start the cycle again. The key is to keep this cycle going. The more you go through the process, the easier it will get and the more skilled you will become at generating new ideas.

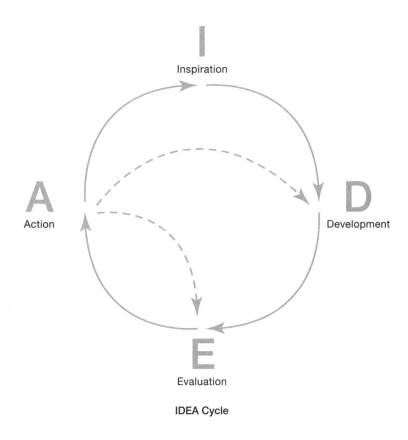

IDEA Cycle

Inspiration: Jump-Start Your Creativity

Every idea cycle starts with inspiration. It's the stage most people think of when they imagine the creative process. But inspiration is just one small piece of the creative puzzle. In fact, it's the least important part of the process, and you can often sidestep it altogether by employing brainstorming techniques or writing prompts.

If you're ever at a loss for story ideas, hop over to DIYMFA.com/writer-igniter and check out the Writer Igniter app. It's like a casino slot machine for writers. Just hit the shuffle button, and it will give you a random character, situation, prop, and setting. The number of possible combinations is practically endless.

One caveat before we continue: Brainstorming is a huge topic. Entire books have been written about it, and I could never cover all the details in just one chapter. To keep things simple, the inspiration techniques that follow focus on helping you generate *story ideas*, with a special emphasis on tools you can squeeze into your busy life. My goal is to give you a few methods to come up with new stories so that your inspiration well never runs dry.

Leave Some Things to Chance

When you leave things to chance, you limit your options in unexpected ways. Using the roll of the die or a coin toss to direct your story forces you to make do with the limited options in front of you. Contrary to what you might expect, these constraints often unleash more creative thinking, not less.

Choose an exercise at random from a book of prompts. Assign options to the numbers one through six, and then roll a die. Flip a coin to decide if your character pursues option A or option B. There's a reason role-playing games rely on dice to determine critical story outcomes. By leaving some elements of the story to chance, it forces the players (who are really storytellers) to find more creative ways to spin their narrative web.

If you find yourself stuck for an idea, use the luck of the draw to decide some aspect of your story, and then follow where it leads.

Engage the Five Senses

Story ideas are all around us, but we often don't notice them. Paintings and photographs can convey entire stories with just one glance. Colors can convey a mood or a character's personality. A piece of music might serve as the "soundtrack" to your story. There are hundreds—no, thousands—of stories around you right this moment. You just need to pay attention.

Writers often focus most heavily on sights and sounds, and they overlook the rich sensory worlds of touch, taste, and smell. The latter senses may in fact lead to even more visceral and emotionally evocative stories if we cultivate them. Smell, for example, is linked to the amygdala, one of the memory centers of the brain, and can evoke more powerful memories than any of the other senses. When we focus our attention on one of these "neglected" senses, we come up with ideas we would never have imagined if we relied only on sight and sound.

Silence Your Inner Critic

You've heard this advice before. It's easy for me to tell you to silence your inner critic, but actually doing so is hard. I've found that the best way to put that inner critic in his place is to laugh at him. This is why I keep a mascot of my inner critic on my desk: a sculpture of a pink alien monster picking his nose with his tongue. Gross, I know, but it makes me laugh, and laughter robs my critic of his power.

Break Out of Your Comfort Zone

Writers are creatures of habit. Our routines can become ruts if we're not careful. For every habit we develop, we want to find that sweet spot where we've become comfortable enough to keep up our momentum but haven't reached the point of stagnation. The key is to notice when a habit has become too comfortable and has outlasted its usefulness.

This comes back to resistance. Many times we stick with habits and behaviors that are comfortable because we're afraid of change. But if we let ourselves get too comfortable, if we don't push ourselves with a new challenge, then we'll never grow as writers.

Practicing the Ten Percent Rule is a great way to push yourself out of the comfort zone without getting overwhelmed. Use your resistance as a guide. If a project scares you, that may be a sign that you need to devote your attention to it. If you're comfortable writing in a quiet room, try working in a public space. The goal here is to shake up your habits once in a while so they stay fresh.

CREATE AN IDEA BANK

When you learn how to generate ideas on demand, you may end up with so many that it's hard to figure out where to focus. It becomes all too easy to jump from one idea to the next and never finish anything.

This is where an Idea Bank comes in. The Idea Bank is a safe space where you store different project ideas until you're ready to work on them. Back in my toy design days, my Idea Bank was a plush toy piggy bank I sewed by hand. Eventually it became too small to hold all of my ideas, so I began to use a ceramic pumpkin jar I found at a thrift store. The pumpkin shape is symbolic because it reminds me to wait until my ideas are ripe before I harvest them.

Using the piggy bank and pumpkin jar as examples, look for or create an Idea Bank of your own. When a sparkly new concept pops into your head and interrupts your current project, jot down the idea and put it in the bank. As with a real-world bank, the Idea Bank will keep your precious inspiration safe until you're ready to put it into action.

Schedule a time once per month or per quarter to take a quick inventory of everything in your Idea Bank. Some ideas may have grown irrelevant and can be discarded. Others may have matured and are now ready for you to invest time and effort in them. Just as you should balance your checkbook

One of the best ways to create a stash of ideas is through writing prompts. Start collecting images, mementos, and anything else that might spark a story. Postcards with paintings, photographs, or interesting scenes can inspire a story. A word box—filled with slips of paper, each with a random word—can lead your project in any number of unexpected directions. And, of course, you'll want to keep a couple of prompt books handy.

I stash all these creative resources in a shrine I lovingly call the ORACLE. (As with everything in my world, ORACLE is an acronym, and it stands for "outrageous ridiculously awesome creative literary exercises.") In the ancient days, people traveled to oracle temples to seek wisdom from their gods. While my ORACLE may not be a temple on an idyllic Mediterranean isle, it's where I go to find creative inspiration.

The ORACLE is different from the Idea Bank. The latter is a place where I store ideas for projects so that I don't have to worry about forgetting or misplacing them. The ORACLE, on the other hand, is not a container of the ideas themselves but a place to go for inspiration. When I need an idea for a new project, or when an existing project has hit a rut, I march to my ORACLE and demand wisdom from the muse.

CREATE YOUR OWN ORACLE

Find or purchase a unique box or container. Paint it. Embellish it. Make it your own. Inside, store different sources of inspiration. In my ORACLE I have a word box, a collection of fortune cookie sayings, an image file, a tarot deck with beautiful illustrations, a kaleidoscope, dice of all shapes and sizes, and a mini notebook where I've recorded some of my favorite writing prompts and exercises.

Don't expect to fill your ORACLE with idea sources overnight. It's taken me years to build the ORACLE I have now. Keep adding to it, and adjust its contents so that it grows with you as a writer. Sign up with your e-mail address at DIYMFA.com/thebook to get a list of recommended resources to add to your ORACLE.

Development: Grow Your Ideas

Now it's time to choose one project and flesh it out. This is the development stage of the IDEA cycle, and you can go about it in three ways: through imitation, improvisation, and incubation. I call these the three *I*'s, and for any given project, you can use one, two, or all three of these techniques.

Imitation

Using imitation to develop a skill is a tradition that spans many centuries. During the Renaissance, artists learned their craft by working under the tutelage of a more seasoned master. The apprentice imitated the master's work until he was ready to branch out on his own and become a master himself. Those years spent copying the master's work taught the artist fundamental skills and helped him understand the "rules" of his craft. It was only once the artist knew these rules inside and out that he could challenge conventions and create something truly new and unique.

Some artists even copied *themselves* to develop their skills and ideas. Edgar Degas spent years tracing and retracing the same ballerina sketches in order to understand the human form. By tracing his own sketches, Degas built up a kinesthetic representation—a muscle memory—of what it felt like to draw a ballerina's shape. This in-depth understanding allowed him to create truly unique paintings and sculptures that challenged the conventions of how his subjects were depicted.

You can use imitation to improve your own writing. One way to do this is to follow in the footsteps of the great writers, like an apprentice learning from one of the literary masters. Choose an author whose voice or style you admire, and then copy a paragraph of one of her stories longhand. Get a sense of how the words feel as you write them on the page. Try to get into the author's mind-set. What was it like to be this author? What was it like to write these words?

You can also try to imitate the voice or style of a writer you admire by applying that style to your own words or stories. In this case, you are not copying the exact text of that author but trying to capture his style on the page. This is an advanced exercise that takes more effort and study, but it is well worth it. When you learn the "rules" of another author's style and gain a deeper understanding of how to re-create that voice, you'll be only a half step away from breaking those rules and crafting your own unique voice.

Improvisation

For three years I played violin with my college's jazz band. As a Suzuki-trained musician, attempting to improvise on a theme was excruciating. I could *hear* what I wanted to play in my head, but when I tried to make my fingers follow along, I'd freeze up. Then my band professor gave me an assignment: Listen to a solo by one of the jazz violin greats and transcribe it note for note. As I transcribed the violin solo from *Suite Thursday* by Duke Ellington and Billy Strayhorn, I started to see the underlying structure of the music. I began to understand how the baseline created a foundation and the chord progression provided a framework for Ray Nance to noodle on his fiddle. The day I handed in my transcription, the band professor cued up the band and said, "Let's see what you've got."

Shaking, I took the stage and started playing the solo I transcribed, each note exactly the way I had heard it on the record. Then it happened: I hit a wrong note. But it wasn't wrong—or at least it didn't sound wrong. It was just different. So I kept going, and before I knew it I was improvising something all my own.

Once you have imitation figured out, improvisation is a breath away. In fact, you may start to improvise without even realizing it. At first it might be a small change, a "wrong note" that leads to another, and yet another, until you're making the piece all your own. In the words of Thelonious Monk: "Whatever you think *can't* be done, somebody will come along and *do* it. A genius is the one most like himself."

Incubation

Sometimes we hit a roadblock in our writing, and, despite our best efforts, we can't navigate around it. This is when incubation becomes crucial. It does you no good to keep pounding on an idea until you squash the very life out of it. Instead, take a break and do something else. This is often when I will make a note to myself about the project and put it in the Idea Bank for a while so it can mature. A mindful break from a project can give you the necessary perspective and distance to gain new insights and eventually make a breakthrough.

Just because you're letting one idea rest doesn't mean you should stop writing altogether. I like to practice "productive procrastination": I procrastinate on a project that needs a break by working on a different project. Letting something incubate until I get closer to the deadline creates a sense of urgency that often helps me get unstuck. There's nothing like a deadline to boost inspiration. But don't procrastinate by watching bad television and eating bonbons. Work on a different project so at least you're making progress on something. This way you're still being productive.

Unplugging from media for a period of time also helps with incubation. In our information-driven culture, it's easy to overfill our heads with videos, articles, blog posts, tweets, books, or anything else. All this sensory input takes up mental space that we need to clear out so we have room to work on a creative problem. Think of it as a cleanse diet for your brain. By stepping away from media for a limited time you give your brain a chance to reset and refocus.

Of course, a complete info-cleanse can be a tall order. Unless you're going on a retreat and taking a vow of silence, it's near impossible to unplug completely. If you stop checking e-mail or mute your phone, you risk getting fired or missing an important call from your kid's preschool. This is why it's crucial to be *strategic* with your information diet. It's not about complete deprivation, but about limiting certain sources so you give yourself the creative space you need.

If productive procrastination and the info-cleanse don't work, it's time to try the most extreme version of incubation: Stop beating your project to death, and do something completely different. Ideally this unrelated activity should be active, repetitive, or restorative. Exercising or going for a walk is a great active way to get your mind off your creative block. Repetitive activities like knitting or coloring allow you to introduce some mental white space into your life without breaking a sweat. And if rest and relaxation are more your speed, do a meditation exercise or take a nap. The point is to break out of work mode and reboot your brain so you can bring a fresh perspective to your creative project.

Evaluation: Test Your Idea

Until now I've talked about generating ideas and gaining fresh perspective on your writing projects. But when do you know if an idea is *The One?* How can you tell when you're ready to commit to a project for the long haul? This is where evaluation and action come in. Once you evaluate whether your idea has merit, you can finally put it into action.

In the tech start-up world, the term *ooch* means to work your way toward a new product one tiny step at a time. This echoes the iteration mindset we've already covered and takes it even further. I realize that ooching might seem like a stretch for writers. It's one thing for a tech start-up to ooch their software, but it's a different proposition for a writer to ooch a book. After all, writing a book takes a long time. How do you iterate on a novel when the first draft alone might take years?

It is precisely *because* writing a book is so laborious that ooching is critical. The last thing you want is to write 250 pages only to discover that you hate your protagonist or you can't stand to write another word of the story. Instead, ooch your way into a book-length project. Hang out with your characters and spend some time in their world before you devote a year or longer to them.

Start by writing a short story. Don't give an overview of your whole idea; you're not trying to summarize your entire novel in a few pages. Instead, take a deep dive into one particular aspect of the larger story. Focus on creating a stand-alone piece with a beginning, a middle, and an end. Use the short story to get to know your characters and to get a sense for your book's world. This exercise will let you see how your characters evolve through an entire story. It will give you insights about those characters that you wouldn't see otherwise, because you're taking them out of the larger context.

Short stories are also a great way to build your platform, boost your writer's résumé, and connect with your readers. Literary magazines won't publish a random chapter from a novel-in-progress, but they will definitely consider a short story if it stands on its own.

Next, give your story to a few readers and ask for their feedback. Here, again, it is so useful to have a stand-alone short story. If you give readers one or two chapters from a larger book, they'll see only a small slice of the overall project. If you give them a short story about those same characters in that same world, your readers will be able to give you much more useful feedback because they'll see the story from beginning to end. Apply the reader feedback you receive to your overall project. From there, you can decide whether you want to stick with this idea for an entire novel.

In addition to reader feedback, you'll also need to get a sense of the market potential for your book. When I worked in the toy industry, we had this saying in the design studio: "Okay, the idea sounds great, but does it have legs?" In other words, can this idea go the distance? Is it just a one-hit wonder, or does it have staying power? While you don't want to write *to the market*, you do need to make sure your story is *marketable*. Don't let trends or fads dictate which story you write, but keep your finger on the industry's pulse by staying abreast of new releases in your genre and reading books with similar topics or themes as your own. These books (often called "comps") will give you a sense of where your book can fit and let you know if your idea "has legs." Remember, this isn't just about expanding your story into a sequel or series. It's also not about writing companion novels. Instead, view your current book as one incremental step in your career as a writer. Make sure that the project you choose to work on today won't paint you into a corner tomorrow.

Finally, when in doubt, extract an outline. In the process of drafting their books, many writers lose track of what they've written and what the story is really about. When that happens, stop and extract an outline from your draft. This outline will show you what you've already written and what still remains. You'll more clearly see redundancies and gaps in your story. In the next chapter, you'll learn several techniques for creating outlines, but for now just remember that the outline isn't just for the planning stage of a book. You can use an outline to test an idea, to take inventory of what you have halfway through a draft, or even to revise.

Action: Set the Idea in Motion

This is the most straightforward part of the IDEA cycle. It is also the most difficult. At some point in this process you have to stop generating, developing, and testing ideas; sooner or later you just have to write. The HABITS you established earlier will come in handy as you crank out those words and get that story on the page. There's no glamour, no easy fix—just hard work. The only caveat I would add is to make sure you set a check-in point (or trip wire) as you're writing so that you know when to step back and look at the project as a whole. When working on a long project, it's easy to develop tunnel vision and lose that broader perspective. Even if you're deep in the trenches of your story, you need to peek over the rim and get a sense of the larger landscape. Use the skills you've learned so far to keep your momentum and write that book.

Even after you've put those words on the page, though, one last step remains. Remember that writing only takes on true meaning when somebody reads it. It's not enough to write a book and hide it away. Stories are meant to be heard. Books are meant to be read. The IDEA cycle only comes to fruition when you finish your story and give it to a reader. It is only when the book passes from the writer to the reader that this circle becomes complete.

This is your goal: having someone read your book. Don't lose sight of it.

07

Outline Your Book Like a Boss

Are you a "plotter" or a "pantser"? In case you're not familiar with these not-so-technical terms, plotters think outlines are the bee's knees, while pantsers prefer to write by the seat of their pants. The plotting versus pantsing debate is an ongoing controversy, one that has raged in the writing world for years.

Plotters live for organization and structure. They color-code their wardrobes, alphabetize their spice racks, and spend hours pouring over The Container Store catalog. Plotters invest a lot of time planning their novels so that when they sit down at the keyboard the story practically writes itself. The one danger with this methodical approach is that all this planning might squelch the life out of your story before you even have a chance to write it. Too much structure can kill the spontaneity. Not to mention, if you know how the story ends you might feel less compelled to write it because the thrill is gone.

Pantsers, conversely, like to "wing it," both in writing and in life. Their creative process is messy, and most of their projects occur organically, often at the last minute. Pantsers love to throw things together and just "see what happens." Whether they succeed or fail, their results are always spectacular. These writers thrive on spontaneity and creative impulse. However, they risk spending days, months, or even years chasing a project only to realize it's a dead end. If you're wondering what type of writer you are, take the following quiz.

For each of these statements, note whether you agree (A) or disagree (D).

1. I believe that there's a place for everything and everything should be in its place.
2. I enjoy making spur-of-the-moment plans.
3. Road trips are more fun when you explore off the beaten path.
4. When I watch movies, I find myself speculating on what will happen next.
5. When I travel, I like to have a detailed itinerary.
6. My world isn't messy; it's organic.
7. Bright colors and organic patterns speak to me.
8. I tend to be punctual.
9. Last-minute plans stress me out.
10. I never lose things. Sometimes it just takes me a while to find what I'm looking for.
11. I don't ask for directions because getting lost is part of the fun.
12. I color-code things.
13. When I read books, I sometimes sneak a peek at the ending.
14. I live for spontaneous moments and unexpected discoveries.
15. I love getting caught up in a good story.
16. When designing my ideal workspace, I like right angles and clean lines.
17. I'm never on time. My friends tell me I live in my own imaginary time zone.
18. I don't ask for directions because I always know exactly where I'm going.
19. I don't care if someone tells me the ending of a movie. I'll still watch it because I want to see how it unfolds.
20. I like to plan things down to the smallest detail.
21. When I travel, I like to look at architecture and visit the landmarks.
22. Games of chance are exciting.
23. When I cook, I just throw ingredients in a pot and see what works.
24. I'm very good at reading maps and finding my way around new places.
25. I love time lines, and I'm great at sticking to a schedule.
26. Deadlines are great motivators.
27. My ideal vacation is all about being in nature.
28. I couldn't bake something to save my life.
29. I enjoy playing games where strategy and skill are key components.
30. I have no sense of direction and couldn't find my way out of a paper bag.

SCORING YOUR RESULTS: (1) A = 1, D = -1; (2) A = -1, D = 1; (3) A = -1, D = 1; (4) A = 1, D = -1; (5) A = 1, D = -1; (6) A = -1, D = 1; (7) A = -1, D = 1; (8) A = 1, D = -1; (9) A = 1, D = -1; (10) A = -1, D = 1; (11) A = -1, D = 1; (12) A = 1, D = -1; (13) A = 1, D = -1; (14) A = -1, D = 1; (15) A = -1, D = 1; (16) A = 1, D = -1;

The plotter/pantser dichotomy is a myth, and most writers fall somewhere between the two ends of the spectrum. In fact, some writers flip-flop between plotter and pantser mode depending on their project or the stage of the process they're in. Even writers stubbornly fixed at one extreme or the other will have to find a middle ground in order to succeed in their writing career. Plotters have to challenge themselves to loosen up or risk writing mechanical, formulaic stories. And because subsequent books or series are often sold based on a book proposal (as opposed to a finished manuscript), pantsers must learn to write an outline if they want their writing career to extend past their first book.

To find a balance between an overly rigid outline and utter chaos, adjust your outline as your story develops and you gain new insights. This is one of the reasons I avoid outlines in a long-list format: Like knocking down the first in a long line of dominoes, making one small change at the beginning of your outline will affect all the subsequent list items. Instead, I prefer modular outline techniques that allow for more flexibility as the story ebbs and flows. Here are a few of my favorites.

Scene Cards

One of best ways to map and organize a narrative book (i.e., a novel or a memoir) is to create scene cards. Each card represents one scene in the story—not a chapter or a sequence of scenes, just one scene. Each scene card needs four pieces of information: a title for that scene, the major players, the action, and the purpose. Any other information is extraneous for the purpose of this exercise and will only get in your way.

The Reaping

Major Players:	Katniss Everdeen, Peeta Mellark, Primrose Everdeen, Effie Trinket
The Action:	Prim's name is chosen from the tribute jar. Katniss volunteers to take her place. Peeta Mellark is chosen from the boys.
Purpose:	This scene forces Katniss into the Games. Katniss is not selected but chooses to volunteer to save her sister. She is the first volunteer tribute from her district, which sets her apart from other tributes.

The Reaping scene from *The Hunger Games* by Suzanne Collins

The title of your scene should be short and catchy. It should sum up the scene in such a way that the minute you read it you remember which scene it is and the overall gist of what happens. For example, "The Reaping Scene" in *The Hunger Games* is where Katniss Everdeen's sister, Prim, is chosen for the games and Katniss volunteers to take her place.

The second item on your scene card is the major players, or characters. You don't have to list *all* the characters, just the ones who play an essential part in that particular moment of the story. Crowds can be treated as a unit, and you don't need to mention individual background characters. In *The Hunger Games* example, the major players in the reaping scene are Katniss Everdeen, her sister, Prim, Peeta Mellark, and Effie Trinket. Yes, many other characters appear in this scene, but these four people are the only ones who matter in that moment. Everyone else is an extra in the District 12 crowd.

Next comes the action, or what happens in the scene. You should be able to sum this up in two or three sentences. In our example, Katniss and Prim stand in the square for the reaping. Prim's name is pulled from the jar, and Katniss volunteers to take her place. Then Peeta's name is chosen, and he joins Katniss on the stage.

Finally, we come to the most important piece of your scene card: the purpose. If you cannot state why a scene exists in your story, then chances are you don't need it. While there are no hard-and-fast rules, most scenes must either contribute to the plot or help develop a character, or both. If a scene is not doing at least one of those things, then it is likely not pulling its weight and you should examine whether you need it at all.

The reaping scene in *The Hunger Games* is an excellent example of a scene that both advances plot and develops character. This moment not only kicks off the action and sets important events in motion, but it also forces our protagonist, Katniss, to make a choice. Katniss is not chosen for the games, which means that she must volunteer to take her sister's place. This might seem like a minor detail, but *The Hunger Games* would be a very different story if Katniss's name had been picked and she had been thrown into the games against her will. Instead, by taking her sister's place, Katniss chooses to embark on the journey that comprises the rest of the novel and the two sequels that follow. This scene exists because it not only moves the plot forward but also establishes Katniss as an active agent in the story.

Scene cards allow you to take stock of your novel even if you don't yet have all the pieces in place. You can create cards for scenes you've already written and scenes you have yet to write. Once you have a stash of cards, you can play with the order and get a sense of your story's trajectory. This outline method is especially useful for writers who don't like to draft their book from beginning to end and prefer to jump between different scenes. It also gives you flexibility to change direction if your book takes an unexpected turn. Instead of throwing away an entire draft, you can eliminate the scenes that are no longer relevant and keep the scenes that still fit.

Mind Maps

I discovered mind-mapping in a creativity seminar I took as a psychology grad student. Until then I had always used linear outline methods (I. A, II. B, etc.), but when I learned how to mind-map I never took notes the same way again. Mind-mapping has been instrumental in helping me organize and structure my ideas.

Here's how it works. First, write the title or broad topic in a circle at the center of a page. Then draw branches extending from the center circle and write the main subtopics on those lines. Separate your subtopics even further by splitting those lines into even more branches. You can also include thought bubbles for ideas and speech bubbles for quotes. You can even doodle or sketch images to supplement the ideas you're mapping. Here's the mind map I used to organize the main topics of DIY MFA.

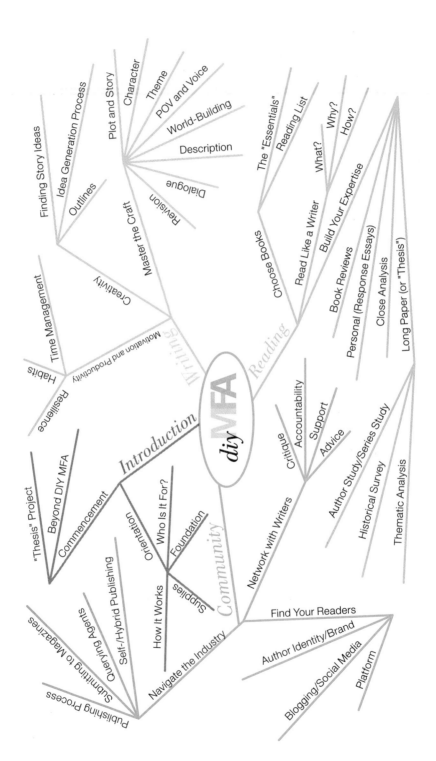

Mind Map of DIY MFA

Mind maps have several advantages. They allow you to capture a huge project or concept on just one page, which forces you to distill your ideas to the most fundamental elements. When you look at your mind map, you'll be able to see the entire scope of the project at a glance. Also, because mind maps aren't sequential, they don't place more significance on one aspect of your project over another. In a linear outline, the items at the top of the list inevitably get the most attention. A mind map outline allows you to see different elements of your book side by side. This approach can help you see connections between elements of your book that you may have otherwise missed.

One caveat is that mind maps do not lend themselves to narratives. Because of its categorical nature, this technique tends to work better for outlining prescriptive nonfiction (i.e., a how-to book) where you split a concept into subtopics or categories. Although mind maps might be clunky for capturing a narrative *story*, novelists and memoirists can use it for world-building or keeping track of different groups of characters. For instance, you might not be able to capture *The Hunger Games* story in a mind map, but the technique can come in handy for keeping track of the twelve districts. You can also use mind maps to organize content for your author website or to plan aspects of your author identity (i.e., brand), which we'll discuss in a later section.

Story Sketch

The story sketch is not so much an outline technique as a tool that captures the overall essence of your project. This tool is especially useful for bringing critique partners up to speed if they are unfamiliar with your book. By including a story sketch at the beginning of a submission, you give your critique partners the information they need to make sense of your story even if they haven't read earlier chapters.

Start by writing the flap copy, or the elevator pitch for your story. This is the summary you find on the inside flap or back cover of a book, and it gives readers just enough of the premise to entice them to read the book. Next, list your five most important characters and give a brief description of each one. Then give a short description of the story's world and narration, and choose a theme song or soundtrack for your story. Finally, sum up your story in a fortune cookie saying. For example, the fortune cookie fortune for *The Wizard of Oz* is "There's no place like home." This exercise forces you to boil down your story to its simplest, most fundamental element: the theme.

 *Story Sketch*

Title of story: ___The Wizard of Oz_ (movie version)___

Flap Copy:___Dorothy has always dreamed of leaving Kansas to go someplace "over the___
__rainbow." When a tornado sweeps her house to the land of Oz, all she wants is to find___
__a way back home. Will Dorothy make it to the Emerald City to see the Wizard of Oz?___
__Will she defeat the Wicked Witch, and will she get back to Kansas?___

Important Characters
(Name)   (Description)

___Dorothy Gale___   Lives in Kansas with Uncle Henry, Aunt Em, and her little___
                                      __dog Toto. She dreams of leaving Kansas and going "over___
                                      __the rainbow."___

Scarecrow, Tinman,
___and Cowardly Lion___   These are three friends who join Dorothy to see the wizard.___
                                      __The Scarecrow wants to ask the wizard for a brain, the___
                                      __Tinman wants a heart, and the Lion wants courage.___

Wicked Witch
___of the West___   Dorothy's house landed on her sister and killed her, leaving___
                                      __behind a pair of ruby slippers. Dorothy now has the slippers,___
                                      __and the Witch wants desperately to get them back.___

___Wizard of Oz___   The Wizard lives in the Emerald City and supposedly has___
                                      __the power to give Dorothy and her friends all the things they___
                                      __want. It turns out he's not as powerful as he appears ...___

_____   _____
                                  _____
                                  _____

World: _Kansas is drab in sepia tonies, while Oz seems magical in its glorious Technicolor.___

Narration:_Third-person omniscient, but mostly following Dorothy's POV.___

Fortune Cookie:

> There's no place like home.

Music:_ "Somewhere Over the Rainbow" performed by Judy Garland___

Images: (Sketch or attach images to reverse side. Include a color swatch if you have one.)

Story Sketch of *The Wizard of Oz*

Story Map

The New York City Subway system was the inspiration for this next outlining method. I'm a New Yorker, born and raised, and subways have always been a big part of my life. When I needed to piece together different subplots and story threads for my novel, I chose the most logical strategy and drew my outline like a subway system. In this way, the story map method was born.

Each subway line represents a different subplot or story thread. The dots (subway stops) represent individual scenes. Black dots (local stops) are scenes that apply only to one storyline. White dots (express stops) are scenes where two or more plot threads intersect. When you map your story in this way, you can tease apart the different threads and test each one for pacing, buildup, and tension. It can be hard to juggle multiple story threads at the same time, but when you use this mapping technique, you can isolate the main plot or one of the subplots and examine it separate from the others.

To create a story map, begin by writing out your scenes. If you've already created scene cards, use those. Then figure out the plot threads, thematic elements, or images you want to track in your story map. Short stories often have only one main thread, but novels can have a main plot plus several intertwined subplots. For each of your plot threads, you need to determine the dramatic question: the question or conflict that drives the story. Your main plot thread will have a Major Dramatic Question (MDQ), while subplots will have Lesser Dramatic Questions (LDQs). Knowing these questions will help you boil down each plotline to one central conflict. As you'll learn in later chapters, conflict is the driving force of your story. If your character doesn't want something, or if there's no obstacle in her way, the story has no point. When you use the story map technique, conflict takes center stage in your outline.

Once you have assigned scenes to different story threads, you're ready to draw your map. Here's an example from *The Hunger Games*.

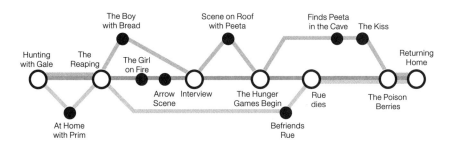

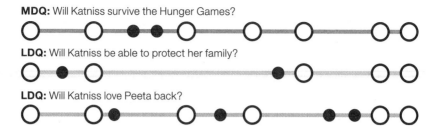

MDQ: Will Katniss survive the Hunger Games?

LDQ: Will Katniss be able to protect her family?

LDQ: Will Katniss love Peeta back?

Story Map of *The Hunger Games* by Suzanne Collins

Mood Boards

This isn't so much an outline technique as it is a method for capturing the mood of your book. You won't see a chapter-by-chapter breakdown in a mood board, but you will get a sense of the overall feel of the story, the characters, and the setting. When I worked in the toy industry, we created mood boards for all our major products. We even had a huge corkboard that served as a communal mood board in the hall outside the studio. Designers would post product ideas on the board, including magazine clippings, prototype pictures, and material samples. Other team members would walk by the board and add their own inspiration or comments via sticky notes. After a few days of walk-by brainstorming, the designer in charge of that project would have a pretty good idea of what the product was and how to build it.

I still use mood boards as part of my creative process, but instead of capturing the mood and look of a physical product, I now use this technique to convey the mood of my story and capture the world of the book. In a pinch, you can use tools like Pinterest or Instagram to create a mood board, but seriously, nothing beats good old-fashioned scissors and glue.

MAKE A MOOD BOARD

Set aside an hour (and only one hour).
    Grab a stack of old magazines, fabric scraps, paint chips (you can get these free at paint stores), and any other materials that might convey the mood of your story. Cut out images and lay them out on a large piece of paper or poster board. Arrange the images until you strike a nice visual bal-

ance that captures the mood or feel of your story, and then glue everything down. Hang your mood board in your writing space to inspire and motivate you while you work.

TIP: Snap a photo of your mood board and use it as your desktop wallpaper. This will help you get in the mood for working on your book and help you stay focused. Even better, make your mood board the lock screen for your smartphone or tablet so that whenever you pick up your mobile device, you'll think about your book.

Now that you have a solid understanding of outline techniques, you're ready to start applying them to different stages of your writing process. Most writers use outlines to plan their books, but there are other ways to use these techniques. You can use your outline as a diagnostic tool while you write your first draft, or you can extract an outline from a finished draft. You can even extract outlines from books you read and get an in-depth look at their story and structure. We covered many techniques in this chapter, each with different strengths. As you iterate and develop your writing process, you will find a combination that works for you.

— 08 —

Create Compelling Characters

Any discussion of writing craft must begin with characters. They are the heart and soul of your story. Without them, your story is nothing more than a sequence of events. Characters give us someone to root for (or against) and make us care about the story. They make the story personal.

Characters also give us a lens through which we experience that story. We can read about World War II, study the different battles, and watch video clips from the era, but those events take on a more powerful meaning when we see them through the eyes of Liesel Meminger, the young protagonist in Markus Zusak's *The Book Thief*. Similarly, we can read about the estate and inheritance laws of Regency Period England, but those details come to life and ring far more true when we see how they affect the lives of the Bennet sisters in *Pride and Prejudice* by Jane Austen. Plot points move a story along, but characters bring it to life.

Create a Cast of Characters

Your cast of characters includes the people, animals, or other sentient beings who populate the world of your story. While these characters are unique to your story, certain archetypes appear again and again regardless of genre or category. To create engaging characters, it's useful to understand these archetypes and how they operate within your story.

The Protagonist

The protagonist is perhaps the most important character in every story—the star of the show, whom your story centers around. Every story must have a protagonist. Without one you don't have a story, just a newsreel or series of facts. The protagonist is your window, your entry point into the narrative.

Readers need a single character to care about and focus on, so a story usually features only one true protagonist. Even books with multiple viewpoints often center around one character who drives that story forward. The only exceptions are long epic series, such as the high fantasy that sprawls across multiple kingdoms or the historical family saga that spans multiple generations. Yet, even in these books, you'll often find that each volume in the series or each plot thread has one—and only one—character at the center.

Your protagonist can be one of two basic archetypes: the ordinary Joe (or Jane) and the larger-than-life hero. The ordinary Joe is an unlikely hero, a "regular guy" thrown into a wild journey. The larger-than-life protagonist on the other hand, is a "chosen one" singled out for a particular adventure. These archetypes are opposite sides of the same coin, and as you will see, the strengths of one are the weaknesses of the other.

The Ordinary Joe (or Jane) Protagonist

This archetype is an everyman character, an ordinary person pulled into extraordinary circumstances. He is normal—even boring—when measured against the norms of the story's world. Ordinary Joes often resist change and adventure and usually get pulled into the story against their will. Examples of this archetype include Bilbo Baggins from *The Hobbit* by J.R.R. Tolkien, Wilbur the humble pig from *Charlotte's Web* by E.B. White, Katniss Everdeen from The Hunger Games series, and Elizabeth Bennet from *Pride and Prejudice.*

Notice that while these characters seem "normal," we see hints of their unique qualities early in the story, and it becomes clear that they may not be as ordinary as they first seem. These hints are crucial because we need to see that these characters have the potential to change throughout the story. The writer must establish the ordinary Joe's special qualities in the beginning so that when the protagonist does something astonishing later, her actions do not feel out of character.

In *The Hobbit,* we learn in the first chapters that Bilbo Baggins is not a dimwit. Thrown into the company of a pack of dwarves, Bilbo's cleverness is a sharp contrast to the burly strength of his counterparts. From the beginning of the quest, it is clear that the dwarves might have the brawn but Bilbo is the brains of their operation. This quality becomes crucial when Bilbo must outsmart bigger and stronger characters—like the trio of trolls—in order to save his friends.

Other ordinary Joe characters also exhibit special characteristics. Katniss Everdeen might at first seem like an ordinary girl from an impoverished district, but she has a deadly aim with a bow and arrow and proves to be a more formidable opponent in the Hunger Games than anyone anticipated. Elizabeth Bennet has the "fine eyes" that capture Mr. Darcy's attention and a lively spirit that captivates his heart. Wilbur the pig is able to win Charlotte's friendship and manages to save the egg sac containing her children at the end of *Charlotte's Web*. It turns out that ordinary Joes are, in fact, far from ordinary and are able to do extraordinary things if given the right motivation.

Notice, too, that a protagonist may start out as an ordinary Joe but can morph into the opposite archetype as the story develops. Katniss Everdeen begins as an ordinary Joe archetype in The Hunger Games series, but as the trilogy develops she transforms into the Mockingjay and becomes the symbol of the revolution. At several points in the trilogy's story arc Katniss resists this new role, but despite her efforts to stay ordinary she eventually becomes a larger-than-life hero.

The Larger-Than-Life Protagonist

At the other end of the spectrum is the larger-than-life protagonist: the classic hero who can face down any obstacle single-handedly. This archetype includes classical heroes like Heracles and Odysseus and comic book superheroes like Superman and Batman. Contemporary literature features larger-than-life characters in thrillers (the tough-guy protagonist), crime novels (the sharp-witted detective), and commercial women's fiction (the "girl who has everything"). Examples of larger-than-life characters include Harry Potter from the series by J.K. Rowling, Odysseus from Homer's *The Odyssey*, Sherlock Holmes from the stories of Sir Arthur Conan Doyle, and Emma Woodhouse from *Emma* by Jane Austen.

Unlike the ordinary Joe who must show early hints of his extraordinary qualities, the larger-than-life protagonist must have some vulnerability, some hint of "normal." Screenwriters show this vulnerability in what they call the "pet the dog" moment. This is a scene that demonstrates the character's potential vulnerability or flawed nature. Imagine a tough-guy protagonist in a shoot-'em-up movie. Our hero is fighting a bunch of bad guys when he suddenly finds himself alone in a dark alley. He ducks behind a dumpster to reload his gun and hears a noise. He whips around, gun at the ready, and sees a scraggly dog poke its head out from behind a trash can. He lowers his gun and extends his hand to the dog, who trots across the alley to sniff and lick his fingers. The hero *pets the dog* and then says something like, "Go on, get outta here buddy. There's gonna be trouble." The dog scampers away just as bullets start to fly, and the hero goes back to shooting up bad guys.

This type of scene is so common in action movies that it's become a cliché. For our purposes, however, a "pet the dog" moment doesn't need to involve an actual dog; it just needs to show that your otherwise-perfect character has an imperfection or vulnerable side. Oftentimes, however, this vulnerability doesn't appear in one isolated scene but slowly unfolds throughout the story. In many cases, while the protagonist is seemingly perfect at the beginning of the story, we see hints of her flaws and vulnerability as the story develops.

Unlike Elizabeth Bennet, whose future is precarious, Emma Woodhouse from Jane Austen's *Emma* lives in a position of great privilege and security. Her father is wealthy, and she is pretty and desirable. Any wealthy, eligible bachelor would be thrilled to court her. While Emma is clever and charming, her overconfident know-it-all nature gets her into trouble. Emma thinks she knows what is best for everyone around her and not only misjudges many of her acquaintances but also gives poor advice to her friends.

In one "pet the dog" moment in the novel, Emma shows bad judgment when she advises her friend Harriet to reject Mr. Martin. Thinking Mr. Martin is beneath her friend, Emma encourages Harriet to pursue the far more eligible Mr. Elton, but it turns out he is not interested in Harriet at all and instead wants to court Emma. Not only must Emma ultimately reject Mr. Elton's affections but she must also accept that her bad advice has caused her friend's heartbreak. Emma does not learn this lesson overnight. It takes several other gaffes and poor decisions before she mends her ways.

Sometimes larger-than-life characters are predestined to do something important. In the Harry Potter series, we know from the first book that Harry is no ordinary wizard child. He is "the boy who lived," the infant who defied the powers of the evil wizard Voldemort. People expect great things from him, and as we later learn, he is destined to save the wizarding world from He-Who-Shall-Not-Be-Named.

Not all larger-than-life characters are preordained to be heroes. Odysseus, for instance, is distinct from other classical heroes because he is not the child of a god. He might be a distant descendant of Hermes (messenger god) and Aeolus (controller of the winds), but he is not a demigod like Heracles or invincible like Achilles. Instead, Odysseus has a cunning and calculating mind, and he relies on his wits to save him from several sticky predicaments. Odysseus devises the horse decoy to help the Greeks breach the impenetrable walls of Troy, and he later uses that same quick thinking to blind and escape the giant cyclops, Polyphemus.

While Odysseus's cleverness nearly defies belief, he has one tremendous flaw: He falls asleep and leaves his crew unattended at the most inopportune moments. In Book 10 of *The Odyssey*, when his fleet is within eyeshot of his homeland, he falls asleep at the helm of his ship. While he is asleep, his crew opens the bag of winds given to them by Aeolus. With those winds unleashed, the fleet is flung across the sea, and the crew must start the journey home again. Odysseus and his men are later marooned for a month on the island where Helios (the sun god) keeps his sacred cows. The men are starving, and Odysseus ventures inland to pray. He falls asleep *yet again* (you would think he'd have learned his lesson the first time), and his men kill and eat the sacred cows in his absence. As punishment for this crime, Odysseus's ships are destroyed in a storm, leaving him the lone survivor.

Larger-than-life characters do not need to be magical or heroic. Sherlock Holmes is a larger-than-life character who does not wield any supernatural abilities, yet his powers of deduction are almost superhuman. In the first paragraph of *The Adventures of Sherlock Holmes*, Watson describes him as "the most perfect reasoning and observing machine that the world has seen." Although he has an extraordinary level of intelligence, Sherlock's arrogance and lack of emotion make him an unlikable protagonist. In fact, it is often difficult for the reader to sympathize with him, which is likely why the author chose to narrate the stories through Dr. Watson's viewpoint. This choice in narration softens Sherlock's edge and allows the reader to see his otherwise difficult personality through the eyes of a friend who likes and respects him.

The "Opposite Is Possible" Theory

In order to make a protagonist—or any character, for that matter—feel real to your reader, you must show that he has the potential to take on opposite traits from those he displays at the beginning of the story. This sets up the possibility for the protagonist to change. It might seem counterintuitive, as if you're dragging your protagonist out of character, but that's not the case.

Your job isn't to make the character the total opposite of who he is but to show that the *opposite is possible*.

This "Opposite Is Possible" theory allows both ordinary Joe and larger-than-life characters room to grow and develop throughout the story. Remember that your story is an emotional journey as well as a physical one. The protagonist must end up different from how he started. In some stories this journey is obvious. Harry Potter begins as an outsider in the wizarding world, one who is unsure of his own abilities, but by the end of *The Deathly Hallows*, he is able to lead an army against the Death Eaters and sacrifices himself for the greater good. The story confirms that Harry is, in fact, the chosen one destined to defeat Voldemort.

In other stories the change is not as clear. It might appear that little has changed in the life of the protagonist and that she has come full circle and has ended up in the same place she started. Even in such stories, the insights the character gains from the journey transform her into a different person. In Nathaniel Hawthorne's *Young Goodman Brown*, the protagonist ends up in the same place he started: the same town, the same house, the same wife. Yet after a tumultuous night in the woods where he witnesses a witch meeting and faces the Devil himself, Goodman Brown is no longer the same man. He is no longer optimistic and hopeful. Hardened by what he discovered in the woods, he sees everything around him enshrouded by darkness. It's ambiguous whether the events of that fateful night were real or just imagined, but it doesn't matter. What's important is that the protagonist has changed—in this case perhaps for the worst—and that he possesses this gloomy and suspicious demeanor for the rest of his life.

Whether your character is an ordinary Joe who rises to the occasion and does something extraordinary or a larger-than-life hero who shows a vulnerable side, the key to bringing your character to life is to make sure that the *opposite is possible* and that your character can change.

The Supporting Cast

As we've discussed, every story has one—and only one—protagonist. Everyone else is a supporting character and exists for a single purpose: to support the character development of the protagonist. This is why I insist on call them *supporting* characters rather than secondary or side characters. These characters are not necessarily subordinate to the protagonist; in fact they may occupy just as much space on the page. Nor are your supporting cast members "fillers" for your story. They have a purpose: to support and affect your protagonist's journey.

While it might be obvious to you, the writer, that the protagonist is the lead in your story and that the others play a supporting role, the supporting characters don't actually *know* that they're supporting characters. Everyone in your story believes she is the protagonist of her own life. You don't wake up in the morning and think, *Gee, how can I be a supporting character in someone else's life today?* Why should it be any different with your characters? This distinction is crucial. Each supporting character must behave as though she thinks she is the protagonist, even if she plays a supporting role.

With this in mind, let's explore five supporting character archetypes and the function they typically serve in a story. You don't need to represent all of these types—or any, for that matter—in your book, but it's useful to know who they are and what roles they play.

The Villain

Most people use the terms *villain* and *antagonist* interchangeably, but they are not the same. While all villains are antagonists, not all antagonists are villains. An antagonist is a force or entity that is at odds with the protagonist. That antagonist can be anything: another person, nature, technology, society, the supernatural, or even the protagonist himself. But only when the antagonist is another human being can he be considered a villain.

When the antagonist is not a villain but a faceless force, like a massive storm or a pack of hungry dinosaurs, the writer must work harder to make the reader care about the conflict in the story. Nonhuman antagonists don't have an agenda or a justification for all the harm they cause. In *The Perfect Storm* by Sebastian Junger, the antagonist is a combination of extraordinary weather conditions that happened to coincide. The storm doesn't have a dastardly evil plan, nor is it trying to kill people. It's just there. Similarly, in *Jurassic Park* by Michael Crichton, the dinosaurs might be the main threat to the characters, but they aren't chasing the humans because of some ulterior motive—they're just looking for lunch. These nonhuman antagonists pose a challenge for the writer because, while they create danger in the story, they don't give the reader somebody to root against.

When you personify that antagonist and make it a villain, suddenly the conflict becomes more interesting, more personal. A villain might do evil things, but on some level he believes his actions are justified. This adds dimension to the conflict because no longer is the protagonist 100 percent "good" and the villain 100 percent "bad." Now we're dealing in shades of gray, and the reader might even begin to sympathize with the villain or at the very least understand his perspective.

One such multifaceted villain is President Snow in The Hunger Games trilogy. At the beginning of the first book, it seems that Katniss is the hero and Snow (along with the tyrannical government he leads) is the obvious villain. We know little about him except that he claims to run the infamous Games as a way to preserve peace in the country of Panem.

As the story develops in the later books, we begin to see the extent of President Snow's manipulative nature, but we also get hints of his vulnerabilities. We learn that he has an illness and that he uses white roses to mask the sour smell. We get hints that his power is not nearly as absolute as he would like and that he manipulates the system because his control over the districts is tenuous at best. However, it is only in the final act of *Mockingjay*—after the Capitol has fallen and Snow has been captured—that the tables seem to turn.

When Katniss speaks to Snow in the greenhouse, he continues his attempts to manipulate her, but she begins to realize that he is not her only enemy and that things are not nearly as black-and-white as they seemed. It turns out that President Coin (the leader of District 13) may also have been manipulating Katniss and that Coin's seemingly selfless drive to liberate the districts has actually been spurred by her desire to claim power for herself. Katniss realizes that while President Snow is still power hungry and manipulative, he is not her only enemy and may even be the lesser of two evils. In the pivotal execution scene—the climax of the entire series—when Katniss is supposed to shoot Snow, she turns her arrow on Coin instead.

A villain can add complexity to a story, but what do you do if your main antagonist is not a villain? How do you create those same layers and dimensions of conflict? One solution is to use a "day-to-day bad guy" to give the antagonist a face. This day-to-day bad guy is not the primary source of conflict in the story, but enhances that conflict and gives the reader a character to root against. The conflict between the protagonist and the day-to-day bad guy might even mirror the larger conflict of the story.

Draco Malfoy in the Harry Potter series is one such day-to-day bad guy. In the first book of the series, *Harry Potter and the Sorcerer's Stone*, the main antagonist (Voldemort) is a disembodied spirit and plays a relatively small role compared to his presence in the later books. In fact, for the first three books of the Harry Potter series, Voldemort hardly appears at all, and instead Draco Malfoy serves as a major source of conflict. In the beginning of the series, Harry's conflict with Draco carries high stakes for him and his friends. Winning the House Cup or beating Slytherin House at Quidditch seem vitally important in the early books, and Draco is often the main obstacle who blocks Harry and his friends from their goals. As the series develops, however, Voldemort regains his human form, and suddenly the competition with Draco feels less significant. Even though Draco continues to be at odds with Harry throughout the series, he becomes a less important adversary. Using Draco Malfoy as a day-to-day villain, J.K. Rowling gives her readers a concrete character they "love to hate," at least until Voldemort takes center stage as the primary bad guy.

The Love Interest

The love interest is a versatile character because, depending on the genre, this archetype can play very different roles. In romance or women's fiction, the love interest is part of the central conflict of the story—will the heroine get the guy in the end? In other genres, though, the love story is often a subplot that enriches the central conflict. Let's look at two examples of the love interest: Mr. Darcy in *Pride and Prejudice*, and Peeta Mellark in The Hunger Games series.

In *Pride and Prejudice*, the love story between Elizabeth and Mr. Darcy is central to the plot. In this book, the major dramatic question—the question that drives the story—is whether Elizabeth and Mr. Darcy will fall in love, and how their love story will unfold, especially since they hate each other at the beginning. Since the book is a romance at its core, the love story is enough to carry the reader's interest throughout.

The Hunger Games trilogy presents a different situation. Here, the love triangle between Katniss, Peeta, and Gale is secondary to the main thrust of the story. Readers want to know if Katniss will survive the Games and save the districts from the oppressive Capitol. Whether she gets the guy—or which guy she gets—is not as important. In *The Hunger Games,* Peeta adds an extra wrinkle to the main survival thread of the story. It is no mistake that author Suzanne Collins has Peeta admit his love for Katniss during the television interview the night before they enter the arena. Until this point, it has been easy for us to root for Katniss, to hope she wins the Games. We haven't gotten to know most of the other tributes, so it doesn't matter as much that Katniss must kill the others in order to survive. The story becomes far more complicated when Peeta admits his love for Katniss, especially since she believes he has an ulterior motive for his declaration. According to the rules only one tribute can win the Hunger Games, which means that these star-crossed lovers ultimately can't be together. This raises the stakes of the book and makes the survival story more interesting. In this case, even though the romance is a subplot, it enhances and adds tension to the central conflict of the books.

The BFF or Sidekick

Including the Best Friend or Sidekick archetype is a great way to counterbalance your protagonist. In most books, BFF characters have qualities that complement the protagonist's strengths and make up for his weaknesses. In the Harry Potter series, for instance, Hermione Granger and Ron Weasley both demonstrate strengths that Harry does not have but sorely needs in order to face Voldemort. Harry might be brave and pure of heart, with a strong moral compass, but he lacks cleverness. This is where Hermione complements him perfectly; whenever Harry needs a crucial piece of information, Hermione has the right book, reference, or legend at her fingertips. Ron, on the other hand, provides comic relief and lightens the tone of the story, especially when Harry is having one of his moody, introspective moments. In his dark periods, his best buddy, Ron, helps raise the mood.

The BFF archetype is often split into a pair of characters so that the protagonist has not one but two sidekicks or best friends. This is important. The protagonist plus two BFF characters make for a more interesting dynamic. In general, an odd number of characters tends to create more tension on the page than an even number. It creates "odd man out" scenarios in which two characters are in conflict and the third must take sides. We see this dynamic from the beginning of the Harry Potter series: Harry and Ron quickly become close friends, while Hermione is the know-it-all dork at the mercy of their mockery. It is only when a troll invades the castle and Hermione takes the blame that Harry and Ron begin treating her as a friend. In later books this two-against-one dynamic returns several times, always with a different character as the odd one out.

Throughout the Harry Potter series, Hermione and Ron are never far from Harry. As BFFs, they add layers of complexity and interest to the otherwise lonely journey Harry must make.

The Mentor

This archetype is one of the easiest to spot, and also one that most often trips up novice writers. The mentor character imparts wisdom and advice to the protagonist, often sharing important tidbits of backstory in the process. Examples include Gandalf in *The Hobbit*, Obi-Wan Kenobi in *Star Wars*, and Dumbledore in the Harry Potter series. While there is nothing wrong with this archetype in general, writers sometimes depend too much on these characters to convey important information to the reader. The mentor does not exist to give the reader information, but to advise the *character* in the story. You can use these mentor moments to sneak in crucial information that you wouldn't otherwise be able to share with your readers—but don't overdo it. Most writers overuse mentor moments to plug up plot holes, and doing so results in clunky stories.

These mentor moments—I call them "Dumbledore moments" because all seven books in the Harry Potter series have at least one—work best when the mentor has flaws and is fallible. Dumbledore, the Hogwarts headmaster and the epitome of a mentor archetype, is far from perfect. He tries to protect Harry, and in doing so he often withholds important information from him. He is also not invincible. The cursed ring cripples his hand before *The Half-Blood Prince* (Book 6), and eventually he dies.

In the first five books of the series, the Dumbledore moments fall toward the end of each volume. Harry and his friends have saved the day and escaped peril, but before they head home for summer vacation Dumbledore gives Harry a pep talk and reveals an important magical secret that explains some aspect of the book. *The Half-Blood Prince* is practically a series of mentor moments, building up to the climactic scene in which Dumbledore is killed. This is the only book in the series that places mentor moments early in the time line, because these moments set up the twist at the climax. In *The Deathly Hallows* (Book 7), just when we think it is impossible for Dumbledore to give his classic mentor moment speech, he *comes back from the dead* and meets Harry in a purgatory-like place to deliver his final pep talk. The author is only able to pull this off because she has fully fleshed out Dumbledore's character and has made the reader care about him. It took the author seven books to build that character and earn the right to bring him back from the dead to deliver his final mentor moment.

Mentor characters can be useful for the writer because they provide a way to explain things that the reader might not otherwise be able to discover. In the Harry Potter books the Dumbledore moments work well because Harry is a newcomer to magic and is unfamiliar with the intricacies of the wizarding world. It makes sense that Dumbledore would step in and explain things to Harry from time to time. The problems arise when a mentor becomes too perfect or infallible, or if that character conveniently explains away all plot holes or complications. This is where the mentor archetype goes from being useful to being a crutch or, worse, an excuse for lazy writing.

The Fool

The fool is a fascinating archetype and dates as far back as the plays of ancient Greece. In those days, the fool's role was filled by the chorus, who would appear throughout the play to add commentary and subtext to the story on the stage. Later, Shakespeare turned the fool archetype into an actual character in several of his plays, such as Feste, the clown in *Twelfth Night*, and the Fool in *King Lear.*

Don't be fooled by the name of this archetype. The fool is usually not a *fool,* but rather the voice of reason in the story. His job is to say the things that the protagonist does not want to know but most needs to hear. In the Shakespearean examples, the fool uses humor and farce to show that the protagonist has made a mistake. A contemporary example is Haymitch in The Hunger Games trilogy. He is not afraid to talk about the harsh realities Katniss and Peeta will face in the arena, and while he often comes across as a bumbling drunk, he is actually the voice of sanity and reason.

Now that you know the different archetypes and how they operate in your story, it's time to talk about how you can bring your characters to life on the page. The next chapter will show you a four-part system to help you do just that, using a simple diagnostic technique.

09

Bring Those Characters to Life

When I first began to teach writing, I collected an arsenal of examples to show different facets of a character's development. One day I stumbled on "The Yellow Wallpaper" by Charlotte Perkins Gilman and realized that this short story is the quintessential example of bringing a character to life on the page. You can get this text as a bonus by signing up with your e-mail address at DIYMFA.com/thebook, and I strongly recommend you print it out and read it before you proceed with this chapter. (There will be spoilers. Read the story first.)

"The Yellow Wallpaper," first published in 1891, is a fictionalized version of Gilman's own struggles with mental illness. Its publication was met with outrage from the medical community, in part because of the realistic story it portrays. The protagonist, a young married woman, falls ill with a "temporary nervous depression—a slight hysterical tendency." We learn that she has a baby and her husband is largely absent. It's likely that this new mother is suffering from postpartum depression, though the medical community of the time labeled all such mood disorders "hysteria," the typical treatment for which was a "rest cure." The patient would spend most of her days in quiet, restful isolation, engaging in as little intellectual activity as possible. Of course, knowing what we know now, this prescription probably would have worsened her depression rather than alleviated it.

In the short story, the protagonist's husband (a doctor) prescribes this rest cure and sends his wife to an ancestral country estate. We get hints throughout the story that there is something mysterious, even sinister, about that house. Our main character spends hours in solitude and is forbidden to engage in any creative endeavor. She's allowed no company. No writing. Nothing. As the hours and days drag on, the protagonist keeps a diary in secret where she recounts her treatment. This diary becomes a record of her mental deterioration as she slowly unravels.

The "TADA!" Method for Showing Character

Writing teachers instruct us to "show" rather than "tell," but they rarely explain what showing is and—more important—*how* to do it. "Telling" is when a writer skims the surface of the story and gives a summary of what happens. "Showing" is when the writer digs into a scene and brings that moment to life. When a writer shows the story, readers feel as if they're right beside the character, watching the scene unfold.

The TADA! method is a tool I developed to help me remember how to show my characters and make them come alive. The acronym stands for Thoughts, Action, Dialogue, and Appearance. When you combine the right amount of each component … TADA! You've showed your character.

Don't feel as though you need to use all four elements in equal amounts for every scene. Some scenes might be more introspective, showing your character's thoughts and very little action, dialogue, or appearance. Other scenes might be action packed and full of conversation. The TADA! elements aren't items you check off a list. Instead, think of them as tools in your toolbox ready and waiting when you need them.

T Is for Thoughts

Thoughts include both what the character is thinking and what she is feeling. In "The Yellow Wallpaper," most of the narrative takes place inside the character's head. Because the story is told in first-person point of view (through the protagonist's diary), every word is filtered through her thoughts.

> It is very seldom that mere ordinary people like John and myself secure ancestral halls for the summer.
>
> A colonial mansion, a hereditary estate, I would say a haunted house, and reach the height of romantic felicity—but that would be asking too much of fate!
>
> Still I will proudly declare that there is something queer about it.
>
> Else, why should it be let so cheaply? And why have stood so long untenanted?

From the first lines, we see that our protagonist has a vivid imagination, an inquisitive mind, and a somewhat quirky personality. Even the way she describes the house and imagines it haunted reflects her creative spirit. But she reins in that side of her personality and corrects herself, thinking, "but that would be asking too much of fate!" Notice that the character both *shows* and *tells* us her thoughts. When she states: "I will proudly declare that there is something queer about it," she is telling us what she thinks about the house. This is the version of her thoughts that she has crafted and filtered for the reader, almost as though it's been rehearsed and prepared beforehand. But when we read, "Else, why should it be let so cheaply?" we aren't getting the protagonist's account of what she thinks; we are seeing her actual thoughts. This is an important distinction, because sometimes what a point-of-view character *says* she thinks and what she *actually thinks* can be two very different things.

The last line in this opening passage lets us infer an additional layer: a feeling. This character is worried, maybe even afraid. This hint of fear is not explicit on the page, but it's implied by the questions in the last line. The character is trying to put on a brave face. She suspects something is wrong with this house, but she dismisses it, merely stating there is "something queer about it." Still, her deeper fear betrays her, and in the next line she can't help but wonder why the house has stood empty for so long.

A Is for Action

The first *A* stands for action. In "The Yellow Wallpaper" the protagonist spends much of her time alone, and her only action is writing in her diary when no one is nearby to see her doing it. However, from the beginning of the story, the wallpaper seems like a character as well, and despite being an inanimate object, it plays an active role.

> I never saw a worse paper in my life.
>
> One of those sprawling flamboyant patterns committing every artistic sin. It is dull enough to confuse the eye in following, pronounced enough to constantly irritate and provoke study, and when you follow the lame uncertain curves for a little distance they suddenly commit suicide—plunge off at outrageous angles, destroy themselves in unheard of contradictions.

The wallpaper is not introduced with a description of its color or overall appearance. Instead, the author gives us action. Look at all the verbs in her description: "confuse the eye" and "irritate and provoke study." The curves of the pattern "suddenly commit suicide"; they "plunge off at outrageous angles" and "destroy themselves." This active description personifies the wallpaper. Only afterwards do we get any description of the color or how the paper looks. The author makes it clear: The paper is an active element first and foremost; its appearance is secondary.

The wallpaper becomes even more active as the story develops. A few journal entries later, our protagonist begins to see something take shape in the wallpaper, something that looks "like a woman stooping down and creeping about behind that pattern." The wallpaper's actions also become more aggressive. The protagonist says the paper's pattern "slaps you in the face, knocks you down, and tramples upon you. It is like a bad dream." While the protagonist is rather passive and inactive throughout the story, the wallpaper is almost confrontational. The more the protagonist stares at the paper, the more it seems to seep into and infect her mind.

As the protagonist's mental state deteriorates further, she makes another discovery: The wallpaper appears to move because the woman in the pattern is shaking it. At this point, the paper has clearly come alive as a character. Its activity is not just a fancy way of describing the hideous pattern. It seems to have a mind of its own—the woman in the pattern *wants* to get out. (Later in this chapter, you'll see that this want is a crucial element in a story, one that bridges the gap between the character and the plot.) The paper's desire comes to light in this crucial moment:

> I really have discovered something at last.
>
> Through watching so much at night, when it changes so, I have finally found out.
>
> The front pattern does move—and no wonder! The woman behind shakes it!
>
> Sometimes I think there are a great many women behind, and sometimes only one, and she crawls around fast, and her crawling shakes it all over.
>
> Then in the very bright spots she keeps still, and in the very shady spots she just takes hold of the bars and shakes them hard.
>
> And she is all the time trying to climb through.

As the story reaches its astonishing climax, our protagonist becomes more active. She develops a kinship with the woman in the wallpaper and begins to mirror that woman's actions until she finally tears the paper down.

D Is for Dialogue

The *D* for dialogue represents everything the character says in the story. Early in "The Yellow Wallpaper," we see very little dialogue on the page. Instead, we get only snippets as the protagonist recounts what was said. From the beginning we see that the protagonist is at odds with her husband. They argue about everything: her "rest cure" in the countryside, even the room of the house where she is confined.

> "You know the place is doing you good," he said, "and really, dear, I don't care to renovate the house just for a three months' rental."
>
> "Then do let us go downstairs," I said, "there are such pretty rooms there."
>
> Then he took me in his arms and called me a blessed little goose, and said he would go down to the cellar, if I wished, and have it whitewashed into the bargain.

We see this type of interaction again and again. The protagonist expresses something that she wants (or needs) only to have her husband say no, then call her a "blessed little goose" or another similarly patronizing epithet. While we often hear the husband's voice in the story, we rarely hear the protagonist speak her mind. Most of the time, the protagonist recounts her side of the dialogue as exposition.

This distinction is important because the way the writer crafts the dialogue in a story can reveal a lot about the characters and can underscore thematic elements. For instance, when the protagonist tries to tell her husband that she is not feeling any better, she states, "I thought it was a good time to talk, so I told him that I really was not gaining here, and that I wished he would take me away." When her dialogue is filtered through exposition, it emphasizes how the protagonist's voice is being silenced by the people around her.

It is only in the final climactic scene that the roles reverse. Now most of the husband's dialogue appears in exposition and the protagonist has finally found her voice. This strength comes at a price: The protagonist finds her voice at the expense of her sanity.

> Why there's John at the door!
>
> It is no use, young man, you can't open it!
>
> How he does call and pound!
>
> Now he's crying for an axe.
>
> It would be a shame to break down that beautiful door!
>
> "John dear!" said I in the gentlest voice, "the key is down by the front steps, under a plantain leaf!"
>
> That silenced him for a few moments. Then he said—very quietly indeed, "Open the door, my darling!"

"I can't," said I. "The key is down by the front door under a plantain leaf!"

And then I said it again, several times, very gently and slowly, and said it so often that he had to go and see, and he got it of course, and came in. He stopped short by the door.

"What is the matter?" he cried. "For God's sake, what are you doing!"

I kept on creeping just the same, but I looked at him over my shoulder.

"I've got out at last," said I, "in spite of you and Jane. And I've pulled off most of the paper, so you can't put me back!"

Now why should that man have fainted? But he did, and right across my path by the wall, so that I had to creep over him every time!

Notice how the husband's voice has become less dominant in the dialogue. We don't hear his actual cries as he pounds on the door and demands the axe. Instead we get: "How he does call and pound! Now he's crying for an axe." When he gets into the room, the husband is astounded by what he sees and faints. The protagonist gets the last word: "I've pulled off most of the paper, so you can't put me back!"

As you can see in this story, dialogue is more than just a record of what a character says. As a writer, you can use dialogue artfully to show who the character is and also to reflect how that character grows and changes.

A Is for Appearance

The second *A* stands for appearance, which includes any description of how a character looks. In "The Yellow Wallpaper," we get no indication of our protagonist's appearance. Except for a passing mention that she has gained "flesh and color," we have no idea what she looks like, and the truth is it doesn't matter. The protagonist's faceless, almost invisible presence only underscores her lack of agency in the story.

The wallpaper, on the other hand, has a very distinct appearance. Aside from the descriptions of how it taunts the observer with its moving patterns, we also learn that "the color is repellent, almost revolting; a smouldering unclean yellow, strangely faded by the slow-turning sunlight. It is a dull yet lurid orange in some places, a sickly sulphur tint in others." We learn more about the wallpaper's appearance in that one line than we do about the protagonist's in the entire story.

Logistically it makes sense that we should learn so little about the protagonist's appearance. In first-person point of view, it's hard to describe her because she is the one telling the story. Unless the protagonist looks at herself in a mirror and describes what she sees (awk-ward), it is difficult to show details of her appearance. Then again, while showing appearance might be a challenge, it's by no means impossible. As you'll learn in chapter fifteen, you don't need to overload the reader with description to capture the essence of a character's appearance. Instead, a few well-placed details will suffice.

The Character Compass

So far, we've looked at TADA! components separately. Now it's time to combine them with a diagnostic tool: the Character Compass. This technique will show you which parts of the TADA! formula you use most often, and it will reveal new insights about your characters. Use this tool to find out if you depend too much on one of the TADA! elements or are ignoring others. You can draw a compass for different characters after writing each scene. Keep in mind that the compass does not have to be perfectly balanced all the time. This is a *diagnostic* tool to give you a sense of what you're doing. It's fine to write an "unbalanced" character, but only if you do so with intent.

To create a Character Compass, begin by drawing a circle. Next, divide the circle in half with a vertical line, and then again with a horizontal line. Label the points where lines cross the circle with the letters *T, A, D,* and *A,* as in the provided image.

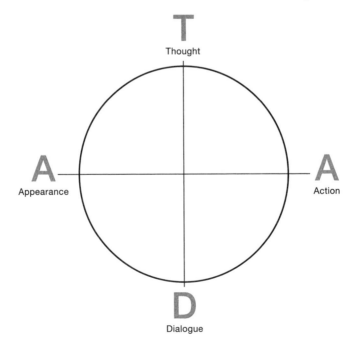

Character Compass

Now fill in your Character Compass by drawing a dot along each of the lines to indicate how much of that component you use in a given scene. The more you have of a given element in a scene, the closer to the edge of the circle you should place the dot. For instance, if your scene has a lot of dialogue and action, you would draw the dots farther from the center on those lines. If the scene doesn't have a lot of thought or appearance, you would draw those dots closer to the center, like this:

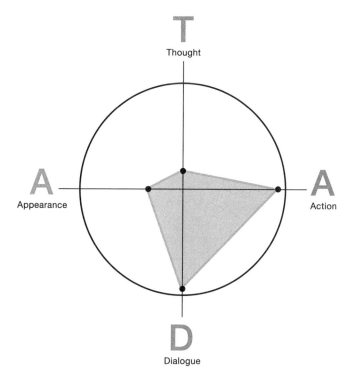

Character Compass: High Dialogue and Action, Low Thought and Appearance

Let's apply the Character Compass to "The Yellow Wallpaper," but here's the catch: We'll draw a compass both for our protagonist *and* for the wallpaper. Remember how the wallpaper takes on a life of its own? For this example we'll treat it like a character. As you know, the protagonist is portrayed mostly through thought and dialogue, with very little action or appearance. The wallpaper, conversely, is heavy on action and appearance, but does not offer any thought or dialogue. (This makes sense, as it is an inanimate object.)

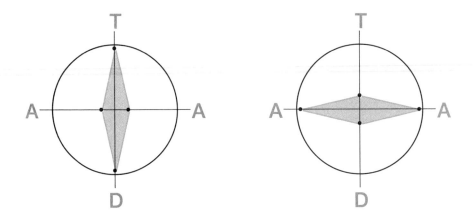

Character Compass: Protagonist (left) and Wallpaper (right)

But wait, it gets even more interesting. Look at what happens when we over-lap the two compasses.

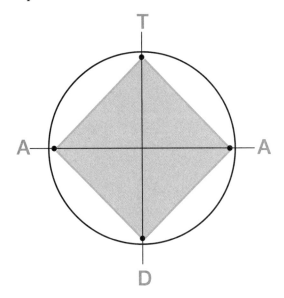

Combined Character Compass

Just as the protagonist and the wallpaper blend together at the end of the story, so, too, do the Character Compasses. When the protagonist and the wallpaper merge, the Character Compasses finally become whole. The way the author brings both the protagonist and the wallpaper to life reflects the way these two characters merge at the end.

What Does Your Character Want?

Before we wrap up our discussion of character, we need to talk about what your character wants and how that desire affects the trajectory of your story. One way to make sense of this is to think of the acronym WORST. Not only will it help you remember your character's wants and desires, but it also will remind you to steer your character toward the worst-case scenario. Stories with happy, comfortable characters are boring. Creating a worst-case scenario for your character will help you write an engaging story your readers won't be able to put down.

> W = What does your character **want**? What is her deepest desire?
>
> O = What **obstacles** are in her way?
>
> R = What will your character **risk** on the quest for this desire?
>
> S = What's at **stake** in your story? What will happen if the character fails?
>
> T = How does your character **transform** or change on this journey?

The Want

A story is not a story unless the character wants something. Your character must have a deep desire, even if it's as simple as a glass of water. The want can be something monumental, like Katniss wanting to survive the horrific arena of the Hunger Games. It can also be relatively minor, like the character in "The Yellow Wallpaper" wanting to leave the house.

The character's desire can also be active or passive. An active desire is a character wanting something to happen or change: For instance, Harry wants to defeat Voldemort in the Harry Potter series. A passive desire is a character wanting something *not* to happen: for example, Wilbur wants to avoid being slaughtered in *Charlotte's Web*. Whether active or passive, your character must have a deep desire and that desire should drive your story.

The Obstacles, Risks, and Stakes

As your character pursues whatever it is that he wants, he will encounter obstacles along the way. This is where your antagonist or villain comes into play. The obstacles can be faceless, like a raging storm, or a person, like the school bully. It doesn't matter how powerful these obstacles are. What matters is that they feel insurmountable to the protagonist. It will take every ounce of the character's strength to overcome them.

When your character faces these obstacles, she must risk something. There must be something at stake. If the character has nothing to lose, then you won't have an interesting story. For instance, there's a reason *The Hunger Games* is told from Katniss's perspective—she is the sole breadwinner for her family. If we saw the story through the eyes of the career tributes, who likely volunteered for the Games, it wouldn't feel nearly as powerful. When Katniss volunteers to take her sister's place in the Games, she not only is risking her own life but is also putting her mother and sister at risk. If she dies, her family will no longer have a source of income. Other characters in the story have various active and passive desires: The career tributes want glory for themselves and their district, and Peeta does not want to be a pawn in the Capitol's Games. However, Katniss can't afford to think like this because dying is not an option for her. She must win the Games not just for herself but for her family.

Even when the stakes are not life-and-death, they need to feel that way. This is the case in many romances and contemporary YA novels. Whether the main character gets the guy is not an issue of physical survival but of social survival. It doesn't matter that the stakes are not life-and-death; to the protagonist they still feel vitally important. For example, in the early Harry Potter books, winning the Quidditch match is very important to Harry and his friends. As the series develops and Voldemort becomes a greater threat, these smaller goals fade into the background. In the later books, it's far more important to defeat Voldemort than it is to win the House Cup.

The Transformation

As your character pursues this high-stakes desire, takes risks, and overcomes obstacles, he *will* change. This is inevitable. Even if the character ends his journey in the same physical place as he began it, the journey will have forced your character to grow. This transformation is crucial because if that desire is not worth changing *for*, then the character has no real reason to pursue it in the first place. This change is baked right into both the ordinary Joe and larger-than-life protagonist archetypes. When you show that it's possible for your character to be something different from what he is, you open the door for him to change.

Now we shift gears and look at the journey that will transform your character. This is where the plot comes in.

— 10 —

Begin at the Beginning

If character is the heart and soul of your story, plot is the road map that will help that character navigate from beginning to end. Many writers struggle with plot, but that's not a reason to fear it. Once you know the basic landmarks, plot becomes easy to understand and put into action. It all boils down to the DIY MFA "secret sauce" formula for story structure.

DIY MFA "Secret Sauce" Formula: 3 + 2 = 1

You read that right. While it might seem to defy the rules of arithmetic, $3 + 2 = 1$; that is, when we talk about story structure. In every story you have the same set of ingredients. You start with *three* acts: the beginning, the middle, and the end. As you transition from one act to the next, you hit *two* crucial points where the character must make a choice. Together these three acts and two decision points equal *one* universal story structure. This structure works for any genre, and people have been using it for as long as the art of storytelling has existed.

Even more important, this formula places the character front and center in the story. Thus, the story is not a set of random events happening *to* the protagonist, but one in which the character is an active agent who makes decisions—for better or worse—that affect what happens. This makes us root for and care about the protagonist. We stand up and cheer when he overcomes an obstacle ("Yes! Show that villain who's boss!"), and we cringe when he makes a stupid choice ("Don't go into that abandoned cabin in the woods when there's a serial killer on the loose!"). The universal story structure encourages the reader to become invested in the protagonist and gives the story a deeper meaning than if it was just a disparate series of events.

Act One: The Beginning

Every story has a beginning that starts at an intentional, specific moment. You want to start as late in your story as possible, just before something happens that shakes up the status quo. You don't need to show dozens of pages where your character goes about her everyday life. Start the day that everything changes.

The Hunger Games opens with Katniss meeting Gale to go hunting. After shooting pheasants and trapping rabbits, they eat a meager breakfast and discuss the reaping. During their conversation, we get a sense for what the reaping is and what it means to these characters. We also learn about Katniss's and Gale's friendship and how it has almost (but not quite) become a romance.

As Katniss walks to the Seam to sell her quarry, we learn more about her world and see District 12 through her eyes. We don't get the backstory of the Hunger Games and the reaping until Katniss and her sister arrive at the district's main square—all that history is not as important as getting to know and understand the characters. Nor do we read about the years Katniss and her family have spent suffering in District 12. The hints we get in the opening scene are enough.

These opening scenes are so seamless that we barely realize the five crucial elements the author sets up—promises that Suzanne Collins makes to us, her readers. We meet the protagonist, Katniss and get a sense for her unique voice as the story unfolds in her first-person point of view. We get subtle details about the world of District 12 and the problems Katniss and her family experience in trying to survive in this unjust system. Finally, we know that a critical event (the reaping) looms large for Katniss and her family.

Five Promises You Make to Your Reader

At the beginning of your novel or short story, you make a series of promises to the reader. You set up rules and expectations that she will rely on throughout your piece. You take her by the hand and lead her into your story. Breaking or stretching these promises creates tension and damages your reader's trust in you. Doing so might get the reader's attention, but as you move ahead in your story you'll have to work much harder to gain back that trust.

Most writers make and fulfill five essential promises within the first five pages of a novel. In the case of a short story, these promises might be made in the first five paragraphs or sentences. Keep in mind that these promises also apply to narrative nonfiction (memoir or biography) as well as prescriptive nonfiction (how-to books).

1. You Promise a Character

From the beginning of your story, your readers want to know who they're supposed to root for, so the first promise you must make is a character—namely your protagonist—and introduce him as early as possible. In most books, the protagonist appears in the first chapter, if not on the first page.

Sometimes an author will artfully delay the main character's entrance to create anticipation or to reflect the character's personality. For instance, in *The Wainscott Weasel* by Tor Seidler, the main character, Bagley, does not appear in the first chapter at all, and we only meet him in chapter two. Bagley is an introverted, shy character, so by making the reader wait to meet him, the author underscores his reticent nature.

Remember, too, that your protagonist is not always the point-of-view (POV) character or the narrator of the story. In some books, the narrator is a supporting character and we see the protagonist through his eyes. You can also have a third-person narrator who has a "bird's-eye view" of the story and allows the reader to see scenes where the protagonist does not appear. With multiple points of view, the reader can peer into the minds of several different characters and see the story from their perspectives. In chapter fourteen, I show you the smorgasbord of POV options you have at your fingertips.

Memoir and other forms of narrative nonfiction have a protagonist, but he or she is a real person rather than a fictional creation. In prescriptive nonfiction the character is *you*, the expert who explains the concepts in the book. Just as changing the main character in a work of fiction will shake up and confuse readers, the same is true for nonfiction. Your central character must stay consistent throughout the book, both in your stance on the subject matter and in terms of your voice.

2. You Promise the Voice

The biggest challenge with voice is that it's nearly impossible to define. When writers ask me, "What is voice?" I have a hard time coming up with an answer; I typically tell them, "I know it when I see it." Even though it's hard to describe, voice is easy to spot, and it is central to establishing the mood and feeling of your story. In chapter thirteen, I'll discuss voice in depth, but for now let's focus on how different authors use voice to establish mood at the beginning of their stories.

In Gayle Forman's *If I Stay*, the protagonist, Mia, is caught between life and death after a horrible car crash. The book is told from the point of view of Mia's spirit as she watches herself in a coma and tries to make sense of what has just happened. Interspersed with these present-moment hospital scenes are various flashbacks that depict what Mia's life was like before the accident. The book's opening line perfectly captures the hazy, dreamy quality of the entire story: "Everyone thinks it was because of the snow. And in a way, I suppose that's true."

Mia's voice is tentative and unsure. She begins by telling us what *everyone else* thinks about the accident rather than offering her own opinion. When she does state her thoughts in the second sentence, she qualifies her statement with phrases like "in a way" and "I suppose." Mia's voice reflects the dream-like mood of the story and also shows us right away who this main character is.

The opening lines of *Feed* by M.T. Anderson set a completely different mood.

> We went to the moon to have fun, but the moon turned out to totally suck.
>
> We went on a Friday, because there was shit-all to do at home. It was the beginning of spring break. Everything at home was boring. Link Arwaker was like, "I'm so null," and Marty was all, "I'm null too, unit," but I mean we were all pretty null, because for the last like hour we'd been playing with three uninsulated wires that were coming out of the wall.

If you haven't read this book (you should), it's about a dystopian society where everybody has a computer chip plugged directly into their brains, from which they can access information on the Internet. Everyone is constantly bombarded with ads and entertainment, so it's no surprise that the narrator, Titus, is bored out of his mind.

The opening lines depict Titus as a dazed and overstimulated kid in this dystopian world. We hear it in his voice, and, more specifically, we see it in the length and structure of his sentences. The first sentence is fairly complex, with a "_____, but _____" contrasting structure in which the first clause conflicts with what happens in the second. The next sentence, however, is less complex. Instead of a contrasting structure, we are given cause and effect: "_____, because _____." It's also slightly shorter than the opening sentence. The next two sentences are simple, single-clause statements and are shorter still. It's as though the protagonist's attention span shrinks with each passing phrase and his thoughts speed up until he can barely process his own words. Finally, the narration devolves into a massive run-on sentence, showing us exactly how bored and distracted he is.

In contrast to Mia and Titus, Holden Caulfield, the protagonist in J.D. Salinger's *The Catcher in the Rye*, immediately takes on an antagonistic stance, almost taunting the reader.

> If you really want to hear about it, the first thing you'll probably want to know is where I was born, and what my lousy childhood was like, and how my parents were occupied and all before they had me, and all that David Copperfield kind of crap, but I don't feel like going into it, if you want to know the truth.

The voice of the narrator perfectly captures the mood of the novel and Holden's struggle to figure out who he is and to resist the conventions of the adult world around him. His defiant words in the beginning not only reflect his personality but also set the tone for the rest of the book. This opening line also makes it very clear that Holden's account of his story will be shaded by his own point of view. He says so himself: "… but I don't feel like going into it, if you want to know the truth." We get a sense that Holden's version of the "truth" might not be completely accurate, and is most likely shaded by his own perspective and what he wants to make his audience believe. The voice of *The Catcher in the Rye* plants us firmly in Holden's point of view, but also establishes that his first-person narration may not be 100 percent reliable.

So far we've looked at first-person narrators because in these stories the narrator's voice is clear. With a first-person narrator, the narrator and the protagonist are one and the same, so the voice of the story is also that of the main character. When the narrator is *not* a character in the story, the voice of the protagonist still comes through loud and clear in dialogue, but the narrator may fade into the background and become almost invisible. Of course, there are instances to the contrary, where the narrator also has a distinct and unique voice, as seen in the first line of Jane Austen's *Pride and Prejudice*: "It is a truth universally acknowledged, that a single man in possession of a good fortune, must be in want of a wife."

Notice the ironic, almost sarcastic tone of this opening sentence. It shows us right away that while the story may be set in Regency Period England, where women were expected to be proper and well behaved, we are most definitely not dealing with a passive narrator. This narrator (who is clearly a woman, simply by her tone) is spunky—snarky, even—and has as much spark and wit as the protagonist, Elizabeth Bennet. We see opinionated narrators in other nineteenth-century novels, such as those of Charles Dickens, and you'll often find a similar type of narrator in biographies or history texts, where the author brings his own slant to the subject.

3. You Promise the World

Promise the world? As in the *whole world*? It might sound daunting to give your readers the world, but it's not just any world you're promising. It's *your* world, the world of your book, the world you know inside and out. Most writers think world-building is only necessary for historical fiction, fantasy, or science fiction. The truth is that every book—regardless of genre—has a world, and it's your job to make it feel real.

John Gardner describes story as a "narrative dream." In other words, when someone is reading a story, he isn't aware that he is reading the story; he's just in that world, experiencing the events along with the character. The moment a reader becomes aware that he is reading is the moment he falls out of the narrative dream and returns to reality. Whether you're writing a contemporary story set in an average suburb or an elaborate fantasy tale set in another dimension, you need to understand your story's world and bring it to life for your reader. He needs to believe that world is real and that he is *there.* And the best way to accomplish this is to believe in it yourself.

When it comes to describing your world, a little detail goes a long way. Writers are often tempted to give as much detail about setting as possible, thinking that the more information they share, the more real the world will become. This is especially true for fantasy stories, where the writer may worry that the reader won't "get" the setting if they don't describe every inch. However, when the writer overloads the world with needless detail, the reader checks out and loses interest. Remember: Your readers are smart, and often a few well-placed details will carry more weight than long passages of description. Just as readers trust the writer to present a world that feels real, the writer must trust readers to invest their imaginations in that world and fill in any gaps.

4. You Promise a Problem

From the first page, you need to establish a problem the character is facing. Whether that problem is explicit (like the family's financial state in *Pride and Prejudice*) or a mystery (like what has happened to the protagonist in *If*

I Stay), readers should know from the first moment that the character is facing a seemingly insurmountable difficulty or challenge. This problem will be crucial in establishing the central conflict for your story.

Note that while the problem that appears early in the story does not have to be the central conflict, it's usually tied to that conflict in some way. In *Pride and Prejudice,* for example, the initial problem is the family's financial situation. In the first chapter we learn that because Mr. Bennet does not have a male heir, his family cannot inherit Longbourn, his estate. If he dies, his wife and daughters will be left destitute. This is a high-stakes problem for the characters, and it explains why Mrs. Bennet is so desperate to marry off at least one of her daughters.

As the story develops, we see that the central conflict actually lies in the relationship between Elizabeth and Mr. Darcy—will the two fall in love, and if so, *how?* This is a very different conflict than the initial problem of not inheriting Longbourn. However, the initial problem opens the door to the potential love-hate courtship between the two central characters and sets the events of the story in motion. After all, if the Bennet family were not facing such a serious financial dilemma, Mrs. Bennet would not have pushed her daughters to meet potential husbands, and most likely Elizabeth and Mr. Darcy would not have been thrown into each other's company.

In chapter seven you learned about the Major Dramatic Question (MDQ) and Lesser Dramatic Questions (LDQs). The MDQ is the question that sums up the central conflict of your story, and the LDQs are the questions that drive the subplots of your story. You might not know all of these dramatic questions from the first page, but that initial problem can eventually develop into your story's Major and Lesser Dramatic Questions.

For example, in *The Hunger Games*, Katniss faces two problems in the first chapter. First, she wants desperately to protect her sister, Prim, who qualifies for the reaping for the first time. This problem spurs her to take her sister's place in the Games, thus leading to the MDQ of the whole book (i.e., "Will Katniss survive the games?"). The second problem she faces is her complicated relationship with her best friend, Gale: There is obvious romantic tension between them, but given their circumstances neither of them acts on it. This romantic tension becomes significant later on when Katniss learns that Peeta is in love with her. In an instant, the complicated friendship with Gale becomes a love triangle that feeds into an LDQ (i.e., "Which boy will Katniss choose?"). The LDQ continues to play out through the rest of the trilogy.

5. You Promise an Event

Every story needs to begin with a significant event, an *opening image*, that nudges the story into motion or gives it a sharp shove. In *If I Stay*, a tragic car crash turns the characters' lives upside down. In *The Catcher in the Rye*, Holden leaves boarding school, an event that sets up the rest of the story. In *Feed*, the characters go to the moon to have fun, and things unravel from there. In *Pride and Prejudice*, the wealthy bachelor Mr. Bingley moves into the neighboring estate, raising all sorts of gossip among the neighbors.

The opening image starts the story at a specific moment, preferably as close as possible to the action of the plot. In *Pride and Prejudice*, we don't need to read chapter after chapter about Mrs. Bennet playing matchmaker for her daughters. Instead the story begins when Mr. Bingley moves in next door. Remember that your reader will be waiting for this opening image, so you need to follow through as quickly as you can. If you delay this first event for too long, your reader will lose interest or, worse, stop reading altogether. Hook your reader by setting the story in motion.

While you want to dive into the meat of your story as soon as possible, those opening pages also play another equally important role: They set up the status quo. Your story is a journey, and as your character faces various obstacles, he will invariably change. This change is meaningless if we don't know where he was when he started. You must use these opening pages to paint the scene and set up the contrast.

Advertisers are great at using contrast to show a journey or transformation. Think of all those infomercials with "before" and "after" photos. The picture of the burly muscleman isn't nearly as powerful if we don't first see the scrawny guy in the "before" photo. Your opening pages are the "before" photo for your character. You need to show us what life is like for the character before everything changes. You need to set up the status quo so that when you shake up the character's world, your reader will feel the impact.

Act One is all about building trust with your readers. They need to trust that you won't go back on your promises or play tricks on them. Likewise, you must trust your readers to be smart and to understand what you're doing. Every stretched or broken promise will test that reader-writer trust relationship. This doesn't mean you can't take risks. You can break any of these promises at any point in your story, but do so with artful purpose.

Decision One: The Point of No Return

When Act One transitions to Act Two, two critical things happen: the *inciting incident* and the *first reversal*. These technical terms are just a fancy way of saying that something happens and your character makes a choice.

The *inciting incident* is the first moment in a story where the status quo changes. This moment is almost always an external event that happens to the protagonist. The character must make a choice after this event, or the story will be nothing more than a series of occurrences that toss her around like a boat on a choppy ocean.

For every external event in the story, your character must make a choice. Sometimes it takes the character pages or even chapters to weigh out her options. Sometimes she makes that choice in an instant. The point is that your character is not a passive agent who gets pushed through the story against her will. Things happen to your character, and she must *choose* how to respond. This decision is the *first reversal*, or what I like to call the *point of no return* because after this moment things will never be the same.

In *The Hunger Games* the inciting incident is the moment when Effie Trinket pulls Prim's name from the tribute jar. At first Katniss is in a haze, unsure of what's happening. Then reality sinks in: Her sister has been picked. She can't let this happen, so she does the only thing she can: She volunteers to take her sister's place. This split-second decision is the point of no return. The element of choice is key. *The Hunger Games* would have been a very different book if Katniss's name had been pulled from the jar. When she volunteers to take her sister's place, that choice gives the story more impact and meaning.

In some stories that choice is almost invisible, but it's still there if you look closely. The inciting incident in *The Wizard of Oz* movie is hard to miss. After all, the tornado that sweeps up Dorothy and her house is a major part of the story and a great visual scene. But the point of no return is quieter, more subtle. When her house lands in Oz, Dorothy faces a choice: She can stay where she is or venture out into this strange but beautiful world. The moment Dorothy opens the door and steps across the threshold is the point of no return. After that, it's very clear that she and Toto are "not in Kansas anymore"; the sepia tones of the film's opening are replaced by vibrant Technicolor as soon as Dorothy steps into Oz.

In *Pride and Prejudice,* on the other hand, the inciting incident is fuzzy, though the point of no return is quite clear. Several events nudge Elizabeth

Bennet into Mr. Darcy's presence. First, Mr. Bingley arrives at Netherfield. Sometime later, Elizabeth encounters Mr. Darcy at a ball, where he snubs her by refusing to dance. Later still, Elizabeth's sister, Jane, falls ill while visiting Mr. Bingley's sister. But these external incidents are not nearly as important as the pivotal moment when, despite the rain and mud, Elizabeth decides to venture to Netherfield on foot to tend to her sister. Until this point, Elizabeth has not had much choice about being thrown into the company of Mr. Darcy and the rest of the Netherfield residents. She has run into them at a ball and in town, but their meetings are always in passing and never her choice. Furthermore, Elizabeth dislikes all of the residents except Mr. Bingley—she thinks the others are snobs and hypocrites. Despite her distaste for these people, however, she still braves the mud and mire to care for her sick sister. This decision forces Elizabeth to stay at Netherfield for several days, putting her in the company of the very man she wants to avoid: Mr. Darcy. Those days together at Netherfield cause Mr. Darcy to begin to fall in love with Elizabeth and open the door for their courtship.

You might say that the inciting incident and the point of no return form a door between the first and second act. Once the character steps through that door, there is no turning back. From here the protagonist must go on the journey and see the story through.

Muddle Through the Middle

The middle of a novel is often the most difficult part for a writer to traverse. While Acts One and Three each take up about one-quarter of the story, Act Two comprises half of the novel. If you are muddling through the middle of your story, know that you are not alone. Many writers struggle to sustain momentum and figure out what happens next in Act Two. This chapter provides some landmarks that can help you steer through the mid-novel slump.

Story Archetypes

Act Two is where the bulk of your story happens. It's where you deliver on the premise of the book. In *The Hunger Games*, Katniss trains for the Games and then fights in the arena. In *The Wizard of Oz* movie, Dorothy explores the world of Oz and meets new traveling companions. In *Harry Potter and the Sorcerer's Stone*, Harry and his friends arrive at Hogwarts and shenanigans ensue.

If you find yourself getting stuck in the middle, ask yourself, "What is the premise of my story?" The premise is the underlying concept that drives your story. In a mystery, the premise is "Whodunit?" and the middle of the book shows the sleuth finding clues and piecing them together to solve the crime. In a romance, the premise is "Will they get together?" and the middle includes all the flirtation, conflict, and sexual tension between the couple after they first meet. Some genres have "rules" surrounding the premise—mystery requires a crime, romance requires a love story—but the author can bend or blur these rules to her advantage. Don't think of story structure as a series of check boxes on a list; formulas can be confining. Instead, look under the hood and tease apart the power struggle or conflict that drives your story.

Story Is About a Power Struggle

Dozens of experts have tried to boil down plot into a handful of labels and categories, claiming that a different number of plot archetypes exist. Even the venerable John Gardner said that there are only two plots in all of literature: "You go on a journey," and "A stranger comes to town" (also known as a "fish out of water" story). Sure, we can shove stories into neat little categories, but what do we do when a story breaks the mold?

In *The Wizard of Oz* movie, Dorothy is swept up by a tornado and goes on a magical journey through the Land of Oz. This sounds like the first of Gardner's two plots. But wait! If we look at this story from another angle—from the perspective of the Wicked Witch or other citizens of Oz—Dorothy is a stranger who arrives in a new land and shakes things up. That's a "stranger comes to town" narrative if I ever saw one. What use are archetypes if a story can be categorized in multiple ways?

Instead of thinking in terms of plot archetypes, think in terms of *power*. Focus on the power struggle at the heart of your story. This will force you to put the conflict front and center. And as we know, conflict is what makes your story interesting. Without conflict you will have a hard time sustaining momentum past the first few pages, much less for the entire book. Remember the problem you promised in Act One? It is the precursor of the central conflict that will drive your story forward, and that conflict is about power.

At the heart of every story, the protagonist must confront an antagonist of equal or greater power than himself. You have one of three options:

- The protagonist confronts an antagonist with more power.
- The protagonist confronts an antagonist of equal power.
- The protagonist confronts himself.

It might seem as if an option is missing. Why don't stories ever feature a protagonist who confronts an antagonist with *less* power? It might seem unfair, but the odds must always be stacked against your protagonist. If your character goes up against someone or something of lesser power, the story will have no conflict or tension, and your reader won't have a reason to keep reading. Not to mention that your protagonist will come across as a bully, and readers don't like to root for bullies. Even if your protagonist has superpowers, she should always face off against an equally powerful antagonist, like Superman battling against the evil mastermind Lex Luthor.

When you focus on power dynamics between your protagonist and antagonist, it doesn't matter if your narrative is in line with the "journey" archetype or the "stranger comes to town" archetype. The key to an interesting story is to put your character in situations where he will be vulnerable. Vulnerability is good. It leads to conflict and tension, which in turn help sustain your story's momentum through that muddle in the middle.

The Protagonist Confronts an Antagonist with More Power

This is an underdog story. While there are different ways of looking at this narrative, the core of the story's conflict is always the same: The underdog protagonist must face a character or entity with more power, and the protagonist may or may not win. Readers will root for the underdog protagonist because they want to see that character come out on top despite all odds.

This archetype can span many genres. A romance could be a rags-to-riches love story in which an unappreciated protagonist catches the attention of the prince. You might also have a Pygmalion-type "makeover" story in which the protagonist creates or improves another character, only to have that character take on a life of her own. Mary Shelley's *Frankenstein* and Jane Austen's *Emma* are great examples of a Pygmalion-type story from two very different genres.

Even in stories where the protagonist is not the underdog, he might portray himself as such. In *The Odyssey* by Homer, during the Trojan War, the Greek armies are depicted as no match for the strong-walled city of Troy, and they are at the point of giving up until cunning Odysseus dreams up the Trojan Horse. Had the Greeks been far superior in battle, the story of the Trojan Horse would not be nearly as compelling. Instead, because that victory comes on the heels of a near defeat, the reader feels compelled to root for the Greeks.

The Trojan perspective in Virgil's *Aeneid* is quite different. In this version of the story, the city of Troy is worn out by siege and war. When the Trojans are at the brink of giving up, the Greeks appear to set sail, leaving behind a horse statue as an offering. Despite omens and warnings, the Trojans are fooled by the "unfair trickery" of the Greeks and bring the horse into their city. That night, the Greeks jump from the horse, throw open the gates, and lay siege to Troy. The reader knows from the beginning that this horse is bad news. We want to yell at the Trojans, "Don't bring that horse into your city, you idiots!" But even though we know they are making a bad decision, we are still compelled to root for the Trojans. We hope against hope that the worst-case scenario won't actually happen, even though it's inevitable. That hope makes us see the Trojans as underdogs.

You will see a similar power dynamic in comeback stories, redemption narratives, and stories where the protagonist is "chosen" to overcome some major adversity. In a comeback story, the protagonist has suffered a huge setback and must work hard to regain his status. The redemption story is similar, but the character is the cause of his own downfall and must redeem himself. The development of Severus Snape's character in the Harry Potter series is a great example of a redemption narrative. For several books in the series, the reader has no idea whether Snape is good or evil. It is only when Harry places Snape's tears in the Pensieve and views the professor's memories that he understands the truth: Despite having a deep dislike for Harry's father, Snape has always harbored love for Harry's mother, and that love has been central to his complicated relationship with Harry.

When you look at stories in terms of power struggle, you will start to see how the same story can span many different archetypes. The Harry Potter series begins as a "fish out of water" story with Harry as the outsider in a strange wizarding world. As the series develops, Harry takes his place as the "chosen one" destined to defeat Voldemort. Alongside this primary story arc, we see the redemption narrative for Snape's character, as well as several love stories and triangles. You can weave together multiple threads—each with a different conflict—to create your story. To see how these threads fit together, use the story-mapping technique from chapter seven.

The Protagonist Confronts an Antagonist of Equal Power

This type of power struggle includes "long-lost twin" stories, "hate to love" romances, buddy comedies, and other such scenarios. This category usually pits the protagonist against another character, because it wouldn't make much sense for a faceless antagonist to have power equal to the protagonist. If your protagonist faces a natural disaster or other faceless antagonists, it must pose a serious threat. "Man is stranded on a deserted island and survives comfortably" is not a compelling story. "Man is stranded on a deserted island and must struggle against all odds to survive"—now *that's* a story.

Though the antagonist of equal power is at odds with the protagonist, he doesn't have to be an all-out villain. In a love story, for example, the protagonist might start out in conflict with the love interest, but eventually the two find common ground and fall in love.

"Long-lost twin" or "hate to love" narratives—even buddy comedies—are all stories where the antagonist is not *evil* but still causes serious conflict for the protagonist. A "long-lost twin" narrative is where two characters—they can be friends or even enemies—start out at odds but eventually discover a hidden kinship or shared likeness. "Switched at birth" or "switching places" stories combine the "long-lost twin" and "fish out of water" scenarios, forcing opposite characters to walk in each other's shoes. In doing so they learn that they have more in common than they first believed.

The "hate to love" narrative is a formula used in many romance stories, including *Pride and Prejudice*. In this case, the protagonist and the love interest hate each other at the beginning, but as the story develops, they discover they had more in common than they thought. Eventually they fall in love.

The Protagonist Confronts Himself

In this narrative, the protagonist is struggling with an inner conflict that must be resolved. Often you will find this scenario in literary fiction, though it is usually combined with one or more of the other power struggles. A story that takes place only in the protagonist's head can quickly become boring. The wife in "The Yellow Wallpaper" by Charlotte Perkins Gilman is a great example of a protagonist who confronts herself, but she appears in a short story, not a novel.

It is extremely difficult to sustain a story for an entire book using only internal conflict. However, as you will discover shortly, every story has at least one moment where the protagonist must confront himself. That moment happens in the middle.

Act Two: The Middle

In Act One of your story, you make several promises to your reader. You promise a problem, one that is usually linked to the central conflict of your story. You also show your reader the status quo of your story's world, and then you turn that world on its head with the inciting incident. At the point of no return, the character must make a choice, and this decision launches the protagonist into Act Two. This is where you let the central conflict play out. Act

Two is where most of your story happens, but what if you lose momentum? What if energy seeps out of your story like air from a balloon?

New Characters and Subplots

One of the best ways to keep your story moving is to add a new character, or two, or ten. In *Harry Potter and the Sorcerer's Stone*, we meet all of Harry's professors and classmates in Act Two. In *The Hunger Games* we get to know Peeta, Rue, and the other tributes participating in the Games. In *Pride and Prejudice* we meet Wickham and the militia, as well as Mr. Collins, Lady Catherine, and Georgiana Darcy. Act One introduces your protagonist, but it's in Act Two that the supporting cast comes to life.

New characters bring new subplots with them. For instance, during his interview with Caesar Flickerman, Peeta Mellark professes his love for Katniss. Not only does this moment open the door for a love story subplot but it also adds an additional layer of tension to the original survival narrative. No longer is *The Hunger Games* just about surviving the arena. Because only one tribute can win, we now have a "star-crossed lovers" story as well.

In Act Two, you can also introduce surrogate supporting characters who take on the roles of other supporting characters. This technique is especially useful when your protagonist is separated from the supporting cast from Act One. For example, in *The Hunger Games* Katniss is separated from her sister, Prim, and her best friend/pseudo-love interest, Gale. To keep the momentum of those relationships, the author created surrogate characters to take their places and play the same roles. Rue, the young tribute from District 11, becomes a surrogate younger sister to Katniss. Similarly Peeta becomes the new love interest, and when Katniss is reunited with Gale in the second and third books, this romance becomes a complicated love triangle.

The works of William Shakespeare are filled with surrogate supporting characters. In *King Lear*, for example, the fool archetype is played by a character named the Fool as well as by Lear's favorite daughter, Cordelia. Just as the Fool tells King Lear the things he does not want to hear, so, too, does Cordelia when she speaks the difficult truth to her father. In fact—and here's where things get interesting—the characters of Cordelia and the Fool never appear in the same scene, and in early performances of *King Lear* the same actor often played both roles. At the end of the play, when Lear learns of Cordelia's death, he even calls her his "poor fool," further establishing the link between those two characters. It's significant that Cordelia and the Fool are interlinked and almost interchangeable because they serve the same purpose in the story.

The Rule of Three

It happens to the best of us: Sooner or later in Act Two, you will likely hit a wall and run out of ideas. When you reach a dead end in your story, one of the best ways around it is to use the *rule of three*. What is this magical, mysterious rule? You probably already know the rule of three and don't even realize it. It is embedded in nearly every narrative and is especially prevalent in children's stories. After all, it's not "Goldilocks and the Two Bears," nor is it "The Four Little Pigs."

The number three gives us a feeling of completeness. Two is not enough to establish a pattern, and four feels like too many. Three is just the right balance. It sets up a pattern but allows room for a twist in the third repetition. Think of the "Priceless" MasterCard commercials: "Two tickets to the baseball game: $46. One autographed baseball: $50. Real conversation with your eleven-year-old: priceless." The rule of three is so deeply ingrained in our psyches that it doesn't even matter what the first two options are and how much they cost. What matters is that the third option is "priceless," and that's what makes it different. This pattern is what resonates with us and makes the commercial so memorable.

You can use the rule of three to keep your story moving in Act Two. For instance, your protagonist can confront three obstacles. The first two times your protagonist might be defeated, but in the third iteration she musters the strength to overcome. *Pride and Prejudice* uses the rule of three by having Elizabeth Bennet navigate through not one, not two, but three courtships, all of which end poorly. First, the awkward Mr. Collins proposes, and Elizabeth turns him down. Next Elizabeth enjoys a flirtation with Mr. Wickham, who reveals that he has been badly treated by Mr. Darcy. While Wickham insists that he will not let Darcy's influence daunt him, he leaves town abruptly, just when Elizabeth has begun to grow fond of him. Finally, in the middle of Act Two, Mr. Darcy proposes to Elizabeth. This proposal is so condescending that Elizabeth not only rejects Mr. Darcy but also confronts him about his awful treatment of Wickham. Mr. Darcy responds with a letter wherein he explains his behavior and also reveals Wickham for the scoundrel that he is. It is only after these three failed courtships that Elizabeth begins to see Mr. Darcy's true character and develop feelings for him.

Similarly, we see the rule of three at work in the "road trip" subplot of *Pride and Prejudice*. In Act Two, three significant trips advance the plot. First, Elizabeth's sister Jane travels to London to visit her relatives, Mr. and Mrs. Gardiner, but also in the hopes of seeing Mr. Bingley, who has left Netherfield for the season. During this trip, Jane corresponds with Elizabeth and recounts how Mr. Bingley fails to call on her and how his sister behaves rudely when she does pay a visit. This first trip establishes that Jane's marriage prospects are not as good as they seemed in Act One.

Later in Act Two, Elizabeth travels to visit her friend Charlotte who is now married to Mr. Collins. During this trip, Elizabeth meets the infamous Lady Catherine and learns that Mr. Darcy has been betrothed to the lady's sniveling, annoying daughter. This sets up the potential for conflict later in the book when Elizabeth develops feelings for Mr. Darcy. This visit to Mr. Collins and Charlotte also provides the opportunity for Mr. Darcy to deliver his first failed proposal. (This key moment happens at the midpoint of the story, a landmark I will discuss in more depth in the next section.)

In the final trip, Mr. and Mrs. Gardiner take Elizabeth on a tour of the Lake Country. They visit Pemberley, Mr. Darcy's estate, and run into the gentleman himself on the grounds. Mr. Darcy is quite cordial to Elizabeth and her relatives, and her opinions of him shift even further. This trip ends with a crucial turning point where Elizabeth receives word from her family that her youngest sister, Lydia, has eloped with Mr. Wickham.

The Midpoint

About halfway through your story is a moment aptly called "the *midpoint*." This moment is more than just a scene right in the middle of your book; it has special significance and often is a turning point. As with all of the significant landmarks in your story, the midpoint has two sides: the external event and the character's internal response to that event. The external event has one of two flavors: the *temporary triumph* or the *false failure*. What is more important, however, is the character's internal response to the external event.

While the midpoint scene usually falls about halfway through the story, remember that crafting a narrative is not an exact science. Depending on your story's genre or overall structure, the midpoint may appear earlier or later than the exact middle of your book. The only major requirement for this moment is that it is firmly planted at the center of Act Two so that it occurs after the *point of no return* and before the major decision point at the end of

Act Two. You have some wiggle room about where you place this midpoint in your story, but it must fall somewhere between those two crucial decisions.

Temporary Triumph

The temporary triumph is that "Yesssss, we made it!" moment where it seems as if the protagonist has finally achieved what she wants. It's a victory, but as you can guess from the term, that triumph is only temporary.

In Jane Austen's *Emma*, the midpoint is when Mr. Frank Churchill pays a visit to Emma Woodhouse. Emma has developed an interest in Mr. Churchill, and she is convinced that he feels the same way about her. In the scenes leading up to the midpoint, Emma plans a ball and looks forward to dancing with this lively young man. As the ball draws near, Emma learns that Mr. Churchill has been called away and must return home to tend to a sickly aunt. He calls on Emma to say goodbye, and his demeanor is awkward and nervous, as one might expect from a young man in love who is forced to leave behind the object of his affections.

The scene culminates with this moment: "He stopt again, rose again, and seemed quite embarrassed. He was more in love with her than Emma had supposed; and who can say how it might have ended, if his father had not made his appearance?" At this point, Emma is convinced that Mr. Churchill is desperately in love with her, and she thinks that given the opportunity he would have proposed. Although Emma is determined not to reciprocate his feelings—she prides herself for not being prone to such trifling emotions—it is clear in the pages that follow that Emma *is* in love. She doesn't love Mr. Churchill per se, but she clearly loves the idea of his being in love with her. This is a huge triumph for Emma's ego, and she spends the better part of Act Two "fighting against" any feelings she has for Mr. Churchill.

This midpoint moment does more than merely boost Emma's ego: It opens the door for Emma to fall in love with *somebody*. At first she believes that Mr. Churchill is her best match, but as the story develops and she suffers several disappointments (including the discovery that Mr. Churchill is secretly engaged to another woman), Emma falls in love with Mr. Knightley, who ends up being her perfect match.

Jane Austen's *Emma* is an example of the "hate to love" narrative in which the couple in question start off at odds but later fall in love. Emma spends the entire story trying to match her friends with each other, and she misreads the affections of three different young men. (Look—the rule of three!) Whether you are writing an action-packed thriller or a character-driven classic, the same rule of three and story landmarks apply. You can also use the 3 + 2 = 1 formula and distill your story's conflict using the same set of power dynamics regardless of genre.

False Failure

Sometimes the midpoint isn't a moment of triumph, but one of failure. This is a place in the story where it feels like things couldn't possibly get worse for the protagonist—but they do. It is a false failure because it seems like the worst-case scenario, but it turns out that the character just needs more time to develop and change before she can turn things around and achieve victory.

Mr. Darcy's failed proposal in *Pride and Prejudice* is a false failure. At this point in the story, romance looks hopeless for Elizabeth. As readers, we're wondering: *How on earth she will ever find happiness?* Her rejection of Mr. Darcy—the love interest—leaves us scratching our heads. Elizabeth and Mr. Darcy are *supposed* to end up together, so when he proposes and she says no it seems like the entire premise of the novel has been turned on its head.

This rejected proposal is crucial for shaping both Elizabeth's and Mr. Darcy's characters. Without it, they would never find the common ground between them to eventually fall in love. This moment forces Mr. Darcy to reconsider his prideful behavior, and his character softens, revealing a kinder, gentler side both to Elizabeth and to the reader. However, Elizabeth's character is affected more by the false failure. After the proposal, Mr. Darcy writes her a letter that explains the reasons for his behavior and reveals the true dark nature of Mr. Wickham. After reading the letter, Elizabeth goes into a moment of deep introspection, leading to this famous passage, which occurs just past the exact middle of the novel.

> "How despicably I have acted!" she cried; "I, who have prided myself on my discernment! I, who have valued myself on my abilities! who have often disdained the generous candour of my sister, and gratified my vanity in useless or blameable mistrust! How humiliating is this discovery! Yet, how just a humiliation! Had I been in love, I could not have been more wretchedly blind! But vanity, not love, has been my folly. Pleased with the preference of one, and offended by the neglect of the other, on the very beginning of our acquaintance, I have courted prepossession and ignorance, and driven reason away, where either were concerned. Till this moment I never knew myself."

One of the primary themes in *Pride and Prejudice* is the idea of truly knowing someone. Throughout the book, we see fascinating contradictions between how characters present themselves and who they are at their core. Until this point, Elizabeth has believed she is discerning and able to see the false aspects of other people. Now, suddenly, she realizes that not only has she been prejudiced in her opinions of Mr. Darcy and Mr. Wickham, but that her pride in being a good judge of character has been false. The character who she has most misjudged is, in fact, herself. This is one of the most delicious moments of thematic irony in all of literature.

Though they might seem opposite, the temporary triumph and the false failure share a common thread: In both cases, the external events lead to an internal moment where the protagonist must decide how she feels about the person she has become. In his book *Write Your Novel from the Middle*, James Scott Bell refers to this as the "mirror moment." This introspection may be a complete turning point where the protagonist reconsiders every aspect of her personality, as Elizabeth does in *Pride and Prejudice*. It might also be a slight shift, as when Emma doesn't change her entire outlook on love, but does become more open to the possibility. As with any aspect of a good story, the external events need to reflect and contribute to the internal journey that eventually makes the protagonist grow and change.

— 12 —

Arrive at the End

Toward the end of Act Two, you hit the second major decision point in the 3 + 2 = 1 formula. This moment, the bridge between Act Two and Act Three, usually occurs about three-quarters into the story. Once you cross into Act Three, the story begins a rapid climb in tension until you reach the climax or "final showdown." Here the central conflict comes to a head and finally resolves.

You can end your story in four possible ways. These resolutions depend on your character's want: Does your character get what she wants, and does she still want it? Successful endings give the reader a sense of closure and don't leave major details hanging. At the same time, you don't need to wrap up every loose end. You can leave room for the story to breathe, so it feels like the world you've crafted extends beyond the last page.

Decision Two: The Dark Night of the Soul

Once you pass the midpoint of your story, the events of Act Two may seem to pick up speed and start rolling toward a resolution. It might even feel like a happy ending for your character is just around the corner. Don't be fooled. You will hit a point where the protagonist plunges to her lowest point. I call this scene the *"over the cliff"* moment because it pushes your character into an abyss of despair and self-doubt. You might think I'm being melodramatic. I'm not.

Every story has an "over the cliff" moment. Consider this: As the writer, it's your job to push your character toward the worst-case scenario. (Remember that WORST acronym from chapter nine?) As your protagonist chases his deep desire, you need to make that quest as difficult and painful as possible. *It's your job to make your characters suffer.* If characters get what they want too easily, the story will either be boring or too short. Struggle and suffering are storytelling gold, so it should come as no surprise that before your character can reach the ending, he must hit rock bottom. You have been leading your character toward this point the whole time.

Once you push your character over the cliff, he undergoes another moment of introspection. Writers often call this the "*dark night of the soul.*" This is the scene where the protagonist feels like all is lost and she cannot possibly go on. In war movies this is where a character says: "Tell my kids I love them." There is no resolution in sight, no light at the end of this struggle. The character feels like he has nothing left to give. At this point she has two choices: give up, or muster one iota of strength and survive just a little bit longer.

In *The Hunger Games* the dark night of the soul is when Rue is hit by a spear and Katniss sings to her as she dies. This is Katniss's lowest point, her moment of despair. Rue is dead, and Katniss could do nothing to save her. She realizes that just as she couldn't protect Rue, she also can't protect her family. Even volunteering for the Games will be meaningless in the end. Engulfed by darkness, she can do one of two things: give up or take a stand. Katniss chooses the latter.

Furious at the injustice of Rue's death, Katniss stands up against the Capitol for the first time in the book. In the past, she has always kept her head down and played by most of the Capitol's rules in order to protect her family. When Rue dies, she finally fights back, with a subtle but meaningful gesture of defiance.

Katniss wreaths Rue's head and hair with flowers, kisses three fingers, and holds them up—a District 12 symbol of support. This isn't a loud, bombastic call to arms; it's an act of kindness and humanity amid all the inhumanity of the Games. Katniss's actions also cause a ripple effect: First, District 11 sends a gift of bread to Katniss as thanks for honoring Rue. This act of defiance (and solidarity) is the start of something that continues to escalate in the districts through the second and third books of the trilogy. In this pivotal moment, even though Katniss feels that all is lost, she still musters the strength to take her first step and stand up to the Capitol. The gift of bread from District 11 is proof that her actions have resonated beyond the arena.

Act Three: The End

Once your protagonist makes that pivotal second decision, she crosses the threshold into Act Three. Though this final act can make up a quarter of the book, it often seems to move much faster. As the tension rises toward the climax, events happen faster and your reader keeps turning pages to see what happens next. While pacing is important throughout your story, in Act Three it becomes vital.

Pacing and Rhythm

Pacing is the heartbeat of your story. It's the rhythm that keeps your narrative on track, scene after scene. Like voice, pacing is an element of storytelling that is hard to define but is easy to spot when it doesn't work. Think of a drummer in a band who keeps time and makes sure the song doesn't derail or grind to a halt. When you master the pace of your story, it will be so seamless that no one will notice, but if you mess up the pacing, it will stand out like a drummer who's on the wrong beat.

Pacing occurs on two levels: on the sentence level and on the scene level. When a story is zipping along, it is because of a combination of sentence-level and scene-level pacing. At the sentence level, pacing has to do with the cadence and lilt of the words, as well as sentence structure. What kind of language are you using? What are the exact words? Are your sentences long and winding, with multiple clauses weaving in and out of each other, or are they short, brusque, and clipped?

The opening sentence of *Young Goodman Brown* by Nathaniel Hawthorne consists of two parts joined with a semicolon. This sentence structure mirrors the threshold where Young Goodman Brown stands. Ahead of him are the sunset and an adventure in the woods. Behind him are his home, Salem Village, and his wife. This opening paragraph is straightforward in both form and meaning, reflecting Goodman Brown's clarity of mind early in the story. The sentences are not simplistic by any means. The author uses a complex and multilayered sentence structure typical of the time period, though overall the writing is straightforward and clear.

> Young Goodman Brown came forth at sunset into the street at Salem Village; but put his head back after crossing the threshold, to exchange a parting kiss with his young wife. And Faith, as the wife was aptly named, thrust her own pretty head into the street, letting the wind play with the pink ribbons of her cap while she called to Goodman Brown.

This opening is a striking contrast to the language used later in the story, when Goodman Brown watches the witches' meeting in the woods. We see a drastic shift both in the sentence-level pacing and in the story as a whole. Words and clauses begin to sprawl across the page, weaving in and out of each other. Not only does this winding narrative slow the pacing but it also lends a sense of confusion and haziness. This paragraph appears in the buildup to the climax of the story:

> Another verse of the hymn arose, a slow and mournful strain, such as the pious love, but joined to words which expressed all that our nature can conceive of sin, and darkly hinted at far more. Unfathomable to mere mortals is the lore of fiends. Verse after verse was sung, and still the chorus of the desert swelled between like the deepest tone of a mighty organ; and with the final peal of that dreadful anthem there came a sound, as if the roaring wind, the rushing streams, the howling beasts, and every other voice of the unconcerted wilderness were mingling and according with the voice of guilty man in homage to the prince of all. The four blazing pines threw up a loftier flame, and obscurely discovered shapes and visages of horror on the smoke wreaths above the impious assembly. At the same moment, the fire on the rock shot redly forth and formed a glowing arch above its base, where now appeared a figure. With reverence be it spoken, the figure bore no slight similitude, both in garb and manner, to some grave divine of the New England churches.

Look at the length of the sentences in this paragraph. Notice how they are broken into multiple clauses layered upon each other. The author uses complex language combined with these multilayered sentences to slow the reader down. It takes an extra moment for the reader to piece together the meaning of the words and make sense of the scene. Even the second sentence—the shortest in the paragraph—is hard to read because the word order is unusual. It doesn't employ a traditional subject-predicate structure, as in "The lore of fiends is unfathomable to mere mortals." Instead we get a reversed predicate-subject structure: "Unfathomable to mere mortals is the lore of fiends."

Pacing is full of contradictions. If you want to build suspense, don't speed things up. Suspense builds as you slow the action down. Think of how movies use slow-motion shots in a fast-paced action scene to extend the suspense for a little while longer. We see the same technique used in stories of every genre. For instance, in a romance, the protagonist and the love interest might gaze into each other's eyes. They inch toward each other, little by little, until their lips connect in an electrifying kiss.

Nathaniel Hawthorne uses this trick, too. In *Young Goodman Brown* the closer we get to the story's climax, the longer and more winding his sentences become. This slows the pace until the climactic moment when Goodman Brown finally realizes the truth: All the people he loves and respects have succumbed to the influence of the evil one. The story cuts away at this moment, and Goodman Brown suddenly wakes up alone in the forest. The language and sentence structure shifts back to the straightforward style from the beginning. The story's climax has passed, and the suspense no longer needs to build as before.

The Three Cs of Endings

As you move toward the grand finale, remember the three Cs of endings: crisis, climax, and closure. The *crisis* is the buildup of tension as the story moves toward the final showdown. Next comes the *climax*, where the central conflict of your story comes to a head and ultimately resolves one way or the other. This is the scene where the Major Dramatic Question that drives the story is decided once and for all. After the climax comes *closure*, or the dénouement. Let's examine two stories through the lens of the three Cs.

Crisis: Building the Tension

In *Pride and Prejudice,* the pivotal moment between Act Two and Act Three is when Mr. Darcy happens upon Elizabeth, who has just heard about Lydia's elopement with Mr. Wickham. Overcome with shame and grief, Elizabeth is unable to hide her emotions and tells Mr. Darcy what has befallen her family. Mr. Darcy leaves abruptly, and Elizabeth travels home to her family.

For most of Act Three, Elizabeth waits impatiently while her father and uncle try to locate Lydia and force Wickham to marry her. Mr. Bennet returns home without success, and it seems as though all is lost and that this misfortune will plague the family forever. Finally, Elizabeth's uncle sends word that he has succeeded, and the newly married couple comes to Longbourn for a short visit before continuing to their permanent home. During this visit, Lydia lets slip that Mr. Darcy was present at her wedding, and Elizabeth realizes that he must have bribed or even coerced Wickham to agree to the marriage. All the while, Elizabeth has developed feelings for Mr. Darcy. The events of the crisis build toward the climactic scene where Elizabeth confronts Lady Catherine.

In *The Hunger Games,* the crisis takes a different slant. After Rue dies and Katniss defies the Capitol for the first time, the Gamemakers announce a change in the rules: There may now be two victors, provided they both come from the same district. This means that it is now possible for both Katniss and

Peeta to survive. Instantly Katniss knows she must find Peeta, and when she finally does, she discovers that he is severely wounded. As Act Three moves toward the climax, their romance develops, as does the horror of the Games. Between battling muttations (mutant beasts created by the Capitol) and fighting Cato, the most ruthless tribute, Katniss and Peeta barely survive. These events serve as the buildup for the final showdown, the climactic moment where Katniss takes her biggest stand against the Capitol.

Climax: Final Showdown

The climax or "final showdown" is the big moment at the end of the story where the central conflict comes together and resolves in some way. Remember the Major Dramatic Question (MDQ), which drives the main thread of your story? This is the moment where the reader finally gets an answer. If your story has subplots, the climax often answers the Lesser Dramatic Questions (LDQs) as well.

In *Pride and Prejudice* the climax is the scene where Lady Catherine visits Elizabeth and demands she break off her engagement with Mr. Darcy. Elizabeth declares that she and Mr. Darcy are not engaged, at which point Lady Catherine tries to make her promise never to enter into such an arrangement, should Mr. Darcy propose. Elizabeth refuses, saying: "I am only resolved to act in that manner, which will, in my own opinion, constitute my happiness, without reference to *you*, or to any person so wholly unconnected with me." One of the main themes in *Pride and Prejudice* is the tension between marriage and happiness. Many characters in the novel believe that marriage and happiness go hand in hand, but Elizabeth does not. It is fitting, then, that when Elizabeth finally stands up to Lady Catherine in the climax, she does so not to claim Mr. Darcy's affection but to protect her own happiness. That Mr. Darcy should eventually become the source of that happiness is irrelevant. Elizabeth is, first and foremost, standing up for herself.

The climax in *The Hunger Games* takes a different turn. After defeating Cato, Katniss and Peeta stand by the Cornucopia, filled with relief. Then the Gamemakers introduce one final, cruel twist: They revoke the rule that allows two tributes to win the Games. After all they have been through, Katniss and Peeta must now fight to the death. In this moment, Katniss decides to defy the Capitol once and for all. Why should they have any victor in their Games? If she and Peeta kill themselves, then no one wins and the Capitol is humiliated. They threaten to eat poisonous nightlock berries and, in this way, force the Gamemakers to declare them both the victors.

What is so interesting about this scene is that while it functions as the climax for the first book of trilogy, it is actually the point of no return for the trilogy as a whole. When Katniss defies the Capitol, she can no longer return to the status quo. There is no way for Katniss to undo this act of defiance and go back to playing by the Capitol's rules. This scene creates a domino effect that continues throughout the trilogy, beginning with small uprisings in the districts and culminating with an epic battle in the final book. When you are writing a series, key scenes will often play two roles: one role in that particular book and a different role within the series as a whole.

Closure: Dénouement

The final element in your story is the dénouement, a fancy word for *closure*. The reader should feel a sense of closure at the end of the novel, even if the book is part of a series or leaves the door open for a sequel. In some cases you can resolve the LDQs later in the series, but the MDQ needs some sort of resolution.

In *Pride and Prejudice,* the closure is intimately tied with Elizabeth's pursuit of happiness. When Elizabeth finally writes to her aunt to tell of her engagement, she focuses on her happiness. She writes: "I am happier even than Jane; she only smiles, I laugh." In this ending we see that marriage by itself is not the ultimate source of happiness; it must be marriage to the right person.

In *The Hunger Games,* many of the LDQs are left to be resolved in the subsequent books, but we are still given a concrete answer to the MDQ. The Games are over, and both Katniss and Peeta are declared victors. The final image of the book shows them holding hands while traveling home on the train. We have no idea what their lives will be like once they arrive back in District 12, nor do we know if their romance will continue or what consequences they will face after their defiant act against the Capitol. These threads keep readers hooked and eager to read the rest of the trilogy. Yet, even though these elements are left hanging, we feel a sense of completeness because the main thread of the story has been resolved.

Four Types of Endings

How you end your story hinges on whether your character gets what she wants, and whether she still wants it. Usually the character's want is tied to the Major Dramatic Question of the book, so when you resolve that question in the climax, you also determine whether the character gets what she wants. In *The Hunger Games* Katniss wants to survive. In *Pride and Prejudice* Elizabeth wants to find happiness. In the latter case, the MDQ is not whether Elizabeth finds happiness but whether she and Mr. Darcy end up together. Still, Elizabeth's pursuit of happiness is closely tied to the central question of the book.

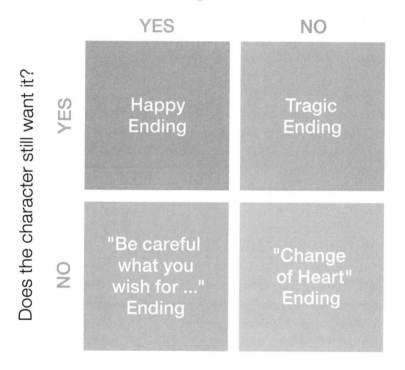

The Ending Matrix

Whether the character gets what she wants is only one facet of your ending. You also need to consider whether your character still wants what she originally desired. For example, in *Pride and Prejudice,* Elizabeth wants happiness, and at first she thinks that her happiness depends on being as far away from Mr. Darcy as possible. As the story develops and Elizabeth changes, however, her want shifts. She begins to realize that being with Mr. Darcy will indeed bring her happiness. At the beginning of the story, Elizabeth thinks that happiness means helping her sister Jane be happily married. She has no intention of getting married herself. As Elizabeth changes throughout the story, her perspective about marriage changes as well. When Mr. Darcy proposes for the second time, she accepts and ends up even happier than her sister.

You can choose one of four possible endings for your story, each depending on your character's want:

- **THE HAPPY ENDING:** The character gets what she wants, and she still wants it at the end of the story. Despite not being particularly upbeat, *The Hunger Games* is an example of a happy ending because Katniss survives and does not have to face off against Peeta.
- **THE TRAGIC ENDING:** The character still wants something, but he doesn't get it at the end. In *King Lear*, Lear wants his daughters to love him most, but his want is not satisfied. Not only do his older daughters abuse him horribly but his youngest and favorite daughter, Cordelia, dies.
- **THE "CHANGE OF HEART" ENDING:** The character doesn't get what she wants, but she is still happy because she doesn't want it anymore anyway. *Pride and Prejudice* has this type of ending because Elizabeth starts out not wanting to get married, but eventually falls in love with and marries Mr. Darcy. In a "change of heart" ending, the protagonist's want usually shifts during the midpoint moment of self-reflection.
- **THE "BE CAREFUL WHAT YOU WISH FOR" ENDING:** The character gets what he wanted, but it's not what he thought it would be. This type of ending is rare; it shows up most often in fables and novellas. Keep in mind that this type of ending isn't as satisfying a resolution for your reader as the other endings. Not only can it seem preachy and moralistic, it can also result in a story that feels incomplete, as though the character's quest for a new want is just the beginning.

There you have it: an in-depth road map of story structure and the landmark scenes in your story. To summarize, in Act One, the beginning, you make five promises to your reader, plus you reach a pivotal moment where something big happens (the inciting incident) and the character must make a choice (the point of no return). This choice pushes the character into Act Two, where she can no longer go back to the way things were.

In Act Two, you deliver on the premise of the story, and your character goes on a journey—literal or metaphorical—and meets new allies or enemies along the way. In the middle, the character experiences either a temporary triumph or a false failure and has a moment of self-reflection. After the midpoint, the story picks up speed, the stakes get higher, and the protagonist hits a rock-bottom moment and feels as if all is lost. She undergoes another moment of self-reflection (often called "the dark night of the soul") and must decide whether to give up or to go on despite all odds. This decision pushes the protagonist into Act Three.

Finally, in Act Three, the crisis builds tension until the climactic "final showdown" scene of your story. Here, the central conflict comes to a head, and the protagonist either gets what she wants or fails. Usually the final showdown is also where the Major Dramatic Question of your story is answered or resolved in some way. After the climax, the story reaches some sort of closure with the dénouement. You can leave the door open for a sequel or series, but it's crucial that you resolve the central conflict of this particular book in some way. Your reader must feel a sense of satisfaction with the ending, but you don't need to tie up all your loose ends.

13

Give Your Story a Voice

Narration is the lens through which your reader experiences a story, and it includes two fundamental elements: voice and point of view. This chapter focuses on voice, and the next one gives you an in-depth look at point of view.

Voice is the sound and tone of your story. It's the piece of you that goes into everything you write. It's your literary fingerprint, your signature style, and it develops over time. As your writing skills grow, you will learn to modulate your voice and adjust it depending on the context. Voice isn't useful in "creative" writing alone, either. It comes through in blog posts, articles, and anything else you write.

Voice is one of the most delicate elements of writing, and if you're not careful, you might squash it. It is one of the few topics I teach without using acronyms, categories, or rules of thumb. Instead, I take a free-form approach that will help you recognize the different facets and layers of voice but give you room to practice and play.

How to Look at Voice

As you recall from chapter ten, voice is one of the promises you make to your reader from the very first page. It is one of the essential elements of your story, and yet it's often the most difficult skill for writers to master.

Many writing craft books try to categorize voice by shoving it into neat little boxes. They claim that one author has a "ceremonial voice" while another has a "conversational voice." This is nonsense. Pigeonholing your voice will only make you want to break free of those shackles. After all, what if your voice doesn't fit into one of these rigid categories? Or, worse, what if your voice *changes* from one book to another (or even changes *within* one book)?

Attempting to categorize your voice won't help you write your book any better, and just because you know what category your book's voice falls into doesn't mean you know how to make the most of it. While labeling character archetypes or plot landmarks can help you understand how those elements operate within your story, when it comes to voice, labels are useless.

In order to make sense of voice in writing, you need to understand two fundamental things:

1. Voice operates on multiple levels.
2. Voice can be obvious or invisible, but it's always there.

Multiple Levels of Voice

Many people talk about the voice of a story, but rarely does a piece of writing have only one voice. In fact, there are usually at least *two levels* of voice in any given work. If you're into metafiction, where the writer offers commentary or uses a story-within-a-story framework, you can have even more levels. For the purposes of this discussion, however, let's focus on a typical two-voice narrative.

The first, most basic level of voice is that of the narrator. This is the voice that tells the story, and we see it in the narration, description, and other non-dialogue segments. The second level contains the voices of the characters in the story, voices we usually hear only in dialogue. Unless a story consists of dialogue alone—like in a stage play—or narration alone, it will automatically have at least these two levels of voice.

Of course, when you're in first-person point of view, the voice of the narrator and the voice of the protagonist overlap because they come from the same person. This doesn't mean that the voices are one and the same. For instance, a protagonist might be very polite in dialogue, but when we read the narration and experience the character's thoughts, we hear a different, snarkier tone. While these voices might be coming from the same character, the dialogue voice and the narrator's voice are completely different.

What about novels with only one level of voice? This happens when you eliminate either all the narration or all the dialogue in a story and constrain yourself to using only one level of voice. Doing so is incredibly hard to sustain, and few books are written this way. Instead, you're more likely to see short stories or essays written with only one level of voice.

"The Tell-Tale Heart" by Edgar Allan Poe is one such short story. Since this story takes place almost entirely in the narrator's mind and eliminates all but a smattering of dialogue, the only thing we hear is the voice of the narrator. This particular example is especially interesting because as the story develops the reader begins to sense that the narrator is, in fact, not completely truthful. Because the story is so deeply entrenched in the character's head, it takes a while for the full extent of the narrator's unreliability to come to light.

In contrast, "Hills Like White Elephants" by Ernest Hemingway relies almost entirely on dialogue. With the exception of a few stage directions and dialogue tags, most of the story is told through the dialogue between the characters. The middle-grade novel *Seek* by Paul Fleischman is an even more extreme example: It is written as a radio play so that most of the story comes through in the voices of the characters.

Another important consideration is whether the narrator's voice is present and distinct, or almost invisible. A first-person narrator is easy to spot, but just because a piece is in third person doesn't mean the narrator doesn't have a voice. Many writers assume that if their book or story is written in third person, they're off the hook and don't have to worry about voice. They're wrong. In fact, the opposite is true: Writing in third person can be even more complex than writing in first person because the author must make conscious choices about how present the narratorial voice will be in the story. The first person is straightforward: A character tells the story as she sees it unravel. The third-person narrator has more wiggle room. The narrator's voice can be in-your-face and opinionated, or so seamless that it's practically invisible. Of course, most stories don't fall into these extreme categories and instead end up somewhere along the spectrum.

The Opinionated Narrator

Sometimes a narrator has strong opinions that slip out as she tells the story. This opinionated narrator is common in eighteenth- and nineteenth-century novels, think of those written by authors like Charles Dickens and Jane Austen. In these cases, an omniscient narrator often "head hops" from one character's point of view to another and shares her true opinions—her agenda, if you will—throughout the story.

A great example of an opinionated third-person narrator is *Matilda* by Roald Dahl. The voice comes through in the first line of the book: "It's a funny thing about mothers and fathers. Even when their own child is the most disgusting little blister you could ever imagine, they still think he or she is wonderful." We can tell right away that the narrator has strong contempt for children (particularly spoiled, unexceptional children) with the phrase "disgusting little blister." In the first few pages of the book, the author establishes the irony of parenting. While some parents blindly adore their mediocre children, others ignore their children despite their legitimate brilliance; the book *Matilda* is about the latter scenario. The opinionated voice of the narrator not only sets up the contradiction between the two types of parents but also establishes the narrator as someone who sees through that absurdity and "tells it like it is" to the reader. The narrator and reader are like allies, discovering together how extraordinary the story's protagonist, Matilda, really is.

In other books, the opinionated narrator might even break the "fourth wall" and address the reader directly. We see this especially in fables or fairy tales, where the narrator might interject with morals or lessons as the story develops. This narratorial choice aligns the narrator and reader but also establishes the narrator as an authority who is imparting wisdom to the reader as the story unfolds. Kate DiCamillo uses this technique in *The Tale of Despereaux*, where from the very beginning we know that this narrator has distinct opinions and an even more distinct voice. Here are the closing lines from chapter one:

> "The last one," said the father. "And he'll be dead soon. He can't live. Not with his eyes open like that."
>
> But, reader, he did live.
> This is his story.

The Invisible Narrator

At the other end of the spectrum are third-person narrators who are so subtle and unobtrusive that the reader hardly notices their presence. The narrator melts into the background so that readers can focus instead on the characters and the story. Of course, invisible narrators don't happen by accident. They're extremely difficult to pull off, and the writer must make a conscious choice to craft the narrator this way.

Having an invisible narrator doesn't mean that you don't have a narrator at all. The narrator is clearly telling the story, but the voice doesn't draw attention to itself. Often this type of narrator is omniscient and can pop in and out of character's heads quietly, without making a fuss. One lovely example occurs in *The Secret of Platform Thirteen* by Eva Ibbotson. The narrator certainly has a distinct tone, but it's so subtle that we hardly notice and are instead carried away by a good story.

If you went into a school nowadays and said to the children: "What is a *gump?*" you would probably get some very silly answers.

"It's a person without a brain, like a chump," a child might say. Or:

"It's a camel whose hump has got stuck." Or even:

"It's a kind of chewing gum."

But once this wasn't so. Once every child in the land could have told you that a gump was a special mound, a grassy bump on the earth, and that in this bump was a hidden door which opened every so often to reveal a tunnel which led to a completely different world.

Notice the subtle choices the author makes in these first lines. She could have started the book by saying: " A gump is a special mound, a grassy bump on the earth ... ." Instead, she uses the invisible—but very present—narrator to engage the reader in a kind of game. The narrator poses the question "What is a *gump?*" and right away the reader wants to figure out the answer. We don't want to be like the kids who give the silly answers; we want to be one of the kids in the know. By the time the author tells us what a gump is, we've become so curious that we're not about to question the existence of gumps. We've already bought into the idea.

Additionally, by presenting the gump as something that was common knowledge long ago but that no one knows about anymore, the author makes the existence of gumps feel plausible. Of course the reader wouldn't know what a gump is—no one does anymore. But that doesn't mean that gumps aren't *real*. Ibbotson crafts this opening with such artful sleight of hand that we don't even notice the narrator gently nudging us into the story, making us suspend our disbelief and embrace a world where gumps—and all the magic associated with them—are real.

EMULATE THE MASTERS

Humpty Dumpty sat on a wall.
Humpty Dumpty had a great fall.
All the king's horses and all the king's men
Couldn't put Humpty together again.

Rewrite the nursery rhyme "Humpty Dumpty" in the voice of one of the authors on this list (or any other author whose voice you admire): William Faulkner, Franz Kafka, Ernest Hemingway, Jane Austen, George Eliot,

Henry James, Edgar Allan Poe, Toni Morrison, Edith Wharton, Charles Dickens, J.R.R Tolkien, Isaac Asimov, Maya Angelou, Chinua Achebe, Sandra Cisneros, Jack Kerouac, Kurt Vonnegut, Samuel Beckett, William Shakespeare, or Geoffrey Chaucer.

The idea is to re-create the story told in the nursery rhyme in the voice and style of the author you choose. It doesn't need to be in poetic form, nor does it need to rhyme. The nursery rhyme is simply a springboard that lets you focus on the voice you have selected rather than on plot or character. Your finished story should be no longer than 700 words.

BONUS: Do the exercise a second time, but with a different author. Try to select an author whose voice is completely different from the one you used before. Then compare the results. Which voice felt more natural to write? When did the words flow more freely? These clues will help you fine-tune your voice going forward.

How to Hone Your Voice

"Find your voice" has become a writing instruction cliché (second only to "Kill your darlings" and "Show, don't tell"), but it turns out that this is bad advice. "Find your voice" implies that your voice is missing and that to improve your writing you must insert more voice into it. Nonsense. You *already have* a voice, and it's present in everything you write. It might not be obvious—it might be almost invisible—but it's there. The key is to shape it with intention.

Unlike fingerprints or DNA, remember that your voice is malleable. When teachers say, "Find your voice," what they really mean is "Hone your voice," or "Understand how your voice works." For better or worse, you already have a voice, but if you're just starting out as a writer, that voice might be mediocre. In fact, your voice might even be terrible. That's okay. You can improve your voice. You can cultivate it, prune it, and shape it so that it will grow into something beautiful.

As you practice and study voice (both your own and the voices of the masters), you will discover something important: While you can hone and improve your voice, you can't force it to be something that it's not. Just as you can't grow roses from sunflower seeds, your voice has a core essence you cannot change. What "finding your voice" really means is that you must uncover that core element, that piece of you that is inextricably woven into your writing. Once you understand your voice's natural tendencies, you can play with it and practice. Eventually, you will learn how to shape your voice and make it the best it can be within those natural constraints.

— 14 —

Choose Your Point of View

In contrast to voice, point of view (POV) is technical and structured. A narrative can be told from several different points of view, and the one you choose will affect all aspects of your story. In this chapter, you'll learn what these POV options are and the advantages and limitations of each. You'll also discover how the verb tense of your story can impact your narrator's perspective and may even affect your overall time line.

Choosing a Point of View

Point of view is one of the trickiest concepts in writing, and one of my favorites to teach. When you first explore POV, it can feel like learning a new language, but don't worry—you are not alone. I grappled with this topic for a long time, as did many of my students, before I came up with a Point-of-View Cheat Sheet to help me keep track of the different POV options and choose the right one for my story. You can download a copy of this cheat sheet at DIYMFA.com/thebook by signing up with your e-mail address.

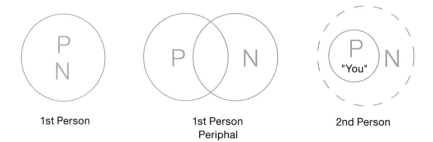

Point-of-View Cheat Sheet

3rd Person
Limited

3rd Person
Objective

3rd Person
Multiple

3rd Person
Omniscient

All Characters

Point-of-View Cheat Sheet

In the cheat sheet, *P* stands for the Protagonist, or the main character in your story, and *S* indicates Supporting Characters. *N* stands for the Narrator, or the person telling the story. Sometimes *P* and *N* are one and the same. Sometimes they are not.

A solid circle in the cheat sheet represents a character inside the story, while a dashed-line circle represents someone outside the story. Notice how *P* is always in a solid circle. This is because the protagonist is always a character in the story. The narrator, on the other hand, can either be a character in the story or someone outside it. This means that *N* can have either a solid or a dashed line. The circles represent what *P* or *N* know in the story—the information and perspective available to each of them.

When using the cheat sheet to figure out point of view, you must consider the intersection between what the protagonist knows and what the narrator knows. For example, in the first-person POV, the protagonist and narrator are one and the same, so the circles overlap completely. Conversely, in a third-person point of view, the narrator is someone outside the story. This means she has access to information the protagonist does not know. An omniscient third-person narrator knows *everything* and can see inside the minds of any character at any time. A multiple third-person narrator can switch perspective from one character to another, but at any given moment that narrator's POV is firmly planted in the mind of one specific character. The *reader*, on the other hand, experiences the whole story from all the different points of view. In piecing those perspectives together, the reader receives a global, big-picture view of the story.

First-Person Point of View: Your Narrator Is a Character

In the first-person POV, the narrator is a character in the story. This is the "I" narrator, where a character recounts what is happening from his perspective. Because the narrator is a character, he has a limited view of the events that occur. The first person has very little ability to zoom out and see the big picture because—for better or worse—that point of view is planted firmly in the mind of one character.

Early writers chose the first-person POV in order to make fiction seem more authentic. The idea was that if a novel was written in the first person, then the reader would feel like it was a true story, something that actually happened. The novel *Robinson Crusoe* by Daniel Defoe is a great example of one of the earliest instances of a first-person narrator. It reads almost like a journalistic account written by a man marooned on a desert island.

> I was born in the year 1632, in the city of York, of a good family, though not of that country, my father being a foreigner of Bremen, who settled first at Hull. He got a good estate by merchandise, and leaving off his trade, lived afterwards at York, from whence he had married my mother, whose relations were named Robinson, a very good family in that country, and from whom I was called Robinson Kreutznaer; but, by the usual corruption of words in England, we are now called—nay we call ourselves and write our name—Crusoe; and so my companions always called me.

First person has an immediacy that makes it easy for readers to relate to the character in the story. It feels almost as though the narrator is speaking directly to the reader. In fact, some stories take that tell-all tone to the extreme by presenting the narration as a confession from the character-narrator to the reader. One example of a confessional-style first-person narrative is *The Catcher in the Rye* by J.D. Salinger, in which protagonist Holden Caulfield tells his story to doctors in a mental institution, explaining the events that led to his breakdown. For another more contemporary example, look at Pete Hautman's *Blank Confession*, in which part of the narrative consists of protagonist Shayne Blank recounting his story to the police as he is interrogated.

The first-person POV has one complication: At some point it may become necessary for the author to explain the existence of the narration. In most situations, the reader will be drawn into the story to such an extent that any inconsistencies surrounding this issue will be irrelevant. As the writer, however, it is important that *you* consider how this first-person narrative came to be. Did the character write down the events as they happened? If so, how did the reader come to possess the text? These are all layers that add dimension to your first-person narration.

"The Yellow Wallpaper" by Charlotte Perkins Gilman accounts for its first-person narrative. In chapter nine, I discussed how this story beautifully illustrates various elements of character development. However, it contains one quirky twist in the point of view. At the beginning of the story, the first-person POV makes sense. The protagonist is writing down her story in secret, in her diary. In fact, at one point the protagonist even says she must stop writing because someone is coming: "There's sister on the stairs!" At the end of the story, however, when "John dear" bursts into the room, the diary style of the narration fizzles away. Suddenly we are no longer reading a diary account of the protagonist's experiences. Instead, we realize that we have been inside the protagonist's psyche this whole time, and as her sanity deteriorates, the diary aspect of the narration disappears as well. The story ends with this line: "Now why should that man have fainted? But he did, and right across my path by the wall, so that I had to creep over him every time!" Where did the diary go? It turns out that it never existed in the first place, and at this moment we realize the truth: that this story exists in a psychological no man's land where wallpaper and woman have blurred together.

Changing the POV is risky. In some cases, your readers might be so drawn into the story that when the POV switches, they will easily accept the change or won't even notice. In other situations, like in "The Yellow Wallpaper," that change can underscore a thematic element of the story. In this example, the disorienting shift in the narrative is effective because it forces the reader to feel some of the protagonist's confusion and madness. Keep in mind, however, that any change in POV will chip away at the trust you have built with the reader. In extreme cases it might feel like you've promised one thing to your readers and then pulled a bait and switch. If you choose to break the rules you've set for your story's point of view, do so with good reason.

The more seamless you make the reading experience, the more likely your readers are to stick with you and not put down the book. When you change the rules too often, your readers will stop focusing on being *in* the story and instead will concentrate on what's happening with the story*telling*. Every time your readers have to pause and wonder about the point of view or the time line, they are no longer immersed in the "narrative dream." You can change your story's time line or try a new point of view, but the more you experiment, the more challenging it will be to make the reader's experience as smooth as possible. Of course, you want to trust your readers to trust you, to "get" what you're doing in the story, but don't make their job unnecessarily difficult. Whenever you jolt your readers out of the story, you give them the opportunity to put your book down. It is your responsibility as the writer to do whatever it takes to prevent this.

THREE THINGS TO CONSIDER WHEN CHOOSING YOUR POV

As you decide whether a particular POV is right for your story, there are three things you should keep in mind. These factors—and how much they matter to your story—will help you determine which POV is the right choice.

1. **VERISIMILITUDE:** To what extent does the POV make this story seem more realistic or true? Does this realism matter to your story?
2. **IMMEDIACY:** Does this narration pull readers into the story and make them feel like they're right next to the protagonist? Is this immediacy vital to the story, or would a bird's-eye view be more effective?
3. **META-NARRATION:** Does the story account for the existence of the narration? If so, how? If not, what is the effect?

Remember, there are no right or wrong answers. These are choices that you must make as a writer; each choice will have advantages and disadvantages. You must learn to train your eye so that you notice the subtleties.

Traditional First Person

In this POV, the most common type of "I" narration, the protagonist is the person telling the story. This POV can use a meta-narration, which accounts for the existence of the story by using a frame. (A frame is a story-within-a-story format that informs the reader of exactly who the narrator is, where or when this story is being told, and—most important—why he is telling the story.) You can also take a more immediate approach by entrenching the POV so firmly in a character's mind that readers don't care how or why the narrative exists; they're just along for the ride. *The Catcher in the Rye* by J.D. Salinger uses the meta-approach, while *The Hunger Games* by Suzanne Collins gives us a more immediate first-person POV, in which the reader experiences the Games along with Katniss.

Notice that in the cheat sheet the circles for *P* and *N* overlap exactly. This is because the narrator and the protagonist are one and the same, meaning that the narrator can only know information that the protagonist has access to—no more, no less.

Peripheral First Person

In the peripheral first person, the narrator is a supporting character in the story rather than the main character. A classic example is *The Great Gatsby* by F. Scott Fitzgerald, in which the narrator is Nick Carraway and the protagonist is, of course, Jay Gatsby.

In the diagram, the circles for the protagonist and the narrator overlap only partially. The narrator has access to *some* information the protagonist knows but does not know everything. The protagonist may have secrets that the narrator is not privy to or must uncover in the story. The narrator also must be present in order to recount the events. This means that if something happens to the protagonist but the narrator doesn't witness it, then the author must find some other way to convey that information to the reader. For instance, Nick is able to give the reader only the details of Gatsby's past that he learns himself.

The peripheral first-person point of view is challenging. The writer must strategically let the narrator discover key pieces of information so that the reader may learn these details as well. The reader can only know as much as the narrator is able to reveal, so if the narrator's view of the story is limited, the reader's view will be equally narrow.

Unreliable First Person

In this POV, the first-person narrator cannot be trusted. There are many reasons why this is the case. Maybe the character is a very young child with an innocent viewpoint who doesn't understand the events happening around him. Or maybe the character's perception of reality is warped because he is insane, as in "The Tell-Tale Heart" by Edgar Allan Poe. Or better yet, the character might be perfectly sane but also a pathological liar.

Gone Girl by Gillian Flynn uses a multiple first-person point of view in order to reveal an unreliable narrator. In this book, we get two alternating first-person accounts from a husband and his wife. The wife has disappeared and is presumed dead, but we get her side of the story from a diary. As the story develops we see inconsistencies between the two versions of reality. Eventually we realize that one of these narrators is lying.

What is so fascinating about *Gone Girl* is how it handles the revelation of this unreliable narrator. In most books with unreliable narrators, the big reveal comes at the end, when we finally figure out that the narrator is crazy or lying. The timing of this moment is crucial; if it comes too soon, readers will stop trusting the narrator and may give up on the story altogether. In *Gone Girl*, however, the big reveal happens in the middle. You might assume that this strategy would kill the story, but with artful plot twists and strong storytelling, the author manages to keep the momentum and retain the reader's trust.

Third-Person Point of View: Your Narrator Is Outside the Story

The third-person narrator can be broad, sweeping, and omniscient, like a voice in the sky. This narrator can also zoom in very close, almost like a movie camera perched on the shoulder of one of the characters. In this close POV (often called the limited third person) the narrator will follow one particular character throughout the story. In some cases the movie camera alternates between two or more characters for different chapters or scenes.

Third person is the "he/she/it" narrator. Unlike the first person, this POV can zoom in and out during a given scene. In some moments the movie camera can zoom in so close to a character that we see the pores on his nose and the sweat on his upper lip. In other moments, the camera can zoom out and give us a broad panoramic shot. This ability to zoom in and out is called *narrative distance*, and it is an important tool in your writing toolbox.

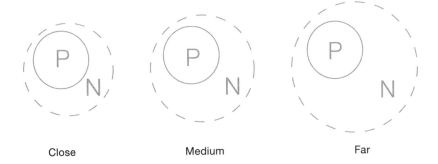

Close   Medium   Far

Narrative Distance: Limited Third Person

This diagram shows how narrative distance can affect your story. The point of view may be the same throughout, but the narrative distance changes. When the narrative distance decreases and zooms in close, the narrator is inside the protagonist's head. This means that even though the narrator is now an entity outside the story, the circles almost overlap. As the narrative distance increases and zooms out, the narrator has access to more information outside the protagonist's viewpoint. This gives readers a more panoramic view, but they also lose some of the detail, that up-close-and-personal feeling they get when the narrative distance is decreased.

As with a movie lens, you should avoid zooming in and out too quickly because it can disorient your reader. Stick with more subtle modulations, and remember that playing with narrative distance will work only in third person. With a first-person narrator, we are locked solidly into the perspective of the character telling the story. Because a third-person narrator is outside the story, you have more ability to vary that distance, so the third-person POV will give you wiggle room that you can't achieve with the first-person POV.

For an example of variations in narrative distance, here is the opening of the sixth book in the Harry Potter series, *Harry Potter and the Half-Blood Prince.*

> It was nearing midnight and the Prime Minister was sitting alone in his office, reading a long memo that was slipping through his brain without leaving the slightest trace of meaning behind. He was waiting for a call from the President of a far distant country, and between wondering when the wretched man would telephone, and trying to suppress unpleasant memories of what had been a very long, tiring, and difficult week, there was not much space in his head for anything else. The more he attempted to focus on the print on the page before

him, the more clearly the Prime Minister could see the gloating face of one of his political opponents. This particular opponent had appeared on the news that very day, not only to enumerate all the terrible things that had happened in the last week (as though anyone needed reminding) but also to explain why each and every one of them was the government's fault.

The Prime Minister's pulse quickened at the very thought of these accusations, for they were neither fair nor true. How on earth was his government to have stopped that bridge collapsing? It was outrageous for anybody to suggest that they were not spending enough on bridges. The bridge was fewer than ten years old, and the best experts were at a loss to explain why it had snapped cleanly in two, sending a dozen cars into the watery depths of the river below. And how dare anyone suggest that it was lack of policemen that had resulted in those two very nasty and well-publicized murders? Or that the government should have somehow foreseen the freak hurricane in the West Country that had caused so much damage to both people and property? And was it *his* fault that one of his Junior Ministers, Herbert Chorley, had chosen this week to act so peculiarly that he was now going to be spending a lot more time with his family?

"A grim mood has gripped the country," the opponent had concluded, barely concealing his own broad grin.

And unfortunately, this was perfectly true. The Prime Minister felt it himself; people really did seem more miserable than usual. Even the weather was dismal; all this chilly mist in the middle of July … . It wasn't right, it wasn't normal … .

He turned over the second page of the memo, saw how much longer it went on, and gave it up as a bad job. Stretching his arms above his head he looked around his office mournfully. It was a handsome room, with a fine marble fireplace facing the long sash windows, firmly closed against the unseasonable chill. With a slight shiver, the Prime Minster got up and moved over to the window, looking out at the thin mist that was pressing itself against the glass. It was then, as he stood with his back to the room, that he heard a soft cough behind him.

He froze, nose to nose with his own scared-looking reflection in the dark glass. He knew that cough. He had heard it before. He turned very slowly to face the empty room.

Throughout this passage, the narrative distance undergoes subtle variations that add texture and depth to the narration and POV. The first paragraph offers a panoramic view of the Prime Minster in his office, then zooms in slightly to get a hint of his thoughts. Despite being in the Prime Minister's point of view, the narration feels like it's at an arm's length.

In the second paragraph, we zoom in closer: The Prime Minister's pulse quickens, and we read his exact thoughts about the bridge collapsing, the murders, and the hurricane in the West Country. In the third paragraph, the lens zooms out again, and we get a view of the Prime Minister stretching his arms, moving to the window, and hearing the cough behind him. Finally, when he turns to face the source of the cough, we zoom out even farther to see the whole empty room.

These shifts in narrative distance are subtle, but they are there. More important, these variations would be nearly impossible to present in the first person. Keep narrative distance in mind as we examine variations in third-person POV.

Limited Third Person

The limited third-person POV is limited to just one character in the story. The narrator only knows what that character knows and only sees what that character sees. For example, in *A Christmas Carol* by Charles Dickens, the story follows Ebenezer Scrooge at all times. In scenes where Scrooge is not a participant in the action—like the Cratchit family Christmas dinner or the party hosted by Scrooge's nephew—he is the observer, and we experience these moments through his eyes as he travels with the ghosts of Christmas past, present, and future.

In the Prydain Chronicles by Lloyd Alexander, the first four books of his five-part series are in limited third person, and the narrator follows the protagonist, Taran. It is only in the final book of the series, *The High King*, that the author shifts from a limited third-person POV to a multiple POV. This shift allows the reader to see the epic battles of that final book from the perspective of several different characters. The multiple POV lets the reader experience scenes where Taran does not appear, adding depth to the story and bringing those broad, sweeping battles to life. Multiple points of view can work with both first-person and third-person narrations, and some books even combine the two. Later in this chapter, we'll look at how to craft a story using multiple points of view.

Omniscient Third Person

The omniscient third person is the "eye in the sky" scenario in which the narrator sees and knows *everything* in the story. The narrator's knowledge isn't limited by what one character knows. In fact, it's almost as if the narrator is an all-seeing god—hence the term *omniscient*. This POV was very popular in eighteenth- and nineteenth-century novels, particularly because it lends more objectivity to the story. While a first-person POV feels *personal*, the omniscient third person is almost journalistic in its objectivity, which adds to the verisimilitude. The voice of this omniscient narrator can be either obvious (like in Jane Austen's *Pride and Prejudice*) or invisible (as with Eva Ibbotson's *The Secret of Platform 13*).

One of the advantages of the omniscient third person is that it allows you to "head hop," or access the thoughts and emotions of any character in the story at any time. While this can work to your advantage, keep in mind that jumping from one character's thoughts to another can be just as disorienting as rapidly modulating the narrative distance. Using the omniscient narrator artfully is quite difficult and should be done with great care.

Also, while this narrator knows all, the "eye in the sky" perspective lends a certain distance to the story. It is quite difficult for readers to relate to the characters if the narrator feels too far away. An omniscient narrator often works best when you follow one protagonist very closely, so that your readers know exactly which character they should root for. *Pride and Prejudice*, which employs the omniscient third person, never follows Jane into London or shows Lydia's elopement directly. Instead, these events occur from Elizabeth's perspective as she reads about them in letters. While the narrator still offers the thoughts and feelings of other characters from time to time, it is clear that Elizabeth is the protagonist because the narration follows her most closely.

Objective Third Person

While the omniscient narrator can hop into any character's head, the objective narrator cannot access anyone's mind. This means that the narrator can only relate information that is easily visible or audible (i.e., the actions or words of the characters). This narrator can't tell the reader about the character's thoughts or feelings because it doesn't know.

The objective point of view is like watching a movie, where the only information conveyed is what is seen or heard. (Disregard movies with annoying voice-over narrators that reveal what the character is thinking—that's cheating.) The objective POV is difficult to sustain for long pieces; in fact, the only example of this POV I can think of occurs in a short story: Raymond Carver's "Little Things." This story, which depicts a fight between a husband and wife as their marriage falls apart, is so emotionally charged that it would be almost too painful for the reader to experience it through either character's point of view. In this case, the objective POV allows readers to keep the necessary distance so that they can see the events unfold without the thoughts or emotions of either character shading their perspective.

Notice how in the cheat sheet the narrator's circle and the protagonist's circle do not overlap at all. This is because the only information the narrator can access is what can be observed externally through the characters' words and actions. The narrator knows no more about the characters than would a casual observer.

Other Point-of-View Choices

In addition to first and third person, there are a few other POV options available: second person, epistolary, and any multiple POV combination. You can also use narrative devices (e.g., letters, diary entries, newspaper clippings, graphic elements, and even footnotes) in your story to add texture, enhance the storytelling, or impart information that the reader might not be able to access otherwise. As with all POV choices, you need to keep three factors in mind: verisimilitude, immediacy, and meta-narration.

Remember, also, that consistency is key. As the writer, you get to make the rules of your story and can break them when necessary, but every time you do so you will stretch your reader's trust. Jump too far out of bounds and the reader might stop trusting you altogether, maybe even stop reading. You must set the ground rules early in the story and give your readers cues so they can follow what you're doing. The more experimental your narrative, the more cues you will need.

Second Person

The second-person POV is the "you" narrator: "You go to the store and realize you forgot your wallet." This POV makes it feel as if the narrator is speaking directly to the reader, but unlike a confessional-style first-person POV, in which the narrator is sharing *his* experiences, the second person makes *the reader* feel like the protagonist.

This narration is common in prescriptive nonfiction, in which the author gives advice to the readers, but when fiction adopts this POV, it takes a very different tone. Suddenly the reader is shoved into the shoes of the protagonist as the narrator gives advice or instructions. Think of the short story "Girl" by Jamaica Kincaid, which begins: "Wash the white clothes on Monday and put them on the stone heap; wash the color clothes on Tuesday and put them on the clothesline to dry." The story continues with a string of similar orders, so that by the end the readers can't help but relate to the protagonist who is forced to do all these chores.

Like objective POV, the second person is hard to sustain, and few novels are written in this way. The most famous example is *Bright Lights, Big City* by Jay McInerney. The author's point-of-view choice makes sense because it forces the reader to suspend disbelief and identify with a protagonist who is not particularly sympathetic.

> You are not the kind of guy who would be at a place like this at this time of the morning. But here you are, and you cannot say that the terrain is entirely unfamiliar, although the details are fuzzy. You are at a nightclub talking to a girl with a shaved head. The club is either Heartbreak or the Lizard Lounge. All might come clear if you could just slip into the bathroom and do a little more Bolivian Marching Powder. Then again, it might not. A small voice inside you insists that this epidemic lack of clarity is a result of too much of that already. The night has already turned on that imperceptible pivot where two A.M. changes to six A.M. You know this moment has come and gone, but you are not yet willing to concede that you have crossed the line beyond which all is gratuitous damage to the palsy of unraveled nerve endings. Somewhere back there you could have cut your losses, but you rode past that moment on a comet trail of white powder and now you are trying to hang on to the rush.

From the opening paragraph we can tell this protagonist has made some poor life choices. Clearly this is not the first time he has ended up in a "place like this at this time of the morning." He does drugs. He parties at all hours of the night. And yet, a small part of us wants to relate to him. The second-person POV shoves the readers into the shoes of this unsympathetic character. Of course, we know that the narrator isn't speaking directly to *us*. We know that this is a story and that we are not this protagonist, but the second-person POV forces us to align ourselves with him.

Epistolary Form and Other Narrative Devices

Epistolary form is a story told in letters. The novel *Pamela* by Samuel Richardson, published in 1740, is a classic example: The protagonist writes letters to her family and recounts the events of her life as a servant in a noble estate.

Through Pamela's letters we get an insider's view of the wealthy household she serves. While it is an entirely fictional account, the epistolary narration gives the story an added sense of realism. There is also something voyeuristic, almost risqué, about the epistolary form, as though the reader is rifling through a character's private correspondence. Similar to the epistolary form are stories told through diary entries, e-mails, text messages, or even blog posts.

These narratives operate like the first-person POV because the main character in the story usually writes the letters, diary, etc. Keep in mind, however, that this form may limit your storytelling options even more than the first person does. For instance, people don't usually write dialogue in their letters or diaries. Your readers might be able to suspend disbelief if you use a little bit of dialogue in this form, but add too much and they may grow suspicious of the narrative.

You can also use epistolary or diary form to supplement another POV choice. For example, Jane Austen often includes letters between characters in her novels. This allows the readers to glimpse information that the main point of view wouldn't ordinarily allow. This technique can be especially useful if you are using a first-person or limited third-person POV and need to convey certain information to your reader. A lost letter, an overheard conversation, a newspaper clipping, or an open diary—you can use these and many other sleight-of-hand tricks to sidestep POV limitations.

Other narrative devices include images or annotations that enhance the story being told in the text. For instance, the doodles in *Diary of a Wimpy Kid* by Jeff Kinney give the story a comedic visual element. While the protagonist might say one thing in the diary text, the pictures show us what really happened, and this contrast often has a humorous effect. Other examples include *Miss Peregrine's Home for Peculiar Children*, in which author Ransom Riggs offsets the narrative with creepy vintage photographs, and Chris Wooding's *Malice*, in which the text shifts into graphic novel sections when the characters enter the world of a comic book. Finally, in *Pale Fire* by Vladimir Nabakov, the story comes to life not in the epic poem itself, but in the footnotes added by the protagonist.

If you decide to use a narrative device to enhance your story, remember the following three things: First and foremost, readers don't care about fancy maneuvers and nifty tricks; they want a good story. The device you choose cannot be an end in and of itself; it should serve a purpose and enhance the narrative in some way. Second, the execution must be seamless. This is especially important with visual elements like illustrations or comics because clunky execution will pull your readers out of the story. Instead, the inclusion of images, drawings, or other visual elements must be flawless so that your readers barely notice all of your sleight-of-hand tricks. Finally, you must consider the context for the narrative device you are using. If the story is epistolary , where did this correspondence come from? Or if the story is told in a journal, how did the reader wind up reading it in the first place? Whether or not you explain the context of the device in the story is up to you. In many cases, the reader may not need to know those details, but as the author you should have some idea about the context of the narrative form you choose for your story.

Multiple Points of View

In multiple POV narration, the story is told from the viewpoint of one character during one scene, then switches to a different POV character in another part of the story. In the multiple first-person POV, the "I" narrator changes from scene to scene or chapter to chapter, as in *Shiver* by Maggie Stiefvater. You can also have alternating limited third-person points of view, like in Lloyd Alexander's *The High King*. To add yet another wrinkle, you can even weave together first- and third-person narrators. For example, *Tiny Little Thing* by Beatriz Williams shifts between the first-person POV of the protagonist, Tiny, and a limited third-person POV of the love interest, Caspian.

When you use a multiple POV narration (whether in first or third person), the artistry lies in presenting the inconsistencies between the different characters' accounts of the story. One character's perception of reality may differ significantly from that of another character, and when you use a multiple POV you can bring to light these conflicting versions of the same story. With a multiple POV we are firmly planted in the head of the POV character, so we get an up-close and personal version of how that character sees the story. When the POV shifts to a new character in a subsequent chapter or scene, we then get a new perspective that puts the previous version of the story into context and gives us a more layered view of the story's reality.

Once you establish the basic "rules" of your POV, you need to stay consistent. If the POV alternates between two characters from chapter to chapter, you should not introduce a third POV character halfway through the book. Remember that multiple POV is more challenging for your reader to follow than a single point of view. Just as our minds need to reset when multitasking, your readers will need to reboot their POV mind-set each time you jump to a new character. The more consistent you can make these shifts and the more cues you can give your reader, the easier and more seamless that reading experience will be.

You can give the reader clues by using the name of the POV character at the chapter header or by including the date with each scene if your story jumps back and forth in time. For instance, *Tiny Little Thing* by Beatriz Williams uses both character names and the year at each POV transition so we know which POV we're in and where we are in the time line. Similarly, Maggie Stiefvater's *Shiver* gives character names and the temperature at the start of each chapter to indicate POV and create suspense, since temperature affects certain paranormal elements of the story.

Verb Tense

When you craft your narrative—be it first or third person—you need to consider which verb tense to use. There are essentially two options: past and present tense. Yes, in *theory* the future tense is also possible, but have you ever seen a novel or even a piece of flash fiction written entirely in future tense? I didn't think so. For the purpose of this discussion, we'll focus on present and past.

The present tense places the reader in the story as it happens. The Hunger Games trilogy begins with the following: "When I wake up, the other side of the bed is cold. My fingers stretch out, seeking Prim's warmth but finding only the rough canvas cover of the mattress. She must have had bad dreams and climbed in with our mother. Of course she did. This is the day of the reaping." Throughout the novel we are with Katniss, experiencing each moment as she does. Not only does the present tense give the narrative a sense of immediacy, it also helps maintain suspense. This is especially important in *The Hunger Games* because Katniss—our protagonist and POV character—is in peril. A past-tense narration automatically implies that Katniss has "lived to tell the tale," but because the author uses present tense, we don't know until the very end of the story whether she will survive.

The past tense, on the other hand, grounds the narrative in the past as opposed to the present moment. This means that the events of the story have already happened and the narrator is looking back as she recounts the events. If the story is told in first person, a past tense narration implies that the first-person narrator has survived and is telling the story as she remembers it.

Herman Melville's *Moby-Dick* opens like this: "Call me Ishmael. Some years ago—never mind how long precisely—having little or no money in my purse, and nothing particular to interest me on shore, I thought I would sail about a little and see the watery part of the world." We can assume that Ishmael has survived his encounters with the great white whale, otherwise he would not be able to tell the story.

With a third-person past-tense narrator, we cannot necessarily assume the point-of-view character's survival, even if the story is told in the limited third-person POV. This is because narrative distance allows the author to zoom out beyond that POV character. Flannery O'Connor's uses this technique in her short story "A Good Man Is Hard to Find." Most of the story is told in the limited third person from the POV of the grandmother. We know we are planted firmly in her mind from the first line: "The grandmother didn't want to go to Florida. She wanted to visit some of her connections in east Tennessee and she was seizing at every chance to change Bailey's mind." Through most of the story, we remain in the grandmother's POV while she and the family drive through the countryside and run into an escaped convict, The Misfit. At the end, the author zooms out from a limited third-person narration to an omniscient narration. This allows the reader to experience the grisly fate of the characters, as those final moments would be unavailable to the reader if the narration stayed in a close third-person POV.

Finally, when using past tense you also need to consider from *where* in the time line the character is telling the story. You can convey this explicitly to the reader by creating a frame for your narrative. The past-tense narrator can also be invisible so that readers don't need an explicit frame to make sense of the story, but even then *you* should have a sense of how much distance the narrator has from the story events. Is he an old man looking back on his early life? Or is he telling the story after just having lived through it? While you don't need to convey such details to the reader, this perspective and emotional distance will affect how your narrator recounts those events, which in turn will affect how you craft your book.

15

Weave Your Story's World

Until now we've discussed the overarching aspects of a story: character, plot, voice, and point of view. In this chapter and the next, we dive into craft elements that play a role at the scene level. Remember John Gardner's "narrative dream"? Like a dream, when you're reading a story, you're not aware that you're reading it—you're just hanging out with the characters. Scenes are where that story unfolds. They carry the narrative dream forward.

Scenes are built from three fundamental elements: exposition, description, and dialogue. This chapter focuses on exposition and description, since these elements exist at the narration level of the story. Dialogue, covered in the next chapter, adds an extra layer by weaving in the voices of the characters with that of the narrator.

The Role of Exposition

It is understandable that writers sometimes confuse description and exposition. Dialogue has its own unique punctuation and is written in shorter paragraphs. However, description and exposition appear similar, formatted in dense, boxy paragraphs. More important, description and exposition both operate on the same narration level of the story, meaning that readers don't hear the individual voices of characters, but instead get all the information directly from the narrator. Despite looking alike, there are key differences that distinguish exposition from description.

Description paints a picture of one moment. It digs deep, often with emotion and detail, bringing that moment to life for the reader. Description doesn't spoon-feed information. Rather, it lets the reader infer meaning and discover different layers within a scene. We've all heard the saying "Show, don't tell." Description shows.

At the same time, you don't want to show *everything*, because your book will be thousands of pages long and your reader will get bored. Too much description can bog down the narrative and distract your reader from the details that really matter. Sometimes you need to skip over the details and get to the juicy parts of the story. Exposition lets you do that. Instead of fleshing out each moment, it gives the reader a series of facts or events. It explains and summarizes. Exposition tells.

Master writers rarely rely on only one element or the other. Instead, they weave description and exposition in and out of each other, creating a complex tapestry that becomes the world of the story. Look at this example from *The Book Thief* by Markus Zusak. The first paragraph is pure description. It paints a picture and shows the scene. It makes us feel like we are *there*, watching the events unfold. The second paragraph, a single line, gives us the explanation. It tells us what we're seeing and why it matters.

> It felt as though the whole globe was dressed in snow. Like it had pulled it on, the way you pull on a sweater. Next to the train line, footprints were sunken to their shins. Trees wore blankets of ice.
>
> As you might expect, someone had died.

"Show, don't tell" is bad advice because it overlooks the importance of exposition. Instead, I urge you to show when you need to show, and tell when you need to tell. Both description and exposition have a place in your writing. The key is to find the right balance between the two.

Techniques for Brilliant Description

Rich, engrossing description is a mysterious combination of imagery, detail, and word choice. To write it, you must become an alchemist of language, but this doesn't mean you should cram as much verbiage as possible into your piece. Instead, you need to strike a delicate balance among different components. You need to engage the five senses and use vibrant language. You must also be specific and remember that less is more. Finally, you can use description to reflect the emotion of your scene. I'll show you these elements of description in action, using the poem "Anthem for Doomed Youth" by Wilfred Owen as an example.

"Anthem for Doomed Youth" by Wilfred Owen

What passing-bells for these who die as cattle?
Only the monstrous anger of the guns.
Only the stuttering rifles' rapid rattle
Can patter out their hasty orisons.
No mockeries now for them; no prayers nor bells;
Nor any voice of mourning save the choirs,
The shrill, demented choirs of wailing shells;
And bugles calling for them from sad shires.

What candles may be held to speed them all?
Not in the hands of boys, but in their eyes
Shall shine the holy glimmers of good-byes.
The pallor of girls' brows shall be their pall;
Their flowers the tenderness of patient minds,
And each slow dusk a drawing-down of blinds.

Engage the Five Senses

While most people have access to five senses, writers tend to rely heavily on sight. In earlier chapters, I showed you how to draw on the other four senses (sound, touch, taste, and smell) to boost your creativity. You can do the same thing to make your descriptions jump off the page.

Different senses will resonate with readers in different ways. Through word choice, alliteration, and rhythm, you can make the sounds of your description come to life. In "Anthem for Doomed Youth" the line "stuttering rifles' rapid rattle" not only conveys a visual image of the guns, but the word choice and lilt of that line also captures the *rat-tat-tat* sounds of the battlefield. Reflecting sensory details through the language not only brings the scene to life but also adds to the emotion of that passage.

Use Vibrant Language

Nouns and verbs are the meat and potatoes of description. Adverbs and adjectives can add flavor, but moderation is key. Beware of adverbs or adjectives that serve as a crutch for weak verbs or nouns. This is especially true with adverbs. You'll often find that you can eliminate an adverb altogether by choosing a more specific verb.

For instance, "He *walked heavily* across the room," takes on a very different meaning if you replace *walked heavily* with *lumbered*, *trudged*, or *stomped*.

These three verbs contain subtle nuances that *walked heavily* does not capture. *Lumbered* implies awkwardness. *Trudged* makes us picture someone struggling to walk, perhaps from exhaustion. *Stomped*, on the other hand, implies a more intentional heavy walking that stems from anger.

Notice how "Anthem for Doomed Youth" uses no adverbs and only a limited number of adjectives. In a poem with 112 words, only ten of those are adjectives, and most of them appear in the first stanza that describes the battlefield scene. Instead, the nouns and verbs create vivid, active images.

In addition to word choice, word order also matters. Remember that emphasis usually falls at the beginning and end of sentences, clauses, or lines. Where you choose to place words can change the meaning or significance of your description. Look at the line "Shall shine the holy glimmers of good-byes." Of course, the poet had to play with the word order to create the rhyme required by sonnet form, but there's more to it than this. The words *shall shine* fall at the beginning of the line, putting extra emphasis on the repeated *sh-sh* sound, almost as if the poet is hushing the dying men to sleep, like a parent soothing an infant. When we reach the word *good-byes* at the end of the line, we feel the gravity and finality of that moment. The men in the scene are dead.

Be Specific

One specific image or detail will often convey more meaning than a vast mosaic of vague information. Gabriel García Márquez said it best: "… if you say there are elephants flying in the sky, people are not going to believe you. But if you say that there are 425 elephants in the sky, people will probably believe you."

To bring a detail to life, make it specific. Harry Potter's wand has a phoenix feather at its core. This specific detail becomes important in later books of the series. Katniss Everdeen wears a gold mockingjay pin as a token from her district. That mockingjay becomes a symbol for the revolution, and the color gold indicates characters who are allied with Katniss in some way.

We see several specific details in "Anthem for Doomed Youth." Most important, though, is the shift from auditory details in the first stanza to visual details in the second. When the *type* of specificity changes, it adds more depth to the description. In the first stanza, we are in the middle of battle, hearing the "stuttering rifles" and the "shrill demented choirs of wailing shells." Then, in the second stanza, all becomes quiet. The battle is over, and we feel the void that comes after the chaos. The images no longer convey the sounds of battle, but show the silent aftermath as dusk falls.

It is easier to keep track of the specific details in a contained poem than in a book-length project. A story map can help you organize the details and images in your novel (see chapter seven). To do so, create a thread or "subway line" in your map for each image you want to trace. This will help you see how that image works both individually and within the context of your story.

Remember: Less Is More

We've all heard that "a picture is worth a thousand words," but this cliché is misleading. Just because a picture can convey one thousand words doesn't mean that you should use that amount to capture its essence. You don't need to create a composite sketch every time you describe something to your reader. Peter Mendelsund explains it best in his book *What We See When We Read*: "Even if an author excels at physical description, we are left with shambling concoctions of stray body parts and random detail (authors can't tell us *everything*). We fill in the gaps."

Many writers worry that if they don't describe every last detail, their readers won't have the information they need to create a mental picture. Often this concern is misplaced. First of all, no matter how descriptive you are, you will never be able to capture every detail. It's impossible. Even if you did manage it, that description would be boring. More important, by letting your readers fill in the gaps in your description, you give them a sense of ownership in the story. Instead of trying to capture *everything* in description, give your readers one telling detail—at most, two—and let them fill in the rest. Trust your readers to bridge those gaps. Let them become active participants in the story. When your readers take on this more active role, they become more invested in your book and are less likely to put it down.

Look to poetry for examples. In "Anthem for Doomed Youth," some lines— "the pallor of girls' brows" and "the drawing-down of blinds"—convey mini stories within the poem. Girls wait at home for their beaus, never to return. Families draw the blinds in mourning for their sons. The poet could write entire stanzas capturing the heartbreak found in those lines, but instead he trusts us to extrapolate on our own.

World-Building

Whatever genre you write, your story has a world. How you craft that world must be intentional. In some cases, this world-building is obvious, as in high fantasy, science fiction, or even historical fiction. In other cases, such as in contemporary fiction or even nonfiction, the world-building might be more subtle but is by no means any less important.

World-building goes beyond the setting (the geography and the time period of your world) to include the culture and societies of your story, how your characters relate to each other, even the dialects and languages they use. World-building is everything that gives your readers a clear sense of your story's universe.

Setting

Setting is the place where your story happens. It can be expansive or tightly contained, a real location or an imagined world. Description plays a part in conveying the setting, but you want to avoid "info dumps" that pile every last detail onto your reader. Remember that while *you* should know all the details of your story's world, your readers do not need to know everything. Instead, focus on the telling details that carry the most weight and let your readers fill in the gaps.

Cultures and Societies

You also need to consider the cultures and societies of your world. Who are the people in your world, and how do they relate to each other? In some cases, you might divide the people into clans, like the twelve districts in *The Hunger Games* or Hogwarts' four houses in the Harry Potter series. You don't need to describe, mention, or name each individual within those groups. Instead, you can treat the groups as a unit. (Think of the nameless "red shirt" characters in *Star Trek*—we know these characters are expendable and that they will mostly likely die during a mission.) Nor do you have to spotlight every group within your world. We learn about the districts in *The Hunger Games* only when we meet significant characters from those districts. Don't overload your readers with information about every group or individual. Focus only on what your reader needs to know in a given moment.

You can also use sensory detail to engage your reader and establish the culture of your world. While food, art, and music are important components, the culture in your world doesn't necessarily need to be foreign or exotic. For example, *The Rocky Horror Picture Show* reenactments in *The Perks of Being a Wallflower* by Stephen Chbosky are a central part of the novel. While this might not seem like a culture at first glance, *Rocky Horror* has unique traditions, costumes, and music that are essential to how the characters in that story relate to each other.

World-building can also include "Easter eggs," which are hidden clues or references that the author slips into the story, often for the benefit of superfans. These details are not essential to the main action of the story, but for readers familiar with the story's world they add an extra layer of interest and engagement. You'll find Easter eggs in books with extensive world-building, like the Harry Potter series, and even in more literary work. For example, in the collected short stories of John Cheever, characters who have bit parts in one story might take center stage in another. As with all aspects of world-building, your job as writer is to give your readers just enough information so they can follow the story. Adding a few well-placed insider details can be a great way to build engagement with your die-hard fans, but it should not be your first priority.

Language and Dialect

Language and vernacular are another important component of world-building. You might create fictional languages, like J.R.R. Tolkien does to enhance Middle-earth, or you might use scientific jargon, like Michael Crichton does in his books. You can also use snippets of foreign language to capture aspects of your characters, just as Junot Díaz uses Spanish phrases in his writing. You can even write the entire book in the vernacular; *Push* by Sapphire and *Tyrell* by Coe Booth are written from beginning to end in urban slang.

Be careful with vernacular and dialect, however. A little bit goes a long way, and if you go overboard it can be hard for your reader to understand what you're saying. Whenever you use vernacular, slang, or other languages in your writing, make sure the reader can figure out the meaning through context clues. Also, narrated vernacular or dialect makes sense only in first-person POV. If the POV character normally speaks in dialect, then it stands to reason that the narration would be in dialect as well. In third-person POV, however, dialect or vernacular in the narration is a stretch. It makes more sense to use it only in dialogue.

"The world serves the story. The story does not serve the world." —CHUCK WENDIG

As you develop your story's world, keep in mind that the details should do more than add ornamentation. Your readers only care about this world because of the characters in it. Your story is what makes that world come to life. Every world-building detail must exist to develop your characters or advance the story. While it can be fun to add quirky languages, funky details, or "Easter eggs" to your world, remember that those details must exist for a reason. Finally, as with every other aspect of writing, you get to establish the rules of your world. Once you make those rules, however, you cannot change or ignore them arbitrarily. If you do decide to let a character break the rules, you must have a good reason and a good explanation.

— 16 —

Deliver Dazzling Dialogue

Dialogue is one of my favorite parts of a story. Don't get me wrong—description and exposition both serve an important purpose, but when it comes to raising stakes and building conflict, dialogue excels at shaking things up. What makes dialogue so interesting are the multiple layers of tension it introduces. What are the characters saying? What are they holding back? What are they thinking, and do their thoughts conflict with what they *say* they think? As you write dialogue, don't forget the role of your narrator. Does the narrator fade into the background and let the characters take center stage? Or does the narrator also play a part in this interaction by sharing editorial commentary on top of the dialogue?

The Nine Nos of Dialogue

Dialogue is fun, but it's also hard to write, or at least to write well. If you try to model written dialogue on real-life dialogue, you'll end up with boring conversations that go nowhere. Instead, you need to find the single nugget of juicy dialogue among all the white noise and blabber, which can feel like a herculean task. So instead of advising you on how to write dialogue, I'll keep things simple and share the mistakes you should avoid. I call these the Nine Nos.

1. Name-Calling

Name-calling is when characters call each other by name in dialogue. For example:

> "So, Bill, how's everything going?" Jill asked.
> "Not too bad, Jill," Bill replied. "Thanks for asking."

Name-calling might seem like a convenient way to establish who's saying what, but it's also clunky and awkward—people don't speak like this in real life. Also, name-calling smacks of distrust, as if the writer is afraid the reader won't be able to figure out who's talking. Your readers aren't idiots. Trust that they'll figure things out, and on the off chance that they don't, know that there are better ways to fix this problem than with name-calling. Things like tags and stage directions do the job very well.

2. Fussy Tags

Tags are the "he said, she said" component of dialogue. If you want to indicate which character is saying what, tags are the way to do it.

Keep your dialogue tags as simple as possible. When in doubt, use *said*, and for the love of all that is literary, don't try to show off by using tags like *chortled*, *grunted*, or *guffawed*. Sure, some of these substitutes for *said* might work in special situations (for instance, if someone is whispering, you can use "he whispered"), but often these fancy tags are distracting.

The beauty of *said* is that it doesn't draw attention to itself. Tags like *asked* and *replied* are also okay in moderation, but when in doubt, use *said*. The *said* tag will disappear into the background, and readers will instead focus on your characters and what they're *saying*.

3. Talking-Head Syndrome

Some dialogue bounces back and forth between the characters, and you have no idea where the characters are or why they're talking in the first place. The characters seem to talk just for the sake of talking, without any actions to ground us in the scene. This is called Talking-Head Syndrome, and there's a simple fix for it: Add stage directions.

If dialogue is the part that's spoken by the characters, then the stage directions are the actions that accompany those lines. Imagine the scene you're writing is part of a play and you're the director. You need to tell the characters when they should shift in their seats or sip their lattes. This can be especially useful if you want to convey that the character is feeling some emotion, but you don't want her to gush about her feelings. Actions can speak much louder than words and can help create subtext, which we'll discuss in the next "no."

4. On-the-Nose Dialogue

On-the-nose dialogue is when characters say exactly what they mean. This type of dialogue is especially strange because in real life people *hardly ever* come out and say what they really mean. As you will see in the example, it's far more interesting when characters force us to read between the lines. You can convey what your characters are thinking by adding subtext, and stage directions are a great way to accomplish this. Here's an example of dialogue that drips with subtext, from Oscar Wilde's *The Importance of Being Earnest*.

> **CECILY.** … May I offer you some tea, Miss Fairfax?
>
> **GWENDOLEN.** [With elaborate politeness.] Thank you. [Aside.] Detestable girl! But I require tea!
>
> **CECILY.** [Sweetly.] Sugar?
>
> **GWENDOLEN.** [Superciliously.] No, thank you. Sugar is not fashionable any more. [Cecily looks angrily at her, takes up the tongs and puts four lumps of sugar into the cup.]
>
> **CECILY.** [Severely.] Cake or bread and butter?
>
> **GWENDOLEN.** [In a bored manner.] Bread and butter, please. Cake is rarely seen at the best houses nowadays.
>
> **CECILY.** [Cuts a very large slice of cake, and puts it on the tray.] Hand that to Miss Fairfax.

In this scene, Gwendolen pays Cecily a visit, and while their conversation begins amicably, after a few minutes they realize they are in love with the same man: Earnest. Of course, since they are upstanding members of Victorian English society, they can't launch into a catfight. Instead they feign politeness, but despite their polished manners their interaction is still quite hostile.

Notice the use of stage directions in this passage. Gwendolen says, "Sugar is not fashionable any more," and Cecily puts four lumps in her tea. Gwendolen says, "Cake is rarely seen at the best houses," so Cecily cuts her a large slice. We sense the hostility between these women not just in the comments themselves but also in the contrast between their words and their actions.

5. Rambling Start

Usually real-life dialogue builds up to the actual meat of the conversation. People ask each other "How are you doing?" and "How 'bout that weather?" and "Waddaya know about the Giants?" It could take several minutes before one of the speakers gets to the real reason they're having a conversation.

We've all been taught to behave this way out of politeness, but on the page you don't have time for such trivialities. If you waste words by having your characters make small talk, you'll lose your readers before you get to the good stuff. Instead, start the conversation when the dialogue gets interesting. Wouldn't you rather read a passage that starts with "Why the hell have you been sleeping with my husband?" than with "Hey Sally, nice to see you again"? Forget the lead-up and get to the juicy stuff as fast as you can.

6. Adverb Overload

Nouns and verbs create vibrant language, but adverbs water it down. While it might seem like adverbs make your writing more descriptive, when you use an adverb it's usually a sign that the verb you have chosen isn't pulling enough weight. "He said softly" becomes much more specific when you say "he whispered," or better yet, "he said, his breath tickling her ear" or "he said, his voice like syrup." The word *softly* doesn't give us a good idea of who the character is or what his intentions are, but the other examples make the character and his actions much more vivid. As William Strunk and E.B. White so eloquently state in *The Elements of Style:* "Do not dress up words by adding *-ly* to them, as if putting a hat on a horse."

7. Exposition in Dialogue

Writers sometimes use dialogue as a shortcut to convey expositional information to the reader. Remember that dialogue is a conversation between your *characters*, and the reader is just a casual observer. One character isn't going to say something to another if he thinks the other person already knows it.

Suppose a character says, "Dude, you've failed all your classes two semesters in a row. Your parents are gonna have a cow." Clearly Dude knows that he's failed his classes two semesters in a row. He was there. He's the one who made it happen. There is no reason for his buddy to tell him this, except that perhaps the writer needs to convey this valuable insight to the reader. We see exposition in dialogue all the time—a super-villain gives the "why I tried to take over the world" monologue, or a mentor character arrives at just the right moment to give the protagonist a pep talk—but that doesn't make it any less clunky.

Unless the character receiving the information truly *does not know it,* there is no reason for exposition in dialogue. Repeat after me: Dialogue is communication between characters, not communication between the writer and reader. Do not confuse the two.

8. Dialogue Blips

In real life people insert blips into dialogue all the time. They say "um," "so," and "well" to give themselves time to think of what to say. But guess what? In written dialogue, you have all the time you need to figure out what your characters will say. This means that dialogue blips are not only unnecessary, they are downright distracting. Think of these hems and haws as red zits on your dialogue's nose. They might seem tiny, but they're so distracting that you can't look at anything else. Nip those blips in the bud. They do nothing but slow down your dialogue.

9. Breaking Character

One of the biggest problems in dialogue is when a character says something that is *out of character*. Often this happens because the writer puts words in the character's mouth that the character would never say. How would the character really speak? What actual language would she use—a ten dollar word or simple slang?

Sometimes you can play with word choice for humorous effect. In the movie *Catch Me If You Can*, con artist Frank Abagnale poses as a doctor and tries to learn the doctor lingo by watching hospital soap operas. The doctors on the show often ask each other if they "concur" with a diagnosis. When the protagonist is playing the role of a doctor himself, he keeps asking the other doctors at the hospital if they "concur," even though it's obvious to the audience that he has no idea what anybody's saying, much less what he's concurring with. In this case, the fact that the character is using fancy language serves to underscore his ignorance about the medical terminology being thrown at him.

Perfect Your Punctuation

Dialogue punctuation can be confusing. Do you use a comma or a period before the ending quotation mark? What if you have a question mark or an exclamation point? It's enough to make a writer avoid dialogue altogether.

Here's a quick primer for how to use punctuation in your characters' conversations.

Scenario 1: Dialogue with a Tag

A line of dialogue plus a tag is one full sentence, so you should use a comma, rather than a period, inside the ending quotation mark and before the tag.

"My name is Susan," she said.

Scenario 2: Dialogue with a Stage Direction

If the dialogue is followed by another full sentence, you should use a period inside the ending quotation mark and begin the new sentence with a capital letter.

"My name is Susan." She extended her right hand.

Scenario 3: Dialogue with a Tag and Stage Direction

Sometimes you have both a tag and a stage direction in one line of dialogue. In this case, the stage direction is usually a subordinate clause, so it's still part of the same sentence as the spoken part. You should use a comma inside the ending quotation mark and before the tag and the stage direction.

"My name is Susan," she said, extending her right hand.

Dialogue with a Question Mark or an Exclamation Point

Question marks and exclamation points are tricky because they can behave either like commas or periods depending on the situation. See the three possible scenarios below for question marks and exclamation points.

SCENARIO 1: "What's your name?" she asked. (In this scenario, the question mark acts as a comma.)

SCENARIO 2: "What's your name?" She leaned in to hear the answer. (In this scenario, the question mark acts as the end of the sentence.)

SCENARIO 3: "What's your name?" she asked, leaning in to hear the answer. (In this scenario, the question mark acts as a comma.)

SCENARIO 1: "Somebody help me!" she screamed. (In this scenario, the exclamation mark acts as a comma.)

SCENARIO 2: "Somebody help me!" She collapsed from exhaustion. (In this scenario, the exclamation mark acts as the end of the sentence.)

SCENARIO 3: "Somebody help me!" she screamed before collapsing from exhaustion. (In this scenario, the exclamation mark acts as a comma.)

— 17 —

Revise in Layers

There are no accidents in effective writing. Every aspect of your story—from the characters and plot to details and dialogue—should appear for a reason. The techniques you've learned thus far are not meant to pigeonhole your writing. Rather the character archetypes, story landmarks, even the nine "nos" of dialogue all exist for one reason: to help you identify different elements of your writing and understand how they work, so you can write with purpose.

As the writer, you get to make (and break) the rules of your story. The key is to do so intentionally rather than by accident. If you understand the different elements of craft, you can write a great story by choosing what to include in your book and what to leave out. But when you first started writing your book, you probably weren't thinking in terms of acronyms, archetypes, and labels. You were wrapped up in writing a good story, and now you have a big mess of words on the page. Don't panic. This is where revision comes in.

Nonwriters believe revision is something you do in an afternoon, manuscript and red pen in hand. They picture it as a cosmetic process, choosing one word over another or transplanting a paragraph to a different page. They believe that once the first draft is done, the book is practically finished. Ha!

Writers know better. They know that a jumbled draft can be even more terrifying than a blank page. They know that revision involves much more than a few red marks on the manuscript. And they know that the first draft is simply the raw material they must shape, carve, and polish into a masterful story.

Revision is hard work, and it requires perseverance. It's not nearly as much fun as writing with abandon, pumped full of the adrenaline that comes from drafting a story for the first time. It's no wonder that so many writers get stuck in a dangerous cycle of producing one first draft after another but never revising anything or following through to the finish line.

No writer wants to send out mediocre work. We want our books to be the best they can be, but the process of cleaning up a manuscript is confusing, not to mention *hard*. It's almost impossible to find a middle ground between marking up your book line by line and completely rewriting it. Plus, it's hard to know what to fix during revision, and even harder to know when you are finished.

Don't worry, I've got you covered.

I have a way to bring method to the madness: *layered revision*. I use this method in my own work, and I've also taught it to countless other writers. In this chapter I'll dig into the details of how to use layered revision and how to apply the craft techniques you've learned thus far to make your story even better.

Draft Zero

Before we discuss the step-by-step process of layered revision, let's address the elephant in the room: your rough draft. After reading this chapter, you might be tempted to discount its importance, but your rough draft is essential to the writing process. It has only one purpose: to exist. This first draft has no other job except to be there, ready for you to shape it into something beautiful.

I call this rough draft "draft zero" because it's a starting point. It's the raw material that you eventually carve into a story. Unlike other crafts where the raw material already exists, writers must create their own. Sculptors can chip away at an already-existing stone to create art. Fiber artists weave or knit threads to craft their unique pieces. Carpenters cut wood and assemble the parts. But what do writers have to cut, shape, and weave? Until we put words on the page in draft zero, we have nothing.

No part of your story truly exists until you put words on the page. You can brainstorm all you like, but until you write a scene you will have *no clue* whether your brilliant idea will actually work. Other craftsmen can inspect their raw material before they shape it; they can choose specific stones, fibers, or wood for their project. Writing is different. In fact it's much more difficult, because before we can judge the quality of our raw material, we must actually create it. Before we write draft zero, our story is just an idea. Whenever the pressure of writing sneaks up on you, remember that draft zero is a starting point. That draft doesn't have to be pretty—in fact, Anne Lamott says it will be "shitty"—and you must learn to embrace that glorious mess. All you have to do is put words on the page. You can always fix them later, using layered revision.

In writing you can fix just about anything, but you can't revise a blank page.

The Revision Pyramid

First, a little history and context. I developed the layered revision method after learning about psychologist Abraham Maslow's hierarchy of needs. Maslow theorized that humans pursue higher needs (like self-esteem and satisfaction) only after more basic needs (like food or shelter) are met. This concept translates beautifully to revision. You first need to address your book's most fundamental needs before you turn your attention to less crucial aspects of the process. Think of it as doing CPR on your writing. You wouldn't patch up your book's scrapes and bruises if it didn't have a pulse, right? This revision method forces you to keep your priorities straight and fix problems in order of their importance. Before attending to less important cosmetic issues, you must address more fundamental aspects in your book, like the narration, character development, and plot.

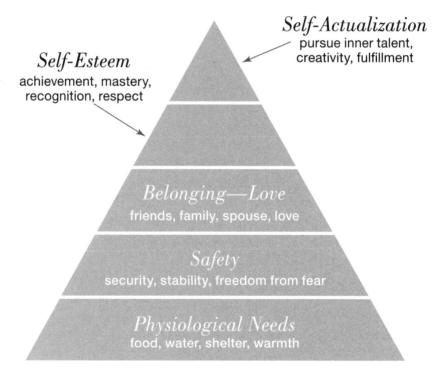

Maslow's Pyramid

Many writers try to juggle all of their revision tasks at once. They examine all the different aspects of the story side by side. They work to improve character development and story structure, all the while being distracted by weaknesses in their setting, dialogue, and theme. Big mistake. This process can be so overwhelming that they give up, in spite of all the countless hours they have already invested in writing that rough draft.

With layered revision, you review your manuscript several times, but each time you focus on one key element. You might zero in on your protagonist in one pass, your villain in the next, and then plot or world-building in a later round. This layered approach means that each individual pass goes much faster than if you had attempted to revise everything at once. The work feels more doable because you're taking it one step at a time. And this approach is more effective, too, because you are more likely to spot problems—and fix them—when your attention is focused systematically.

Just as Maslow's hierarchy places basic needs at the base of his pyramid and higher-order needs at the top, you want to address the fundamental elements of a story first, because changes to these areas will have a broader impact on your manuscript. You also want to resist the urge to make small, superficial changes in the beginning of the revision process. This is because you might end up deleting entire chapters later on and all your cosmetic work will have gone to waste. Instead, start at the bottom of the revision pyramid and work your way up.

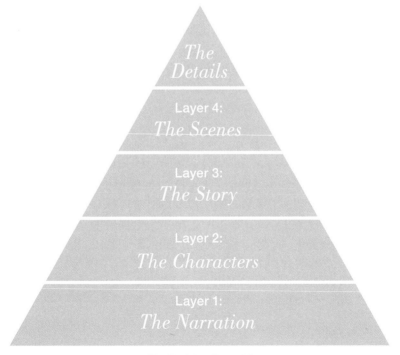

The Revision Pyramid

The beauty of layered revision is that not only will you avoid fixing problems that might end up on the cutting-room floor but your editing process will also go faster with each subsequent layer. As you strengthen your story at each level, you will also solve problems further up because you have addressed the root cause behind them. Finally, with each pass through your manuscript, you will feel more confident and motivated. You'll be less likely to give up and more likely to finish your revisions—all the way to a polished final draft.

Let's look at the pyramid layer by layer.

Layer 1: The Narration

Narration—the way you choose to tell your story—includes the voice of the narrative as well as the point of view of your characters (we covered these topics in chapters thirteen and fourteen respectively). Deciding the narration strategy of your book is one of the most important choices you make for your story, though you might not have realized it when you first started writing. In most cases, the process of writing draft zero forces you to home in on your voice and POV, because it's during draft zero that you test out different approaches and make adjustments as you write.

Sometimes, though, that almost inevitable experimentation with finding your voice can leave your narration scattered and unfocused.

The first step of any revision, of course, is to reread your work and make some overall notes on what you do and don't think is working in the story as it stands. Once you have decided which type of narration you want, you will need to reboot the scenes that depart from that style or POV so that all are consistent. Read over each scene in question, then set the original aside and rewrite it from memory in the newly defined voice or POV. When you write a scene from memory, your brain holds on to the parts that work but lets go of the rest. This allows you to give that scene a fresh voice—as opposed to tweaking or tinkering with the scene until you break it.

Altering voice and POV might seem minor compared to revisiting characters or changing plot points. Don't be fooled. Narration is, in fact, the most important component of your story, because it affects *how the reader experiences it*. In reworking the narration, you refocus the reader's lens for viewing your story, a task that can have a domino effect on all other elements of your book.

Layer 2: The Characters

The next layer in this revision process is character—the heart and soul of your story. Your characters give your readers someone to root for (or against) and give your story meaning. Without characters, a book is nothing more than a series of random events. Characters make us care about the events of your story; they make those events matter. For tools and techniques to help you truly understand your characters, look back at chapters eight and nine, where I show you how to create characters and bring them to life on the page.

By now you should know your protagonist almost as well as you know yourself. In crafting draft zero, you likely answered the three central questions that drive the main characters:

1. What does this character want, and to what lengths will he go to get it?
2. What obstacles stand in the way, and what is at stake if the protagonist fails?
3. How will the protagonist change in the pursuit of this desire?

In the course of putting that journey onto the page, you've spent hours, maybe years, with this person. You've watched him struggle and overcome against all odds. You know his strengths and, yes, his flaws, too. Still, sometimes no matter how well you think you know your protagonist, when you finally review your work and see him anew on the page, suddenly he feels … flat. Unmotivated, even, though you know the motivations are there. When this happens, I recommend using what I call the sandbox technique.

Take your character out of the story, and put her in a different situation. The idea here is to remove your character from her usual environment and "comfort zone" and put her someplace new. If your story takes place in her hometown, send her on a road trip. If the story happens during the school year, show her enjoying a summer's day. By moving your character out of the "normal" world of your story, you can experiment and write a few scenes that occur in a different context.

Open a blank document or grab a clean sheet of paper, and label it "sandbox." Here, you can play and make a mess. The reason for this approach is twofold: First, you're more likely to discover something new about your protagonist by seeing him in an unfamiliar environment. Second—and more important—when you experiment with your character in sandbox mode, whatever you do stays in the sandbox (unless, of course, you decide you want to apply your discoveries to your story). When you test things out in the sandbox, you eliminate the risk of accidentally breaking anything in your manuscript. This technique gives you the freedom to see how far you can take your character, but it also offers a safety net. My experience has been that you're more likely to have breakthroughs in the sandbox than when playing within the confines of your story. And when you return to your completed draft with those breakthroughs in hand, suddenly you will see new ways to bring your character more vividly to life.

Of course, revision isn't confined to your protagonist. One of the big challenges with supporting characters is to portray enough depth that they resonate with readers, but not so much that they steal the show. Naturally, we want our supporting cast to feel fleshed out instead of one-dimensional. All characters, if we have developed them well, believe they are the heroes of their own lives. As you revise, however, remember that the primary function of each supporting character is to *support* the development of the protagonist. Ask yourself what necessary role each character plays in the story. If two or more serve the same function, consider eliminating one or merging them together.

If any of your supporting characters need a little extra TLC, a great way to flesh them out is to follow those characters "off stage." Your story centers on your protagonist, so naturally things will happen to your supporting cast that fall beyond the scope of your story. While these scenes might not make it into the final version of your story, it is sometimes useful to dip into these scenes so that you can better understand a particular supporting character. Take inspiration from Tom Stoppard's play *Rosencrantz and Guildenstern Are Dead*, which follows two minor characters from Shakespeare's *Hamlet* and delves into "missing scenes" we never see in the original story. Similarly, if you need to better understand a supporting character from your own story, follow him off the page and write one of those missing scenes. You never know what you may discover.

Also, watch out for characters who behave or sound the same. You don't want your supporting players to blur together in the reader's mind. If, in spite of your best efforts, you find that your characters still sound similar on the page, I recommend a process called *method writing*. Like method acting—in which an actor steps into a character's skin and "becomes" that character—you need to get inside the mind of the character you want to understand. Imagine you *are* that character. Feel what he feels, see what he sees, think what he thinks. Write a few paragraphs or pages from that character's POV. Once you have truly stepped into that character's mind-set, you'll be able to make him more distinct.

Layer 3: The Story

The next level of revision focuses on the story. By this point you should have a firm grasp on who your characters are and what motivates them, and these insights will drive the events of the story. Now it's time to make sure your plot actually works.

As we discussed in chapters ten, eleven, and twelve, plot boils down to a simple equation: $3 + 2 = 1$. Traditional story structure has *three* acts and *two* crucial decisions the protagonist must make, which fall at the end of Acts One and Two respectively. Together, the three acts and two decisions yield *one* universal story that has been used ever since humans began telling stories.

One of the biggest mistakes writers make in revision is tackling plot and story structure too early in the process. They go through their mental list of plot elements, filling them in like they're painting by numbers. Inciting incident? Check. Point of no return? Check. Denouement? Check.

The danger with this approach is that it ignores the fact that *characters* are the driving force of the story. When you fixate on a rigid plot structure, you leave character by the wayside. But your story exists *because* of decisions your character makes.

Whenever I see a writer struggling to plug up holes in the plot, that's usually a telltale sign that something is amiss on a more fundamental level, usually with the characters. The best plots are often the simplest ones, so if you find yourself overcomplicating things in order to make the story work, that may be a sign that you need to return to the character layer and get a better handle on who those players are and what motivates them.

If your characters are sound and the plot still isn't working, try this: Regardless of whether you drew up an outline before you wrote your first draft, extract an outline now from the manuscript you have written. Go scene by scene, using the scene card method from chapter seven. For each scene, list which characters are present, what happens, and why that scene is important. As you already know, the latter is critical because if you can't think of a good reason for including a particular scene, it may be redundant or extraneous. Breaking down your story in this way can help you see more clearly where you still need to revise to make the plot layer cohesive and strong, with a logical flow and high notes that hit all the right places.

Next, you can use the story map technique from chapter seven to parse out your scenes based on different character arcs or thematic elements. I do this by drawing color-coded dots on the different scene cards. For instance, if

I want to track the love story subplot, I might draw a red dot on all the scene cards that include the love interest supporting character or otherwise advance that story thread. Then when I map out the whole book, I can include one "subway line" for the love story, allowing me to see how that thread works both on its own and in conjunction with the rest of the story.

Layer 4: The Scenes

In this layer, your job is to look even more closely at your scenes, one at a time, and zero in on elements such as world-building, description, dialogue, and theme.

First, examine the world of your story. Does it feel real, or do you throw a lot of information at the reader but fail to show the world in action? Remember, also, that depending on the POV you have chosen, your narrator's state of mind may affect your description of that world. If a character is terrified and fearing for her life, she will see the world around her with a much darker perspective than if she's giddy with puppy love. This is another reason why understanding your voice, POV, and characters early in the revision process can help you with description and world-building later on.

Next, it's time to look at the dialogue that drives your scenes. There are two keys to strong dialogue: understanding your characters and recognizing that written dialogue is not real-life dialogue. By this stage of the revision, you should instinctively know how each character speaks. In any scenes where those conversations don't flow easily, return to the method writing technique from Layer 2. If your dialogue still doesn't ring true, often you need to tighten what's being said. Remember that in reality, people hem and haw, talk in circles, and take forever to get to the point—but none of that works on the page. Trim your dialogue to the barest minimum that still captures the essence of each scene.

The same minimalist approach will serve you well with other elements at this layer. When it comes to making your scenes sing, keep your reader on a need-to-know basis. Give the least amount of information necessary to understand what's happening. We all know that old adage "Show, don't tell," and often our response is to overload our scenes with useless details. Instead, show just enough to keep your reader in the know and tell (use exposition) when you want to cut to the point. A well-crafted scene should be like a house of cards: Each part of the scene is essential, and if you remove one piece, the whole thing comes crashing down.

By this point you likely have a good idea of what your theme is and how it fits into your story. Now it's simply a question of making sure that every scene you've written relates to that overall theme. You don't have to wallop your reader over the head with an explicit message, but if you find a scene that has no relation to your theme whatsoever, that's a sign that you need to give the scene a closer look and may have more work to do.

When this layer is complete—and only then—you can begin to make cosmetic changes, proofreading and editing at the line level. Then go celebrate, because you've reached the top of the pyramid.

REVISING NON-NARRATIVE WRITING

The techniques in this chapter apply to narrative work: short stories, novels, essays, and memoir. For non-narrative writing (how-to books, nonfiction articles, blog posts, and so on) the revision process is a bit different. Instead of focusing on character and story layers, you want to start with big-picture issues and drill down to smaller nitty-gritty details. If you are working on a non-narrative project, here are some guidelines to help you prepare your work for submission:

- **STOP DRAFTING.** That's right. Stop writing the draft of your piece because you do not need to submit a finished manuscript (yet). Instead, focus on writing a book proposal (basically an outline plus a marketing plan) or crafting a pitch for your article. In addition, because the size of your audience is more important for non-narrative projects, you should focus on building your platform.
- **PUT CONCEPTS INTO "BUCKETS."** You likely have a lot of ideas you want your book or article to cover. Don't start by writing down the actual content. Instead, focus on putting concepts into "buckets." I love index cards or mind-mapping for this step because it allows me to see how different concepts relate to each other. Don't worry about organizing the ideas yet; that's the next step. Just focus on which concepts go together.
- **GIVE YOUR CONCEPTS AN OVERARCHING STRUCTURE.** Narrative work is all about the story, but prescriptive nonfiction is about the organization. While the concepts you present in a non-narrative book might be significant in and of themselves, what matters even more is the information architecture. Thousands of diet books, fitness books, and self-help books already crowd the bookstore shelves, and articles about six-pack abs and de-cluttering your life are a dime a dozen. What

makes your book or article unique (aside from your voice) is the way you organize and present the ideas.

- **BETA-TEST AS YOU BUILD YOUR AUDIENCE.** While blogging and social media may not be as intuitive for novelists and memoirists, these tools are *essential* for authors of non-narrative work. Use these tools to build an audience and connect directly with your readers. These platforms will also give you a way to beta-test different concepts before you include them in your book.

If you approach a non-narrative project in this way, you will solve two problems at once. Not only will you build an audience before publication and position yourself as an expert, but you will also be able to beta-test everything— from your voice to your ideas—before immortalizing it in a finished book.

Learning how to revise is only half of the process. You also need to learn when to stop. Think of the revision process in terms of the law of diminishing returns. In the early rounds of revision, you will see a lot of progress from draft to draft. After several passes through your manuscript, however, the improvement will become almost imperceptible. Somewhere along the curve, the improvement that you see from revision no longer justifies the effort you put in. When you reach this point, stop. Send it to some colleagues and gather feedback. Continuing to revise on your own won't help you make any more progress.

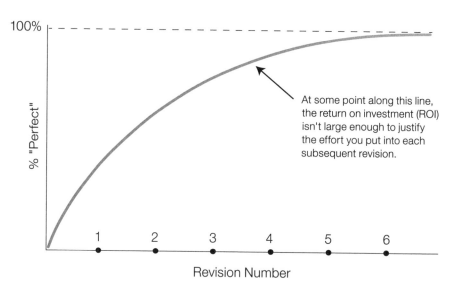

The Return on Investment (ROI) Curve for Revision

Just as there are no accidents in writing, there are also no hard-and-fast rules. The tools and techniques you've learned in the Write with Focus section exist for one reason: to help you identify aspects of your book that may need more work. This does not mean that you can't break these so-called rules; in fact some of the greatest works of literature artfully bend the rules and challenge our expectations of what a story "should" be. You might even argue that challenging the rules is part of what makes many classics so great.

Just remember one thing: Any time you break the rules of writing, you must *earn* it. Want to include an awesome car-chase scene even if it has nothing to do with the theme of your story? Have at it. Want to delay introducing a protagonist until chapter two of your novel? No problem. (Tor Seidler pulls this off beautifully in *The Wainscott Weasel*.) Want to kill off your protagonist in the first book of a long series? Totally fair game. (Ahem, *A Game of Thrones*.) You're the boss of your book. Just ensure that every choice you make is for a reason.

The craft elements you've learned thus far are not meant to limit your options. Instead, think of them as lenses that help bring the different layers of your story into focus. Revision is all about making artistic choices in your writing. As you inspect each layer, ask yourself two questions:

1. What effect does this choice have on the reader's experience?
2. More important, is this the effect that I *want*?

As long as your story is achieving the effect you desire, anything is fair game.

The purpose of layered revision isn't to follow a set of rules or check items off a list. Your goal is to write the best book possible. In the end, this is *your* book, and you get to decide what to eliminate and what to keep. These should be active choices, not decisions made by default. Every character, every scene, every word in your story should be intentional. Know the rules so that when you break them, you do so with purpose and panache.

read with purpose

18

Be a Reader First

Most traditional MFAs have a literature component built into the curriculum. So, too, does DIY MFA. If you're an avid reader—and you must be, if you're a writer—you've likely read many of the classics. This is good, because in order to create fresh, new work, you must understand and appreciate what has been written before. You need to know where literature has come from in order to see the possibilities of where it can go and how *you* can take it there. Reading puts your writing into context.

A basic grasp of the literary canon is only a starting point. To be an effective writer, you must read more than just books written by dead white guys. You must read broadly, choosing from a diverse group of books and authors. And I don't mean "diverse" just in terms of ethnicity and culture—you must read across a wide range of genres and different subject matters as well.

This might sound like a tall order. It's not enough to study the craft of writing and to write your manuscript. Now you also need to build your knowledge of literature, and you need to do it within that tiny "reading" slice of the DIY MFA pie. How are you supposed to develop a command of literature and still fit in time for your writing, not to mention your life? What happened to honoring reality?

The DIY MFA approach to reading is not about reading anything and everything; it's about reading with purpose and strategy. You must read books that will teach you the craft and help improve your writing. You must go beyond reading for pleasure and learn to read like a writer. Finally, you must respond to books—take notes, analyze—so that you truly understand and remember the things you read.

Why You Should Read with Purpose

To a writer, there's no such thing as "casual reading." Reading with purpose helps you retain and learn from what you read. Of course, learning from what you read doesn't mean you can't read for fun. You can learn something from every book. You learn what makes a book engaging and what encourages the reader to turn the page. Or you learn what makes a reader lose interest in a book and put it down. But don't rely solely on the serendipity of "pleasure reading"; you must be intentional in your literary education.

When you read with purpose, you make the most of your reading time. There are so many books in the world that you'll never be able to read them all. This means you must be strategic about the books you choose. In this chapter you'll learn how to select books based on how they contribute to your overall knowledge as a writer. Ideally, books should be fun to read *and* should improve your mind. In a pinch you can choose one or the other, but if partway through the book you realize you're not getting something from it, put it down and read something else. Life is short, after all.

The Essentials

As a writer, you should invest your money (and your shelf space) in a handful of books that will give you the most return on investment (ROI). Everything else you can borrow from a library or read in e-book form. However, all writers should own three essential books in hard copy and keep them close at hand. I call these books "The Essentials." To remember them, think of your ABCs.

> A = Anthology of Short-Form Literature
> B = Book of Prompts
> C = Craft Reference

Anthology of Short-Form Literature

The first of your essential books is an anthology of short-form literature. If you are writing a novel, look for a book of short stories. If you are writing memoir, look for a collection of essays. Poetry is the language of the gods, so it won't hurt to pick up a verse anthology as well.

Short-form literature is anything you can read in one "gulp." It includes poems, essays, short stories, and even picture books. Any piece that you cannot consume from beginning to end in about an hour is too long to be considered short-form literature. This means no novels, novellas, memoirs, epic poems, plays, and so on.

Short-form literature is an important part of your writing library for several reasons:

1. **IT LETS YOU SEE THE FULL STORY DEVELOP FROM BEGINNING TO END.** When you read short stories, essays, or poems, you can see the entire piece develop from start to finish. This gives you a global view of the story arc, and you can see how all the elements fit together, from inciting incident to denouement. A novel has those same story elements, but your reading experience is broken into chunks, and you will not be able to see the elements work together in one sitting. For that reason, short-form literature gives you better insights into how the author crafted a piece.

2. **YOU CAN STUDY THE CRAFT ON BOTH MICRO AND MACRO LEVELS.** With short-form literature, you can look at nitty-gritty details, like word choice and grammar, as well as overarching aspects of the story, such as character development and plot. Writing teacher Barbara Baig (author of *Spellbinding Sentences*) distinguishes these layers as "small craft" versus "big craft." Small craft is the artistry that happens on the sentence or word level. It includes grammar, syntax, word choice, and punctuation. Big craft is the big-picture part of storytelling and includes character development and story structure. Not only does short-form literature give you both detailed and big-picture views of the work, but you can see how various elements on the micro level affect things on the macro level. You can study small craft and big craft side by side. Book-length works force you to look at one aspect at a time, while stories, essays, and poems let you look at both together and see the interplay between them.

3. **YOU WILL SEE THE CHARACTER DEVELOP AND CHANGE FROM BEGINNING TO END.** Every protagonist must change over the course of a story. In short-form literature you can see that change occur from one page to the next, or even over a short span of sentences or words, making it easy to spot. Because you can experience the story in one sitting, you won't have to read hundreds of pages in order to witness the transformation.

4. **THE STORIES ARE FOCUSED AND TO THE POINT.** Short-form literature doesn't have room for subplots or tangential characters. Backstory is limited to the most essential facts. A novel or memoir has the room to sprawl and take its time, but short-form literature must be leaner, meaner, more focused, and to the point.

5. **THE PIECES ARE SHORT, SO EVERY WORD COUNTS.** In short-form literature, you have a limited word count. This means you must find the right

word—not the almost-right word, but the absolute right word—to convey your meaning. You must be daring but precise. Great writers are precise whether they are writing long-form or short-form pieces. They put as much artistry and care into each word of their novels, memoirs, histories, and epic poems as they put into their flash fiction, short essays, and haikus. Economy of words is what distinguishes the great writers from the almost great. So study the great writers.

Book of Prompts

A book of prompts is a key component of every writing library. These handy books are jam-packed with dozens—sometimes hundreds—of story starters and exercises. A prompt book is an instant cure for writer's block because it prevents you from running out of ideas or being stumped about what to write. Open a prompt book, choose an exercise, and start writing. Problem solved.

Not all prompt books are the same, however. While books with prompts arranged at random can be useful, sometimes you want to find exercises that will help you fine-tune a particular aspect of your craft. Look for a prompt book that arranges the exercises according to technique, such as *The 3 A.M. Epiphany* by Brian Kiteley and the Now Write! series edited by Sherry Ellis. Because these books organize prompts by theme and technique, you can use them to apply "the Petri dish technique" and improve different elements of your craft.

Writing is a living, breathing organism with many complex layers and components. This complexity often makes it hard for writers to tease apart how different aspects of writing work together. Just like a biologist must sometimes extract cell samples and study them in isolation, sometimes writers, too, must transplant a sample of their work to a Petri dish for further study. The idea behind the Petri dish technique is that you extract a specific technique or element of writing, and study it separately from the other layers of your work-in-progress. When you have mastered that technique, you can then apply what you have learned to the larger "organism."

The Petri dish technique allows you to focus on the element of craft that needs work. By eliminating all extraneous levels of complexity, you isolate the problem and focus on mastering that one skill. In addition, when you practice a writing technique outside the confines of your work-in-progress, you won't risk breaking your story. Too many writers tinker their books to death or make so many changes at once that the story becomes unrecognizable. Instead, practice outside the context of your project. Then, once you have mastered a skill, apply it to your work-in-progress.

THE PETRI DISH TECHNIQUE

STEP 1: FIND THE PROBLEM

When you hit a roadblock in your writing, you must first determine the heart of the problem. Sometimes the reason is obvious: Your dialogue feels stilted, or your descriptions are flat. Other times the problem is sneakier and harder to spot. Maybe a specific character doesn't "feel right" to you. Maybe you've written a scene that won't gel with the overarching narrative, no matter how many times you rewrite it.

Determine which element of the craft is at the core of the roadblock. Is this a character problem? A POV problem? A plot or story problem? If you can't find the source of the problem yourself, get a mentor or critique partner to read a sample and weigh in.

STEP 2: CHOOSE A PROMPT

This is where it can be useful to have a prompt book that's organized according to theme or technique. Look for an exercise that focuses on the technique you need to strengthen. Does one of your characters feel flat? Do some prompts with that character as the focus. Is the dialogue stilted? Try your hand at a few dialogue prompts. If nothing specific seems to require help, but you do need an overall boost to your creativity, open the book to a random page and try the first prompt you see.

STEP 3: PRACTICE, PRACTICE, PRACTICE

The best way to master a technique is through focused and sustained practice for one solid week. This does not mean you must spend hours on these exercises; fifteen or twenty minutes will do. Surely you can find a few extra minutes per day for one week. Your writing will thank you.

As you work on the exercises, use the iteration steps from earlier in this book to track your progress. Keep the environmental variables constant so that you can observe the changes in your writing and see clear results of this focused study. The only element you should vary is the context of the prompt. Apply the prompt to different characters or circumstances in your story. Everything else should stay as consistent as possible. If you have a work-in-progress, use characters or settings from that project when you do the prompts. Not only will this make it easier for you to get started but you will also make some valuable discoveries as you do these exercises. When you are finished doing a prompt, date it and file it away. *Do not reread what you wrote.* You need to allow some distance between when you do the exercise and when you review it and evaluate the results. When you have finished your week of focused study, take a week off before you look at what you wrote.

STEP 4: REVIEW AND APPLY WHAT YOU LEARNED

After your week off, review the writing that resulted from those exercises. Look at the progression from the first prompt to the last. Focus especially on the specific technique you worked on. Have you improved, or do you need further study? If you feel confident after this week of isolated practice, apply what you learned to a scene or passage in your work-in-progress.

Craft Reference

The final book in your essential collection is a craft reference. You need a book that answers basic writing questions and explains fundamental techniques. This book counts as a craft reference, but if you would like some additional recommendations, go to DIYMFA.com/thebook and sign up with your e-mail address to gain access to the bonus resources, including a recommended reading list.

Build Your Reading List

Reading must be central to every writer's life. If you don't read, you won't know what other books exist on your subject or in your genre. You won't see how your book fits within the greater body of literature. Reading gives your work context, allowing you to learn from writers who came before and also helping you figure out what makes your book stand out from others in the same genre. A writer who doesn't read is like a chef who doesn't eat, and that is a recipe for disaster.

In most traditional MFA programs, the literature courses focus on an area of literature that interests a particular professor. If the faculty's expertise doesn't overlap with the interests of the students, then oftentimes the students are stuck reading literature that is irrelevant to their writing.

This is not to say that you should ignore the literature canon. Writers should possess a baseline knowledge when it comes to literature and books, and most of them will acquire it in high school or college. You must challenge yourself to raise your reading level beyond that baseline. You must read literature that not only entertains you but also helps you improve your writing. Unlike a literature course, in which someone else tells you what to read, in DIY MFA you get to set a reading list that is unique to your interests and writing projects.

On a side note, I realize that not all high school and college English departments are created equally. I myself was blessed with a very comprehensive and intense literature experience as a teenager, but I recognize that not all writers have enjoyed the same. If you goofed off in high school English or never got around to reading all the "classics," don't panic. When you sign up with your e-mail address at DIYMFA.com/thebook, you can access a recommended reading list to help you fill any gaps.

Learn the Art of "Did Not Finish"

One of the most important things about reading with purpose is knowing when to put down a book and pick up another. You are the professor, and you determine the reading list. If a book does not resonate with you, don't read it. It's that simple.

DNF stands for "did not finish," and it is one of the most powerful tools in your writing arsenal. Many writers start out as English majors and avid readers. They love books and feel a sense of obligation to finish each one they start. When they don't finish a book, they feel guilty. Reading is almost like homework, and as dutiful students of literature, these writers feel compelled to muscle through a book even if it kills them.

If you can relate to this description, know that you are in good company. I feel the same way, which is why I will say—from one bookworm to another—stop. Seriously. Stop.

It is the *author's* job to make readers want to keep turning pages. It is not the reader's responsibility to suffer through a boring tome. Read the first ten pages. If you *really* want to give the book the benefit of the doubt, read the first 10 percent. If the book doesn't hook you by then, and if you have a compelling reason for why it does not resonate, then put it away. Choosing to go the way of DNF is not a sign of weakness, and it doesn't mean you are not smart enough to understand great literature. When you DNF a book, you are showing respect for your time and efforts. Life is short. Read with purpose.

Your Personalized Reading List

To read like a writer, you must first create a reading list. This list contains four types of books, and you must commit to reading them in a timely fashion. Two of these categories center around and help inform your current writing project, while the other two challenge you to read broadly and understand literature as a whole. Together they constitute the Four Cs, and they stand for *competitive titles*, *contextual books*, *contemporary books*, and *classics*.

Competitive Titles

This category (also called "comps") includes books that compete directly with your own. Comps are in the same genre and category as your work-in-progress and cover similar themes or subject matter. It's important to read competitive titles so that you know what other books are similar to your book. You must also consider what makes your book unique and different from the competition.

This list of comp titles is essential, and you will return to it over and over. When you pitch or query agents, you will need this list because they will sometimes ask about comp titles. If you are writing nonfiction, you must include a list of competitive books in your book proposal. Finally, when you begin to put together your platform or "author identity," this list of comp titles will help you find published authors whose readership is similar to your own.

Finding the first comp title can be challenging, but once you have that bread crumb, it is easy to find others. Look up that first competitive book on Amazon, Goodreads, or LibraryThing. Scroll down to where the website cross promotes other similar books. (On Amazon this is the section that says "Customers Who Bought This Item Also Bought …".) Look at the other books listed. Preview the first few pages of each and decide if it seems like a good comp for your project. If so, put it on your list.

Contextual Books

This category encompasses all the books that put your current project into context. This includes references and research materials. These contextual books might have a similar theme or subject matter as your own but fall in a different genre, or target a different group of readers. For example, if your book tackles a complex subject, study a picture book on that same topic. When you see how an author distills the information for very young readers, it can pinpoint which aspects are truly important.

You might also read contextual books that use a particular storytelling technique, even though in terms of subject it is completely different from your own book. For instance, if you are planning to use an unreliable first-person POV, you must read Gillian Flynn's *Gone Girl* as well as Henry James's *The Turn of the Screw*. Whenever possible, you should track down the earliest book that uses the technique in question. Dig back through the literary canon and study classics as well as more contemporary examples.

Contextual books might not impact your work-in-progress directly, but they will help inform your writing and expand your vision.

Contemporary Books

Of the four categories, this one fluctuates more than the others. Every day there are new books hitting the shelves, and something will always rush to the top of your "To Be Read" (TBR) list. To stay current, I recommend reading a few recent books in your genre each year. By "recent" I mean books published in the last three years. Given how quickly publishing changes these days, anything older than three years is ancient.

Don't panic and feel like you must read *all* the newest books. Read just enough to help keep your finger on the pulse of what's new in your field. The point is to stay aware of new trends so you can see where your genre or niche is going. Not sure where to start looking for contemporary books? No problem. Ask a librarian or bookseller.

In addition to reading these books, you should also look at how they are launched and marketed. How is the book being promoted? Is there a book trailer? Is the author doing a book or blog tour? Don't go crazy with all these marketing details, but do make a note of any good ideas you find. These kernels will help you cultivate your own promotional ideas when the time comes.

Classics

Classic books are different for each reader. I like to focus my reading of classics on short fiction because it allows me to get a taste of different writers' styles without committing to a long book. Also, by reading short fiction classics, it helps me double down and meet two reading requirements at the same time: classics *and* short-form literature.

Some genres or categories are relatively new. For example the young adult (YA) category only came into its own in the 1960s. Most experts and historians of YA consider *The Outsiders* by S.E. Hinton (1967) as the first true YA novel. Earlier books like J.D. Salinger's *The Catcher in the Rye* (1951), William Golding's *Lord of the Flies* (1954), and Harper Lee's *To Kill a Mockingbird* (1960) were originally intended for adult readers and only later appropriated by teens as YA. Compared to other areas of literature, YA is relatively new, so books published as recently as the 1990s or 2000s might be considered classics for this category.

If possible, try to find at least one book written by an author who is considered a founder of your chosen genre. If you're writing mystery, read Edgar Allan Poe. If you're writing a romance, then at least one Jane Austen book should be on your list of classics. If horror is more your speed, then H.P. Lovecraft may be your new best friend, but you'll also want to explore nineteenth-century horror like Mary Shelley's *Frankenstein*, Robert Louis Stevenson's *Strange Case of Dr. Jekyll and Mr. Hyde*, and Bram Stoker's *Dracula*. You may even want to go as far back as the gothic horror novels of the eighteenth century so you can get a broad view of where your genre started.

You've Got Your List, Now Start Reading

As you can probably tell, there is a lot of overlap between the four categories on your reading list. One book might be both a comp and a contemporary, while another might be both contextual and a classic. The goal is to maximize your productivity and avoid spinning your wheels by reading books at random. Choose books that serve a concrete purpose for your current project and will help you reach your goals. Reading is one of the best ways to learn how to write, and you can get the most out of your reading by being strategic.

Make a list of twelve books, with at least two books in each category. Make a goal to read through your list within one year. This means reading a minimum of one book per month—a manageable goal. If you can read more, that's great, but use this baseline as a starting point.

Take time to reevaluate your list every month or every quarter, and make adjustments as your writing projects grow or change. Use the iterative process you learned earlier to help you hone your reading process and fine-tune your list. In the next chapter, you'll learn how to approach your reading with a writer's eye and get the most out of each book you read.

19

Read Like a Writer

Reading for pleasure is great. There are few things I enjoy more than lying on the beach with a mai tai in one hand and a Kindle in the other. If you want to be a writer, though, you need to *read like a writer,* and that is a very different proposition. Reading like a writer means that you don't read just to find out what happens next in the story. You must read to figure out what the writer is *doing* and how she achieves a particular effect. But before we get to *how*, we must answer two fundamental questions: "What?" and "Why?"

Let's Start with the Basics

When you read like a writer, you must first determine *what* the author is saying. Who are the characters? What's happening in the story? When and where does the story take place? This is the first layer of reading, and it is the way most casual readers approach books. They're not trying to dissect every theme and detail; they just want to get lost in a good story. Readers collect information as it's pertinent to the story, but if the writer does her job, the readers won't consciously ask these questions. Instead they get caught up in the events of the story as if they are experiencing them in real time. This is the most basic form of reading, and most people are quite content to read everything at this level.

Collecting information is just the tip of the iceberg, however. The saying goes, "First we learn to read, then we read to learn," but the truth is that reading to learn is only the first step in a much more complex process. Writers must take two additional steps in order to understand a piece of writing at a truly deep level.

The second layer of reading goes deeper into the story. Instead of asking *what* the author is saying, now we want to understand *why*. This is the type of "close reading" we learn in high school when analyzing the classics. At this level, the reader's job is to interpret the writing, to figure out why the author wrote it and what it means.

I remember wondering as a teenager: *How do we* really *know what Shakespeare meant? I mean, he's been dead for hundreds of years. It's not like anyone asked* him. All those English class discussions felt futile, like we were stabbing into the void, trying to pin down what some dead guy meant when he wrote his plays. In truth, we can't know with absolute certainty what an author means unless we have the benefit of asking him or her. The best we can do at this level is infer meaning from the words on the page. Because words on the page are all we have to go on.

Right?

Reading Like a Revolutionary

This brings us to the level that turns the previous two on their heads. It's not enough to understand what the author is saying and why. We must go even deeper and focus on the *how*. We must look at a piece of writing and ask, "How did the author *do* that?" This is what I call "reading like a revolutionary," and it is a half breath away from creating the same effects in your own writing.

Reading like a writer means understanding that every author has an agenda and that every piece of writing has a purpose. If we read with an eye toward that purpose, we see how writers shape and craft their words to accomplish certain goals and elicit certain responses. We see writing not just as a form of communication or a record of information but also as a method of *manipulation*.

When you read like a writer, you will start to notice that the author is trying to make you respond in a certain way, that the piece is intended to elicit a certain thought or feeling. When you realize this, you can consciously decide whether you want to play along. It is only in being aware of a writer's craft and influence that you can form your own opinions without getting pulled into that web.

Don't misunderstand—most writing is not this sinister. I do not use words like *manipulate* and *agenda* because I think writers have dark ulterior motives and are trying to brainwash their readers. Rather, I want readers to be aware that there is more to a piece of writing than just the words on the page. Even in the most innocuous writing, sleight of hand is at work, drawing our attention from one part of the story and toward another. Understanding how a writer pulls this off not only makes you aware of the artistry but also shows you how you might be able to do it, too.

You do not need to read like a revolutionary all the time. In fact, you will likely find it exhausting to do so for more than a few paragraphs or pages. Sometimes you just want to get swept away by a good story, and that's perfectly fine. The key is to know how to "flip the switch." This way, when you come across an interesting technique or passage, you can understand it at a deeper level. Usually you will need to read the passage in question a few times before your brain clicks into revolutionary mode.

How deeply you dive into your reading also depends on the subject matter and content. When I read anything with a distinct slant or opinion (blogs, news, or current events), my brain automatically switches to revolutionary mode. I start to notice *how* writers use their words to influence or persuade. I challenge myself to read many conflicting accounts before I form an opinion or decide where I stand on a particular issue. This takes a lot of effort, which is why I'm very careful about how much political or issue-driven information I consume. In fact, I have decided that if I can't read and understand all sides of an issue, I would rather not engage with it at all. This is a personal choice and one that I have made to preserve my mental energy. You must decide what works for you.

For fiction or less opinion-driven pieces, I tend to get lost in the story. I only turn on revolutionary mode when I'm struggling with a particular technique. For instance, if I'm having trouble with dialogue in my work, I might read a few dialogue-heavy passages from various authors. I look at how the authors use dialogue to convey different elements of the story. How do they use stage directions? How do they capture the different characters' voices? I try to isolate the technique in question and use my reading to gain a better perspective.

When a piece elicits a powerful emotion from me, I pause and look at the passage with my writer's eye so that I can understand how the author made me respond as such. Similarly, if something in the writing catches me by surprise, I look at the last few pages in revolutionary mode so I can figure out how the author accomplished it.

Reading like a writer is like trying to figure out how a magician performs his tricks. Most of the time you just want to sit back and enjoy the show. Every so often, however, you should take a look behind the curtain to discover how the magician pulled it off. In those moments, I reread portions of a book to see if I can discover the secrets of the trick.

The main goal of this approach is for your reading to inform your writing. Reading with a writer's eye takes effort, and you should expend that effort only when you really need it. For the most part, you will skim the surface of a piece, reading to find out what happens next in the story. But when something affects you, when a paragraph, sentence, or turn of phrase takes your breath away, you must shift gears and read like a revolutionary. Because the moment you figure out how the author pulled off her trick, you'll be able to start applying it to your own work.

READ LIKE A WRITER: A GUIDED EXERCISE

"The Story of an Hour" by Kate Chopin is one of my favorites. Published in 1894 by an American author, it is especially impressive because in two short pages, Chopin shows us a sweeping range of emotions and reveals a lifetime of misery and joy. "The Story of an Hour" is proof that detailed portraits can be painted with an economy of words.

Because this story is so tight and concise, it is great for practicing the different layers of reading. You can see word-level nuances while also looking at bigger elements like character development and plot.

Read the story below, and then delve into its various layers. Notice how the different layers of reading work together. Begin by looking at the *what* of the story. What happens? Who are the major players? When and where does the story take place? Next, shift your focus to the *why*. Why does the author tell this story? What is the deeper meaning? Is the author trying to convince us of something? If so, what is it?

Finally, examine the *how* of the story. Does the story elicit some sort of response from you? What is that response, and more important, how does the author make you feel that way? What specific words or phrases spark those particular emotions? Keep in mind, also, that my interpretations are just that: interpretations. Your reading can be different, but as long as you have evidence from the text to back up your claims, it is still valid.

THE STORY OF AN HOUR

KATE CHOPIN (1894)

Knowing that Mrs. Mallard was afflicted with a heart trouble, great care was taken to break to her as gently as possible the news of her husband's death.

It was her sister Josephine who told her, in broken sentences; veiled hints that revealed in half concealing. Her husband's friend Richards was there, too, near her. It was he who had been in the newspaper office when intelligence of the railroad disaster was received, with Brently Mallard's name leading the list of "killed." He had only taken the time to assure himself of its truth by a second telegram, and had hastened to forestall any less careful, less tender friend in bearing the sad message.

She did not hear the story as many women have heard the same, with a paralyzed inability to accept its significance. She wept at once, with sudden, wild abandonment, in her sister's arms. When the storm of grief had spent itself she went away to her room alone. She would have no one follow her.

There stood, facing the open window, a comfortable, roomy armchair. Into this she sank, pressed down by a physical exhaustion that haunted her body and seemed to reach into her soul.

She could see in the open square before her house the tops of trees that were all aquiver with the new spring life. The delicious breath of rain was in the air. In the street below a peddler was crying his wares. The notes of a distant song which some one was singing reached her faintly, and countless sparrows were twittering in the eaves.

There were patches of blue sky showing here and there through the clouds that had met and piled one above the other in the west facing her window.

She sat with her head thrown back upon the cushion of the chair, quite motionless, except when a sob came up into her throat and shook her, as a child who has cried itself to sleep continues to sob in its dreams.

She was young, with a fair, calm face, whose lines bespoke repression and even a certain strength. But now there was a dull stare in her eyes, whose gaze was fixed away off yonder on one of those patches of blue sky. It was not a glance of reflection, but rather indicated a suspension of intelligent thought.

There was something coming to her and she was waiting for it, fearfully. What was it? She did not know; it was too subtle and elusive to name. But she felt it, creeping out of the sky, reaching toward her through the sounds, the scents, the color that filled the air.

Now her bosom rose and fell tumultuously. She was beginning to recognize this thing that was approaching to possess her, and she was striving to beat it back with her will—as powerless as her two white slender hands would have been. When she abandoned herself a little whispered word escaped her slightly parted lips. She said it over and over under her breath: "free, free, free!" The vacant stare and the look of terror that had followed it went from her eyes. They stayed keen and bright. Her pulses beat fast, and the coursing blood warmed and relaxed every inch of her body.

She did not stop to ask if it were or were not a monstrous joy that held her. A clear and exalted perception enabled her to dismiss the suggestion as trivial. She knew that she would weep again when she saw the kind, tender hands folded in death; the face that had never looked save with love upon her, fixed and gray and dead. But she saw beyond that bitter moment a long procession of years to come that would belong to her absolutely. And she opened and spread her arms out to them in welcome.

There would be no one to live for during those coming years; she would live for herself. There would be no powerful will bending hers in that blind persistence with which men and women believe they have a right to impose a private will upon a fellow-creature. A kind intention or a cruel intention made the act seem no less a crime as she looked upon it in that brief moment of illumination.

And yet she had loved him—sometimes. Often she had not. What did it matter! What could love, the unsolved mystery, count for in the face of this possession of self-assertion which she suddenly recognized as the strongest impulse of her being!

"Free! Body and soul free!" she kept whispering.

Josephine was kneeling before the closed door with her lips to the keyhole, imploring for admission. "Louise, open the door! I beg; open the door—you will make yourself ill. What are you doing, Louise? For heaven's sake open the door."

"Go away. I am not making myself ill." No; she was drinking in a very elixir of life through that open window.

Her fancy was running riot along those days ahead of her. Spring days, and summer days, and all sorts of days that would be her own. She breathed a quick prayer that life might be long. It was only yesterday she had thought with a shudder that life might be long.

She arose at length and opened the door to her sister's importunities. There was a feverish triumph in her eyes, and she carried herself unwittingly like a goddess of Victory. She clasped her sister's waist, and together they descended the stairs. Richards stood waiting for them at the bottom.

Some one was opening the front door with a latchkey. It was Brently Mallard who entered, a little travel-stained, composedly carrying his grip-sack and umbrella. He had been far from the scene of the accident, and did not even know there had been one. He stood amazed at Josephine's piercing cry; at Richards' quick motion to screen him from the view of his wife.

When the doctors came they said she had died of heart disease—of the joy that kills.

Layer 1: What?

Begin by collecting basic information about the story. Who are the characters? What happens? What is the story structure? Don't worry about interpreting the information just yet. For now, just collect the facts.

Who Are the Characters?

Use the tools from chapters eight and nine to understand who these characters are and how they operate in this story. There are four major players: Louise Mallard (the protagonist), Josephine (her sister), Richards (the friend), and Brently Mallard (the husband, presumed dead).

From the beginning, it is clear that Louise is the protagonist. Not only does she occupy the most space on the page but the author employs *focalization* to center the narrative chiefly around Louise and her thoughts. With this technique, the story is told in the omniscient or an otherwise diffuse POV, but the narration tends to focus around one particular character. We will dig into POV in a moment, but for the time being, it's important to note that Louise is the focal character of the story. This is *her* story, and all the other players contribute to her character development.

Notice, also, that Louise is the only character who changes in this story, which again confirms her role as the protagonist. In short stories, it is not uncommon for the protagonist to be the only character who changes. In novels, however, you often see similar development in the villain or in some of the major supporting characters. In these situations it can be tricky to pinpoint who the protagonist is, especially if several characters get similar amounts of time on the page. Look for the character who changes *most* throughout the story. He or she is likely the protagonist.

We have established Louise as the protagonist, but what else do we know about her? In the first line, we discover that she is "afflicted with a heart trouble," meaning that the people around her must be careful about how they break the news of her husband's death. When her sister Josephine tells her of the train accident, Louise does not behave the way most women in her situation do, that is, with a "paralyzed inability to accept its significance." In other words, when most wives hear of their husband's death, their initial response is denial. In contrast, Louise cries violently, and "when the storm of grief" is over, she goes to her room alone.

Right away, we realize that Louise is not a typical wife from the nineteenth century. In the paragraphs that follow, we see additional hints that she is different from the average young woman of her status. Most women of the time period are interested only in commanding their households, wearing the latest fashions, and pleasing their husbands. Intelligence was not a trait to be cultivated in women, and heaven forbid a proper young wife pursue education or entertain any independent thoughts.

In this case, Mrs. Mallard goes into solitude to sort out her thoughts. She doesn't succumb to denial when she learns the news of her husband's death, and instead she responds with reasoned acceptance. As we sit with her alone in that room, we realize that she is not the frail little thing from the first sentence of the story. She possesses an inner strength that only the reader is privy to; none of the other characters see it. Or at the very least, none of them *want* to see it.

Now that we have a sense for Louise Mallard, let's switch gears and look at the other characters in the story. Brently Mallard is nothing more than a name for most of the story. Interestingly enough, even though he is presumed dead throughout the narrative, he is always mentioned by his full name, whereas we only get Mrs. Mallard's first name, Louise, when her sister Josephine uses it in dialogue. This is an important detail, and we will come back to it later. For the time being, just make a note and keep collecting information.

Josephine and Richards appear to serve parallel functions. Josephine is Louise's sister, and Richards is Brently Mallard's friend. Both are present when Louise learns of her husband's death and again when Mr. Mallard walks through the door at the end of the story. Both Josephine and Richards are protecting Louise Mallard in some way, but their motives seem to deviate.

Josephine appears to care genuinely for her sister. She and Louise are certainly close; in fact, when she breaks the news to Louise about Brently, it's almost like she's speaking in sister code: "broken sentences; veiled hints that revealed in half concealing." Josephine knows her sister well enough to communicate the news in the gentlest way possible. At the same time, she is concerned about her sister's fragility and worries when Louise spends too much time alone.

Richards's involvement, on the other hand, seems more sinister. His actions are not so much about protecting Mrs. Mallard, but of serving his own interest. We learn that Richards had been among the first to learn of the train accident and that he confirmed the news only with a second telegram before he "hastened to forestall any less careful, less tender friend in bearing the sad message." In other words, he sees himself as someone who *is* careful and tender enough to share this news with Mrs. Mallard, and he is determined to be the first to bear that news.

This detail hints at a few possibilities. On one hand Richards might be one of those controlling, dominating friends who always wants to be in charge and at the center of attention. Alternately, he may harbor secret feelings for Mrs. Mallard and wants to position himself strategically close to her. This way, when she hears the news of her husband's death, he will be the first of her husband's friends to comfort her and perhaps win her affections. We can't know for sure what Richards' motives are because we get only short glimpses into his mind. But the urgency with which he rushes to bear the news—so much urgency that the news he shares is ultimately *wrong*—hints that he has an ulterior motive.

Notice, too, that Richards stays in the house after Louise retires to her room. Propriety dictates that unless Richards is a member of the family, he should deliver the news, pay his respects, and express his condolences, but then take his leave when the lady of the house has left the room. Yet he remains in the house and is present when Brently Mallard enters later on. In fact, Richards even goes so far as to try to shield Brently Mallard from his wife's view. A true friend would be ecstatic that his friend is alive and would greet him warmly, not jump between him and his supposed widow. Again, because we get very few of Richards' thoughts, the best we can do is infer his motives from his behavior. Clearly, however, something about him and his behavior is not quite right.

What Happens? What Is the Story Structure?

"The Story of an Hour" is short and tightly written. This means that many of the story landmarks discussed in chapters ten through twelve are lumped close together. The inciting incident is the news of Brently Mallard's death, and it occurs in the first line. Thus, Act One of the story is nonexistent, and we never get to see the status quo, the world before the inciting incident. Instead, we get snippets of the Mallards' marriage throughout Act Two in the form of memories. The point of no return, which leads us into Act Two, is Mrs. Mallard's reaction to the news. She does not respond with denial as expected, but cries violently and then retires to her room to grieve.

Act Two takes place with Mrs. Mallard sitting alone in her room, looking out the window. This is where we gain insight into the Mallards' marriage. We learn that Mrs. Mallard loved her husband only sometimes; often she did not. To Louise, this marriage has been like a prison, and now, with her husband dead, she has gained her freedom. In fact, the line where she whispers "free, free, free!" falls almost exactly at the middle of the story. This midpoint—that moment of self-reflection—is when Mrs. Mallard realizes that she is not grieving her husband, but is actually relieved that he is dead.

After this realization, the pace of the story picks up. Josephine begins knocking at the door, convinced that Louise is making herself ill. Mrs. Mallard's conviction grows stronger. She is not ill, she is "drinking in a very elixir of life through that open window." We reach the second turning point when Louise opens the door to her sister. There is something eerie about her now; she has "a feverish triumph in her eyes and she carried herself unwittingly like the goddess of Victory." This moment is a subtle shift. Until this point,

Louise has been blissfully imagining her freedom. Now she has decided to rise up and claim it. Her actions are decided and firm. She clasps her sister's waist, and they descend the stairs together.

We reach the climax, the moment when everything comes to a head. The suspense builds quickly in a few short lines. Someone is fumbling with the key in the front door. Who could it be? It's Brently Mallard, who is not dead after all. Josephine shrieks. Richards tries to hide Brently from the view of his wife. Then the story abruptly cuts away.

The final line is our denouement, the punch line that ties it all together and shows us what really happened. "When the doctors came, they said she had died of heart disease—of the joy that kills." We never see the actual moment of Mrs. Mallard's death. Instead, it is inferred through this last line. The doctors assume she has died of her fragile heart, that seeing her husband alive was too much joy for her to take. Is that really why? To find the answer, we must dig down to the next layer of the story.

Layer 2: Why?

Without cause and effect, you don't have a story. A writing teacher once explained story causality with the following example:

> This is not a story: "The king died. The queen died soon after."
> This *is* a story: "Because the king died, the queen died soon after."

The first line gives us a sequence of unrelated events, a newsreel. This happens, and then this other thing happens. There is no causality. The second line has only one additional word, but that word makes all the difference. "Because the king died, the queen died soon after." We now have a causal relationship between the two deaths. The king dies, and because of his death, the queen also dies. Maybe she died of grief? We don't know the details behind the queen's death, but we do know that it is related to that of the king. This causality gives us the makings of a story.

When reading at this second, deeper level, our goal is twofold. First we want to understand *why* the characters act the way they do and what their motives are. Second, we need to figure out why the author is writing this story in the first place. What's the purpose and message of this story, and—more important—why should we care?

Given the time period, we know that this story is of the same era as Charlotte Perkins Gilman's "The Yellow Wallpaper." Chopin is likely making a similar commentary on the role of women in society. They have little agency and control over their own lives. They have no freedom and depend completely on their husbands. The frustrations caused by this dependence might manifest in physical frailty, such as Mrs. Mallard's heart affliction. While we don't know the author's exact motivations, we do sense her disapproval of the societal norms that repress women to such an extent that they might collapse under the pressure.

The climax reinforces the author's slant in this story. The doctors assume that Mrs. Mallard has died from the extreme joy of seeing her husband alive, and presumably the other characters in the story believe the same. But we know better. The author has given us access into Louise's head, and we know that she did not die of joy at all, but of panic-stricken grief at the loss of her newfound freedom. That last line is like a wink and a nudge from the author, a secret that she shares only with us. How do we know this is the author's intent? Look back to the pivot point between Acts Two and Three:

> Her fancy was running riot along those days ahead of her. Spring days, and summer days, and all sorts of days that would be her own. She breathed a quick prayer that life might be long. It was only yesterday she had thought with a shudder that life might be long.

Note the repetition of the word *days*, which appears four times in this short paragraph. Look closely at how that word operates: "Spring days, and summer days, and all sorts of days that would be her own" is a classic example of the rule of three in action. We start with days belonging to particular seasons and then shift to include "all sorts of days," with the added twist that these days would now "be her own." It doesn't matter if the days are in spring and summer; they can be any sort of days as long as they are her own. This line shows us that Louise isn't excited that life will be *better* now that her husband is dead—just that life will be *her own*.

The repetition doesn't stop there. The next two sentences end with the same five words: "that life might be long." First she says a quick prayer "that life might be long," and we infer that she wants to live long so that she can enjoy her freedom as much as possible. Then the next sentence takes a dark turn. We discover that "only yesterday she had thought with a shudder that life might be long." Clearly Louise has been so unhappy with her life that it pains her to imagine enduring it for a long time. Is it so bad that she would contemplate ending her life prematurely? We don't know, but we do know that death has crossed her mind.

This twist adds another wrinkle to the climactic death scene. Did Mrs. Mallard die of joy from seeing her husband alive? Or did she die of grief at the loss of her freedom? *Or* did she throw herself down the stairs in a moment of panic and despair, thus ending her own life? We can't know for sure, but we get an unsettled feeling that there is more to the story than first appears.

Layer 3: How?

One of the reasons I love "The Story of an Hour" is because most of the narrative occurs with one character alone in a room. From the fourth paragraph until three paragraphs from the end, Louise sits at the open window, alone with her thoughts. From a writer's perspective, putting a character alone in a room can be the kiss of death. How can a story remain engaging if your character doesn't do something or interact with someone? This challenge is what makes "The Story of an Hour" so masterful. Kate Chopin places her character alone in a room for the bulk of the story, and it works. In this deepest layer of reading, our job is to figure out how she pulls it off.

From the first line, we realize that while the story might be tightly contained, it's not as though there is no action whatsoever. Things happen in the story; they just don't happen on the page. Most of the major events happen offstage, and we learn about them through exposition. For instance, we don't see the train accident or its immediate aftermath. Chopin doesn't include a scene at the tracks, with the wounded passengers and the rescue workers digging through the wreckage. All we hear is that a "railroad disaster" has occurred and that Brently Mallard was one of the first names on the list of the deceased.

Several other actions happen off the page as well. We never see Richards' efforts to confirm Brently Mallard's death; in fact we might even venture that he doesn't make much effort at all. The dialogue where Josephine breaks the terrible news to her sister is also hidden from the page. We get a few lines of exposition telling us *how* Josephine related the news to Louise, but we never hear the words themselves. Most important, the moment of Louise's death happens offstage. We see her descend the staircase and then learn the supposed cause of her death in the last line of the story, but we never see the actual moment in a scene.

Why does Chopin tell the story in this way? Why doesn't she paint these significant moments of action in vivid scenes? Clearly this story is not about these action moments. It is not about Mrs. Mallard's reaction to her husband's death, or about Richards sending the telegram, or even about Mrs. Mallard's actual death. Rather, the heart of this story is the *transformation* that happens in Louise as she discovers her newfound freedom. This story belongs to Louise Mallard, not to Josephine or Richards or even Brently Mallard. The only action we see on the page revolves around the protagonist. This, of course, ties closely to Louise Mallard's sense of identity, or lack thereof.

I noted earlier that we only learn Mrs. Mallard's first name as we approach the climax of the story, when Josephine knocks at the door and calls out, "Louise, open the door! I beg; open the door—you will make yourself ill." This moment happens after Louise whispers over and over: "Free! Body and soul free!" Until now, Louise has only been identified by her married name, as though her identity exists only in relation to her husband. But after she begins to recognize her freedom and independence, we learn her first name. It is as if this is the first moment when Louise claims her identity. Before then, she was just Brently Mallard's wife. The way Chopin withholds Louise's first name underscores the shift in her character in this significant moment.

Most of Chopin's techniques are so subtle that it is easy to get caught up in the show and forget that a master puppeteer is pulling the strings. There is one moment, however, where Chopin's artistry jumps off the page, and it is in the pivotal line in which Brently enters the house and Richards tries to get between him and Louise. Look at how Chopin crafts that phrase: "He stood amazed at Josephine's piercing cry; at Richards' quick motion to screen him from the view of his wife." I could write a dissertation on the structure of that sentence alone and what it reveals about the author's intent. Let me break it down briefly.

Begin by dissecting the second part of the sentence, where Richards tries "to screen him from the view of his wife." Chopin deliberately uses the phrase "from the view of his wife" to create ambiguity as to who is looking at whom. We can surmise that Richards is trying to block Brently from viewing his wife or block Louise from viewing Brently, or both. This ambiguity is not an accident. Chopin could have crafted the sentence any number of ways to make it smoother to read. She could have written "screen him from seeing his wife" or "screen him from being seen by his wife," but instead she engages in grammatical acrobatics to preserve the ambiguity.

The ambiguity at the climax of the story is crucial because it leaves us wondering about the true cause of Louise's death. Is it shock and fear from seeing her husband, who was presumed dead? Is it overwhelming joy at seeing her husband alive and well? Or is it something else? We can't know for sure—Chopin makes certain of that—but she hints that there is more to this moment of death than meets the eye.

Notice, also, that in the climactic paragraph, all of the characters are named, save Louise Mallard. Brently Mallard enters the house. Josephine gives a piercing cry, and Richards intercepts Brently before he can reach his wife. In one fell swoop, Louise goes from being "Free! Body and soul free!" and walking like a "goddess of Victory" to merely being Brently's wife again. By withholding Louise's name once more, Chopin shows us that Brently's unexpected return robs Louise of her freedom and her identity. With a simple action—turning the latchkey and entering the hall—Brently Mallard takes away that "very elixir of life" that Louise had just begun to experience. In the next line we learn that she is dead. Of course she is dead! His very presence kills her.

Where Do We Go from Here?

When most people read, they stay at the surface level, skimming the top and allowing themselves to be carried away by a good story. By diving a little deeper, you can uncover more meaning and understand not only why the characters are behaving the way they do but also why the author has crafted the story in this way. The real treasure, though, is when you dive deeper still and look at *how* the author has created various effects.

But while you can only find pearls on the ocean floor, you can't stay in the depths forever—eventually you have to come up for air. You do not need to read at this detailed level all the time. Instead, dive deep only when you spot something important. When you see a pearl glistening down below, make a focused effort and venture to the depths. The rest of the time you can bob along the surface and enjoy the ebb and flow of the story.

— 20 —

Build Your Expertise

By now you have learned how to build a reading list and choose books that will help you improve your writing. You have also discovered how to read like a writer and flip the switch to revolutionary mode so you can engage with a book on a deeper level. But what do you do after you finish reading? This chapter shows you how to respond to what you read, so that you can build your expertise not only as a reader of literature but as a writer in your niche.

Why You Should Respond to What You Read

Responding to what you read *in writing* accomplishes several things. First, you will remember the books in greater detail. When you run into trouble with some aspect of craft, literary examples of those techniques in action can guide you. Remembering what you read will help you come up with relevant examples and references more easily.

Also, writers excel at thinking on the page. We work through ideas with pen in hand, and we internalize what we learn by writing it down. This means that written responses are one of the best ways to work through what we read. Why not play to your strengths and make use of this skill?

Finally—and this reason is the most important by far—when you respond to what you read, you have a *written record* of your initial reaction to a particular book or story. Even though you can return to a book again and again, each subsequent reading is shaded or tainted by that earlier response. In other words, you can reread a book, but you will never experience it the same way twice.

Sometimes when we gain a deeper intellectual understanding for a story, we are able to set aside our initial gut response. Goodness knows I have read many books that felt flat and dull at first, but as I peeled back the nuanced layers below the surface, I gained respect for both the book and the author. With other books, no matter how many times I flog myself into reading them, that initial response never goes away. Sometimes our initial response to a book is spot-on, and sometimes we're wrong and need to reevaluate our opinions. In either case, it is useful to record that initial response because we will never experience the book in quite the same way again.

Short Responses to Individual Works

You can respond to what you read in two ways: either by writing short responses to individual books or by responding to a body of literature. Both types of responses can be useful, but they serve different purposes. Short responses to individual works allow you to dive deep and examine a piece of writing in detail. Looking at a body of literature, on the other hand, gives you a broader understanding of a niche in literature and how the books within that niche relate to each other.

In a literature course, you must submit essays for a grade, but the point of these short responses is to help enhance your understanding of literature. These are not exercises in futility. In this section you will find a few different approaches for responding to what you read. If a particular method is not useful to you, try something else.

Reading Journal or Book Reviews

Perhaps the most straightforward method for writing short responses is to keep a reading journal. When you finish reading a book, record the title, the author, and the date you finished, and then jot down a few sentences that capture your initial response. If you'd like to add an interactive layer to your reading journal, you can publish it as a blog and encourage comments from fellow readers. Many book bloggers start their blogs as a way to keep track of the books they read. These online journals sometimes grow into review sites, and some of these bloggers have become major influencers in the book world.

The line between an online reading journal and a book review blog can blur quickly. You might start by using a personal blog or online community like Goodreads to record the books you read, but it can rapidly turn into a way of reviewing books. However, it is important to consider the implications of writing book reviews and make a mindful decision accordingly.

Before I founded DIY MFA, I reviewed books on my personal blog. When I decided to delve into DIY MFA full-time, I decided that I would no longer review books on the site or allow contributors to review them under the DIY MFA brand. I might *recommend* books I enjoy, but straight up reviews are a no-no on my site.

Here's my reasoning: As an author, I am well aware of the impact negative reviews can have on a book or an author. I have seen too many friends and colleagues burned by poor reviews, and in the interest of good karma I have decided I will not inflict that pain on anybody. Because of this, a few years ago I stopped reviewing books unless I could give them a four- or five-star review. If I didn't have something nice to say about a book, I wouldn't say anything at all.

This Golden Rule approach worked for a short while, but then I realized that it, too, was problematic. By posting only positive reviews, I was not providing a balanced perspective on literature for my students and readers. I also began to wonder whether reviews were the best format for intellectual discussion and analysis. My goal in discussing books with my students has never been to recommend specific books, but to use literature as examples of what is possible. For this reason, I have moved away from book reviews and instead focus on doing a close analysis of the craft.

This doesn't mean that book reviews are bad. If you review books—particularly if you do so under your own byline—you just need to be aware of the implications and set ground rules for yourself. Will you review all books, or only ones that you like? Will you state your review policy publicly on your site? Also, will you refrain from reviewing books written by colleagues or friends? Remember, also, that if you receive free review copies, you must disclose that fact on your site as part of FTC regulations. In the end, set ground rules, stay consistent, and be as transparent as possible.

Close Analysis

Nothing gets me more excited than closely analyzing a story or passage. I love delving deep and playing with words, trying to guess what the author wanted to do with a particular turn of phrase or plot twist. For many writers (and readers), this type of analysis is baffling, but it's actually quite easy. Let me teach you a secret trick to help you analyze any piece of writing, on any subject, and in any genre. Whenever you need to do a close analysis, ask this question:

HOW does the WHAT reflect the WHY?

This question is like magic. It can turn the most banal piece of literature into something worth studying. It can also result in a college or graduate English paper that practically writes itself. I discovered this formula at the tail end of high school, and oh, how I wish I had figured it out sooner. Once I uncovered this gem, I have recycled it for dozens—no, hundreds—of essays, and it works every time. The best part is, this formula doesn't just work for English papers; with a little tinkering, you can use it for *any* assignment on just about any subject.

The magic of this question lies in the way it brings together all three layers of revolutionary reading. When you craft an essay around this question, it challenges you to understand *what* an author is saying, *why* she is saying it, and *how* the way she says it reflects that deeper meaning. After that, all you need to do is find specific phrases or words in the text to use as evidence to support your claim. The result is a critical analysis that English teachers can't resist.

When I first discovered this formula, I used it because it practically guaranteed an easy A on any paper, but after a while I realized that the question is about more than just gaming the academic system. If you're reading this book, your days of English essays are probably long gone, and you aren't reading just to jump through a professor's hoop and get a grade. The goal of a close analysis is to gain a deeper understanding of what you read so that you can *write better*. All the more reason to use this formula. When you connect the *how*, the *what*, and the *why* of a book, you will see connections between those layers, and you will understand how the author works his storytelling magic. Once you figure that out, you will be one step closer to being able to work that same magic yourself.

Here's how to use this question to spark your analysis and guide your reading. First, choose a short passage to analyze. If the piece is under two pages, read the whole thing; otherwise select an excerpt. Next, use the techniques from chapter nineteen to sort through that passage. Look at the three layers of the story: *what*, *why*, and *how*.

Begin by focusing on the *what* and collecting information. What is the author saying? What is the story about? Who are the characters, and what do they do? Make notes and pay attention to specific words, images, phrases, and punctuation. No detail is too small, no nuance too subtle.

Now switch gears and look at the *why* of the story. Why did the author write this piece? What are some of the overall themes or issues the author addresses? In other words, aside from pretty language, what's the point of the piece? Why should a reader care? Why do *you* care?

Finally, put the *what* and *why* together. Look at the deliberate choices the author made, and determine how those artistic decisions support the purpose of the piece. How does the author use elements of the craft (the *what*) to reflect or underscore the meaning (the *why*)? Use evidence from the text to support your claims about how the *what* affects the *why*.

For example, in "The Story of an Hour," Kate Chopin deliberately withholds Mrs. Mallard's first name until a significant moment: when Louise realizes that she is "Free! Body and soul free!" This sense of identity is short-lived, however, and a few paragraphs later, when her husband returns home, she goes back to being a nameless "wife." How Chopin reveals Louise Mallard's name emphasizes the character's sense of self, and when her husband returns and her freedom disappears, so, too, does her name. The more you practice reading and responding to literature in this way, the better at it you will become. This will not only make you a stronger reader but a better writer as well.

Personal Essay

If book reviews or close analyses are not your style, you can also respond to what you read through a personal essay. Look at the major themes in a book you recently read, and consider how those themes apply to your life. Use specific imagery from the book as a springboard to discuss something from your own experience. For example, you could use the imagery of death and dying in *Charlotte's Web* to discuss a loss or death in your own life. Similarly you can respond to *The Hunger Games* by reflecting on how even in the most inhumane situations, people can show a deep humanity. Look for a theme in the book that resonates with you, and write about how it applies to your experience.

Unlike the previous types of responses, the personal essay uses the book itself as a starting point. In fact, you need not discuss that book in detail at all. Instead, focus on applying thematic elements from the story to your experience and use it as the foundation for a larger, more personal examination of that theme. While this response may not relate directly to the book itself, it will help you internalize and remember its themes. Also, because this type of response can grow into something that stands on its own and does not rely on the original work for its meaning, you may be able to repurpose the essay and even submit it for publication.

Build Your Own Literature Anthology

For a long time, I have searched for the perfect literature anthology: a collection of poems, stories, and essays that provides examples of the most fundamental writing principles and techniques. I'm looking for a textbook of sorts, not for a generic English class, but rather for the writing life. Some anthologies and collections have come close to meeting my requirements, and over the years I have managed to find a few anthologies that, taken together, are an adequate solution to my quest. Still, no single volume fulfills all my needs.

Until such a resource exists, I do the next best thing: I create a "personalized literature anthology" pieced together from reading resources specific to my own tastes and preferences. What began as a way to fill the gap on my bookshelf is now a technique I teach to all my students.

The idea behind the personalized anthology is simple. As you read books, stories, poems, and essays, make note of passages that illustrate particular techniques. Photocopy those passages, mark them up with comments, and then file them away in a binder. At first, you will have only a few pages, but after a while, those pages will accumulate. When that happens, sort the passages according to elements of craft. Put passages that illustrate character development in one section, including examples of different character archetypes. Stow plot-related passages in another section, and be sure to include examples of different story landmarks. Collect samples of the different points of view. After a few months—maybe a year—you will have a binder filled with examples of writing techniques, pulled from sources you have read and drawn from genres or subjects that interest you. This collection will be sorted based on different writing techniques, so if you need an example, you can find it quickly in your binder.

This is a powerful tool for a few reasons. First, it forces you to pay attention when you read because you will be motivated to find useful examples to add to your binder. The more you pay attention when you read, the more you will learn and the stronger your writing will become. What is more, unlike required reading compiled by a professor, this collection of examples is personalized to *you*. It reflects your tastes as a reader and writer, and draws from genres or subjects you like to read. The pieces you include in this personalized anthology are not only useful examples, they are relevant to you and your interests.

Finally, when you sort your selections according to technique, you'll find it easier to pull up useful examples when you need them. Most anthologies or collections are organized chronologically or alphabetically by the authors' last names. This method is only useful if you want to find works by a specific author or look at literature from a historical perspective. If you want to locate examples of specific techniques, most anthologies are useless. By categorizing your personalized anthology according to technique, you won't waste time locating relevant examples.

Long Responses to a Body of Literature

Short responses allow you to delve deep into individual stories and can help you understand specific techniques, but your study of literature should not end there. It is also important to look more broadly at a body of literature and uncover how different works relate to one another. In fact, some traditional MFA programs require students to submit a literature thesis in addition to a creative manuscript. But you don't need to write a thesis-length paper to develop your expertise about a certain genre or topic. In fact, you can get many of the same benefits simply by reading broadly and thoroughly on a subject or niche that resonates with you.

Start by reading as many books as you can on that topic. Be obsessed. Geek out. Record everything you can find, and piece the information together. Use that material as a springboard to craft short essays or articles. You can submit or pitch these smaller pieces to build your publication credits. Publishing smaller pieces reinforces your credibility, and you might even get some freelance income as a bonus. Also, if your work appears on a bigger, more prestigious site, this can send Web traffic and new readers your way, helping you build that much-coveted author platform. Finally—and perhaps most important—when you explore a particular topic or niche in depth, you can eventually position yourself as an expert and thought leader on that subject. This type of credibility can lead to interviews, speaking engagements, and other publicity opportunities.

Before any of those wonderful results can happen, you must develop your expertise and position yourself as *the* person who can speak on a particular topic. This is where diving into a body of literature is crucial. Essentially, you can take one of three approaches: a thematic analysis, an author study, or a historical survey. Each of these approaches will teach you different skills and help you gain a different set of insights about the literature in your chosen niche.

Thematic Analysis

With a thematic analysis, you choose a topic, read books by various authors, and formulate a series of questions or arguments based on what you learn. You can write a thematic analysis based on a certain type of imagery, a particular setting, or any other thread that the books you select have in common. Though this is my favorite type of longer response, it may also be the most challenging. With nothing but a common theme, it can be hard to narrow your focus, and the sheer number of books you need to read can be overwhelming. In the beginning, focus your thematic analysis within a particular genre or category. Later on you can expand beyond those limits, but at the start it is helpful to focus on a specific niche.

To illustrate what a thematic analysis might look like, here is an example from my own MFA thesis topic. I have always been obsessed with design and human behavior. Before I turned to writing, I got a master's degree in developmental psychology, with a focus on how toy design influences children's play behaviors. So, when it came time to choose a topic for my literature thesis in the MFA program, I knew I wanted to explore the relationship between the physical design of various books and how those design choices affect the reading experience.

I started by looking at middle-grade literature and spent weeks reading every book I could find that used unique storytelling devices. I wanted to understand how the interactive elements of those narratives contributed to the greater themes of those stories. But I didn't stop there. I started looking at verse novels and how the words themselves create a designed experience for the readers. Eventually, middle-grade literature was not enough. I branched out into young adult literature, genre fiction, even literary fiction like Nabokov's *Pale Fire*.

If my professor hadn't stopped me, I would have spent the year researching and writing that paper and likely would have submitted a book-length manuscript on the subject. To this day, I continue to obsess over this topic. Over the years, this material has found its way into various blog posts I have written and has even snuck into some of my fiction projects.

If you want to write a thematic analysis, find something you love just as passionately as I love design. Read everything you can find that contributes to your knowledge on the subject. Learn the topic inside and out. Be obsessed. What starts as a passion project will not only help you build your reading chops, it can make you a better writer as well.

Author Study

In an author study, you read an author's work (either all, or a representative selection) and then draw inferences about that body of work. When you read several books by the same author, you will begin to see similar themes come up again and again. You will start to understand what topics matter to the author. You may notice patterns between the books. Certain books may be mirror images of each other, different sides of the same literary coin. Other books might stand out and feel very different from the rest of an author's work. If you read an author's work alongside her biography, you might even see parallels between the creative work and real-life events that affected the author.

By looking at an author's entire body of work, you will not only get a deeper understanding of that slice of literature, but you will also gain insights about that author's process. For instance, as a lover of Jane Austen's work, I have spent a good deal of time looking not only at her various novels but also the order in which they were written and at which stages of her life. You can see a clear development in Austen as an author from her first book, *Northanger Abbey*, to her last, *Persuasion*. While her books always center on a love story, her interest in other themes shifts and changes throughout her life. By looking at the overall arc of an author's work, you get a better sense of how that author's interests and skills develop over time.

For a slight variation on an author study, you can focus on one particular series written by an author. For instance, you could look at how the characters and storytelling develop throughout the course of the Harry Potter series, in which the author took several years to develop and write the entire story from beginning to end. Every series has a distinct arc, and with Harry Potter we know, based on author interviews, that J.K. Rowling spent a lot of time pre-planning the books and tying details and story threads together. By doing a close study of such a tightly plotted series, you can observe how the author ties different elements together across various books, giving you insight on how to do the same in your own work.

Other series develop more spontaneously over time and have more of an episodic feel, with a recurring main character who goes on a new adventure or faces a new challenge in each subsequent book. We often see this pattern in mystery series, where the main character sleuth must solve a new murder in each book. While the individual storylines might be self-contained, over the course of several books you will notice changes and shifts in the recurring characters. This type of in-depth study can also help you solve certain problems or challenges in your own writing, especially if you write episodic-style series yourself. For instance, how does an author keep within the conventions of his particular genre without becoming formulaic and predictable? The best way to find out is to study a series that does this well.

If you are a fan of a particular author or series, this type of study will come easily to you. Read a broad selection of that author's work, and get a sense of how it changes over time. How do the author's early books compare with more recent ones? Do you notice any shifts in themes or subject matter? At any point, does the author break into a new genre or category, or shift gears in some other substantial way? Many authors start by focusing on a particular genre, but after a time they may try writing for a different audience. Look at how they make that shift, and the types of projects they choose in their new niche. How do the books in this new area compare to that author's signature style or category?

Studying an author's career and body of work is like a virtual apprenticeship. You will gain insights about books from a writer you love, and you will also learn about his process and may even be able to make inferences about his artistic or professional choices. One writer friend refers to this exercise as "studying mentor texts," and I think that phrase is apt. By doing an in-depth study of an author's body of work, it's almost as if that author is mentoring you from afar or from centuries past.

Historical Survey

The goal of a historical survey is not to focus on a particular theme or author, but to understand the history of your chosen genre. This type of survey is crucial because you need to understand how your genre or niche came to be and how it has changed over time. There are always books that buck trends or break patterns, but having a sense of the history in your chosen genre or niche allows you to see how your own writing fits within that context.

In addition, if you use a particular narrative device or point of view in your writing, it can be useful to trace the history of that particular technique. For example, if you are writing a book using journal form, look for the earliest books that use this structure. Why do you think authors choose that form in the first place? What does it accomplish? You should also study books in journal form that were bestsellers in their time. What made those books successful? When you understand the historical context of a particular technique or device, you can make a more informed choice about whether it will work for your own writing.

Maintaining Balance

This chapter's message may seem overwhelming, as if it's saying you need to read anything and everything that comes your way and then write long, involved responses or notes.

Don't panic.

Remember, DIY MFA is not about reading *all the books*; it's about reading with purpose. These responses are not meant to be assignments or exercises in futility. Try the different options, and iterate. If something doesn't work, *don't do it.* Do not waste time reading a book if it doesn't serve you or your writing. Similarly, don't spin your wheels writing responses that don't help your writing in some way. At the very least, reading these books and writing responses should be *fun.* The benefit to your writing is a bonus, but if you aren't enjoying the process, stop.

This chapter offers several options for how to respond to what you read. This does not mean you must use all of them. In fact, *I* don't even use all these methods. Some techniques, like the personalized anthology, I use all the time. Other options come and go, depending on the project I am working on or the mood I am in. The important thing is that you are aware of your options and that you choose a combination that works for you. The idea isn't to become the most well-read person on the planet (though wouldn't that be nice?). Instead, focus on improving as both a writer and a reader.

Have fun. Learn something. And if writing responses isn't enjoyable or informative, stop.

Seriously, stop. Reboot. Then try something else.

build your community

21

Establish Your Circle of Trust

In this last section of *DIY MFA*, we turn our focus to building a writing community. Until now, we have looked at skills and techniques involved in *creating* written work and *consuming* books in a way that serves your writing. Now we focus on the human piece of the puzzle: When you build your community, you are *connecting* with other people: writers, readers, and professionals in the book industry.

Many writers are tempted to skip this section. You might be thinking: *I just started writing. Why should I worry about marketing or publishing or building a platform?* I urge you to keep an open mind. Even if you don't take action right away, read the information and let it wash over you. It is never too early to start learning the business of writing. Even if you don't use this knowledge right away, you will know what lies ahead, and you won't be surprised when the time comes to implement these concepts.

You might notice this section is far more streamlined than the previous two. I did this on purpose. Instead of focusing on the minutiae of publishing, marketing, and social media, I want to emphasize *strategy*. The business of writing changes fast, so unless you are ready to implement these concepts now, it makes no sense to overwhelm you with nitty-gritty technical details. Instead, I would rather you understand *why* you should adopt certain strategies so you can ask smart questions and make informed decisions. Plus, you can find a lot of great books and websites on those topics anyway. You should also check out the up-to-the-minute list of these resources at DIYMFA.com/thebook; sign up with your e-mail address to get them.

But first, allow me to wax nostalgic for a moment. Before I started at the MFA program at The New School in 2008, the publishing landscape looked very different from how it looks now. Kindle was a newfangled technology that most readers barely knew existed. Self-publishing was synonymous with "vanity publishing." Borders bookstore was still in business. The "slush pile" was an actual *pile* of mail because most agents still read query letters in hard copy. If authors wanted a response to their query, they had to enclose an SASE (self-addressed, stamped envelope) with their letter.

In just the few years since, the publishing industry has turned on its head. The Kindle has gained traction, and competing e-readers like Nook and Kobo are now on the market. Amazon launched its Kindle Direct Publishing program, and self-publishing is now a viable business model for some authors. If you decide you still want to go the traditional route, don't bother sending snail mail to agents, because e-mail queries are now the norm.

And let's not forget the constantly changing landscape of social media. Myspace, which was top dog in 2008, is dead. Facebook reigns supreme with over 1 billion registered users. From Pinterest to Periscope to podcasts, you can find a social medium where you can connect with your audience, no matter your niche or interest. Not only is it easier for writers to publish their work, they have many more channels available to spread their message.

If you want to build a career in writing, the most important skill you must develop is the ability to learn and adapt. You can bury your head in the ground and pretend the world isn't changing, or throw your hands up in despair and wail about the downfall of publishing's golden age. Or you can choose to build a community that will help you grow with the times—and help you stay miles ahead of writers who ignore or bemoan the inevitable changes in our industry.

In this section, I have opted for a more learning-based approach, inspired by the words of Eric Hoffer: "In a time of drastic change, it is the learners who inherit the future." Understand the big picture. Focus on the overall concepts: *what* you need to do and *why* it's important. When it's time to take action, you can figure out the *how* or find someone to do it for you.

The chapters that follow cover the fundamental tools for building your community. You will learn the three types of people you must connect with as an author: writing colleagues, your readers, and members of the publishing industry. Cultivate these relationships, and more important, understand why they are essential to your career. While specific action steps and tactics come and go, the overarching strategy is often the same. Who knows where the publishing industry will be in another eight years? We might have technology that lets us absorb books via osmosis, or the Internet might be permanently implanted in our brains, à la M.T. Anderson's *Feed*. However, the underlying strategies for how we connect with our readers and colleagues will stay consistent no matter how much the publishing business changes.

Writing Friends: Your Circle of Trust

Writing is lonely. You sit in isolation, interacting with characters who exist only in your mind. When you finish pouring your heart and soul onto the page, you release your precious work into the world only to have it rejected and criticized. Even if you receive accolades and critical acclaim, one nasty review can kill your confidence and leave you shaking in your shoes. This is why you need to surround yourself with people who understand what it is like to travel this wild and crazy road.

There are two types of people in the world: writers and nonwriters. Because I'm a huge Harry Potter fan, I call the latter group "muggles." Writers are word wizards; they create magic with language. Nonwriters are everybody else. They are the nonmagical folk who go through life oblivious to all the magic and mystery that surrounds them. I believe all humans are born with writing magic, but somewhere along the way it gets squashed out of most people. Some writers are told that they're not "good" at writing. Others come to that conclusion on their own. Slowly the magic fades, and they shift into the daily grind of living and being normal.

Then there are the select few, the ones who cling stubbornly to writing like castaways clinging to a raft on a choppy ocean. Maybe it is because they can't let go of writing—or maybe writing can't let go of them—but whatever the reason, they hold on. And after a while, they figure out how to paddle.

In his book *Show Your Work!*, Austin Kleon talks about the importance of being an amateur, of creating and holding fast to your art because you love it. He shares a profound quote from Clay Shirky, from the book *Cognitive Surplus*:

> On the spectrum of creative work, the difference between the mediocre and the good is vast. Mediocrity is, however, still on the spectrum; you can move from mediocre to good in increments. The real gap is between doing nothing and doing something.

From this perspective, the difference between being a great writer and a newbie is not nearly as huge as the difference between being a word wizard and a muggle. Despite their disparity in skill level, both beginners and seasoned writers share something in common: They write.

For this reason, one of the most important things you can do is create a network of writing colleagues and friends. These fellow word wizards will support you in a world where most people don't even realize that magic exists, much less understand what it's like to conjure it. The industry might ebb and flow, publishers can come and go, but writing friends can last a lifetime. Your fellow word wizards are your writing family. They are your "circle of trust." They will be your source of support during challenging times and will celebrate your success. Most important, these colleagues help you remember that as lonely as this writing existence may be sometimes, you are not alone.

Your circle of trust has four important roles or functions: critique, accountability, support, and advice or apprenticeship. I use the acronym CASA because it means "home" in Portuguese, and the people in your *casa* are like your writing home. Not every writing friend will fill every role; in fact, few ever do. You will likely need to mix and match, assembling a group of colleagues to fill these different needs.

> C = Critique
> A = Accountability
> S = Support
> A = Advice or Apprenticeship

Critique

Giving and receiving critique is the foundation of most creative writing courses, and the workshop approach is the cornerstone of the traditional MFA system. While feedback is certainly useful, be careful not to depend too heavily on this element of your writing network. Critique is only one small piece of the *casa* puzzle. While it can help you identify aspects of your work that need improvement, it is a reactive approach to writing rather than a proactive one. Rather than learning the fundamentals and avoiding basic pitfalls in the first place, the workshop approach uses trial and error to find and fix mistakes that have already been made. This means it can take a long time before you figure out what works and what doesn't. You have to try different things—and fail—before you discover the best solution.

The workshop approach can become problematic if a writer starts to depend too much on feedback. I've seen many writers lean on workshops and critique groups like a crutch—to the point where they can't write anything without the approval of the group or the teacher.

In the next chapter I delve further into the critique process and show you how to use it to improve your writing proactively rather than after the fact. For now, let's look at the three other equally important components of your writing network.

Accountability

Despite being frequently overlooked, accountability is a crucial component of a writer's circle of trust. While critique, support, and advice help you improve the quality of your work, accountability forces you to do that work in the first place. As you learned in chapter seventeen, the first draft has only one purpose: It exists. It doesn't have to be pretty, and it doesn't even need to make sense. It just has to be words on the page, a jumbled mass of black and white. Accountability is what helps you write those words.

Psychology researchers have long studied different types of social influence. From hazing in fraternities to the power of reciprocity, it is clear that peer pressure is a powerful way to influence people's thoughts and actions. You can use accountability to harness the power of peer pressure and fuel your own creativity and productivity.

Before looking at examples of how to build accountability into your writing network, it's important to define what accountability is and isn't. Accountability is a statement of fact. It is objective and nonjudgmental. In the Orientation section for this book, I discussed the difference between failure and guilt. As you recall, failure is an objective result, while guilt is the emotion that compounds that outcome. Accountability is a record or measure of whether you have met a certain goal. It does not judge the quality of that goal. Nor does it push you toward a "better" goal. It is just a binary outcome. Did you reach your goal? Yes or no? It's that simple.

You likely have some degree of internal accountability: You are able to motivate yourself because you feel compelled to reach the goals you have set. This is called *intrinsic motivation*, and most creative people possess it. If they didn't, very little art, music, and literature would exist in the world. In fact, many creative people feel *less* motivated to create art when they start receiving compensation (money, fame, and so on) because it starts to feel like work.

At the other extreme, some writers, when left to their own devices, spend years perfecting their books and never release them into the world. They are master tinkerers. This is why external or social accountability—a.k.a. peer pressure—is so important.

Social accountability requires you to report to someone other than yourself about whether you have met your goals. When you only have to answer to yourself, it is easy to let deadlines slide and grant yourself a silent extension on a project. No one else will know if you don't meet your goal, so the sting to your ego is relatively small. In fact, master procrastinators develop an immunity to internal goals and become skilled at rationalizing and excusing their lack of progress. Accountability forces you to make your goals public, so that when you succeed or fail, that outcome becomes public as well. Suddenly it is not so easy to fall behind on a project, because other people are watching. Even if you are an intrinsically motivated person, you can use social accountability to push yourself toward your goals.

Keep a Log

You already know how to use a Writing Tracker to log, iterate, and improve your writing *process*, but keeping a record of your writing *progress* serves an additional purpose: It makes you accountable. Not only does this log force you to observe the daily nuances of your process, it pushes you to make progress so that you have something to record in the first place. Keeping a log is often the first step in staying accountable.

Make Your Goal Public

When you announce that you're going to do something, people hold you to your word. This means you are more likely to stop whining and work toward making that goal a reality. Tell someone your goal and suddenly it will feel more urgent, more real. Social media is a great way to share your goals and update people on your progress. Post the goal on your blog or announce it in your newsletter.

If you prefer a more low-tech approach, share your goal with one or two trusted writing friends and play "catch." I discovered this approach when writing my MFA thesis. For the first two months of writing, I needed time to crank out pages without worrying about whether it was any good. I knew if I got feedback from my advisor, I would get hung up on getting it "right" and would stop actually writing. But I also knew that if I didn't submit anything for two months, I would procrastinate for seven weeks and then cram all my writing efforts into those last few days. I needed a way to pace myself and stay motivated without letting feedback derail my momentum. I needed to produce quantity without worrying about quality, accountability without critique.

I discussed this dilemma with my advisor, and we came up with a plan: We would play "catch." At the end of each week, I would e-mail my pages to her. She didn't have to read them or even open them. She just "caught" them and sent me a short reply to keep me motivated. If I missed a week or was late sending my pages, she would send me a virtual nudge. After two months, we would weed through the mass of pages together and decide where to go from there.

This process was miraculous, and in those two months I produced some of my best writing. Since then, "catch" has been a staple in my writing process. Sometimes you don't need feedback on your work; you just need someone to be on the other end of the computer waiting to receive it.

Writing in Tandem

There is a reason the word *dead* appears in *deadline*. It instills just enough fear to make me stop complaining and get to work. To this day, if I don't have a deadline I will procrastinate and tinker with my projects forever. Ironically, deadlines keep me from squashing the life out of my projects and force me to click the "submit" button.

Deadlines are meaningless, though, if you don't schedule actual time to work on your projects. This is where writing in tandem can be lifesaving. A few years ago, some friends started gathering in a coffee shop one night each week to write. They called it Write Nite, and for a while I joined them. Over the years, word about the writing group spread, and more people came. In fact, for a while our group took over an entire section at a cafe. As time rolled on, most of us got new jobs, new babies, or new homes outside the city, and the group parted ways. Still, the discipline and creative energy of Write Nite has remained with me, and I've found new ways to re-create that environment.

Writing in tandem is powerful because it forces you to work. You don't want to be the only slacker in the group who is checking Facebook or playing Solitaire. Working side by side with other writers makes you focus, and you end up accomplishing more than if you were writing by yourself. The peer pressure of seeing other people hard at work keeps you accountable and motivated. No glancing at social media just for a second. No checking your in-box and tumbling down an e-mail rabbit hole. You just write. I still use this technique. In fact, as I write this I am sitting in a coffee shop near my son's school working side by side with a fellow mom-writer.

You also don't need to be in the same geographical location as the other writer in order to write in tandem. One of my writing buddies lives hundreds of miles away, but we'll sometimes open up a video call on our computers and work "across the desk" from each other, even though we're sitting in different cities. With today's technology, you could be writing in tandem with someone on the other side of the globe. The key isn't *how* you do it, but that you find a routine that works.

Support

This aspect of the *casa* equation is perhaps the most obvious, but many writers overlook it. Maybe it's our puritanical culture, or this glorified image we have of the "starving artist" suffering for his work, but often we forget to build a support system into our writing networks. Support is essential for survival.

Writing is hard. It can be fun at first—getting to know new characters and discovering your story's world—but after a while the novelty wears off. You have to keep digging deep and drawing from your inner creative well, even when it feels like you have nothing left to give. By the time you've gone through several rounds of revisions and have what you think is a "finished" manuscript, you might be tempted to call it quits. But no, the process has only just begun, and now it's time to submit your work and brace yourself for the potential pain and rejection that may follow.

When I tell someone I am a writer, the other person usually asks me what I've published or what my book is about. After these initial pleasantries she adds, with a sigh, "I've always wanted to write a book … if only I could find the time."

I often have to bite my tongue to stop myself from saying, "Yeah, I've always wanted to be a neurosurgeon and cut people's brains open … if only I could find the time."

Writing is a strange vocation. It seems like everyone in the world wants to write a book, yet relatively few ever make it to the finish line. Nonwriting folk operate under the misconception that writing is easy and that anyone can do it, unlike string theory, nanotechnology, or other fields people think are "difficult." The truth is that just about anyone *could* be a string theorist if they put in the time and focused study. The same is true about writing.

And yet, writing also holds a certain power over our hearts. It seeps into our souls in a way that few other vocations can. You never hear a neurosurgeon say, "Wow, I haven't given anyone a lobotomy in three days! I just don't feel like myself." But, as writers, we feel like we lose a part of ourselves if we stay away from our work for too long. I know if I'm away from my writing for more than a few days, I get cranky. I lose my temper. I yell at the cat. Writers become their best selves when they do the work they love.

When your work looks like play, others are quick to forget that it's still a job. This is why a support network is so important. Despite their good intentions, the nonwriters in our lives will never truly understand the writing life, so we must surround ourselves with fellow word nerds who *do* "get" it. Just because writing is hard at times doesn't mean we have to suffer alone.

There are many places to find support. You can join a writing association or attend a conference and meet other writers. If social media is more your speed, you can chat with like-minded writers via Twitter hashtags or Facebook groups. Sign up with your e-mail address at DIYMFA.com/thebook for suggestions and ideas. And, of course, you can connect with other DIY MFA word nerds by subscribing to the newsletter and joining our private Facebook community.

Advice or Apprenticeship

Most writing classes and MFA programs use the workshop model, in which you learn by receiving critiques on your work. Yet, rather than endure an endless cycle of submitting work, getting feedback, and resubmitting ad nauseam, why not get it right the first time? This is where advisors and mentors can be instrumental to your career.

Advice can come from any number of sources. If you need to solve a specific problem or learn a particular technique, you can take a class or hire a consultant. Your mentors or advisors can also assist from afar. They can be people whom you've never met in person but whose work you have observed and studied in detail. It is useful to adopt an apprentice mind-set, in which you learn by watching those who are better at a particular skill. Beware, however, two apprenticeship pitfalls: being a copycat and becoming codependent.

Copycatting

Copycats copy the work or system of someone they admire without understanding the underlying concepts. They focus on the surface-level details but don't realize the process that went into it. This approach is dangerous because you risk looking like an idiot when someone calls you out. These days, with the Internet and social media, it is virtually impossible to stay "under the radar," so if your work is an imitation of someone else's, readers are bound to notice. More important, copycats don't learn the deeper strategy or the concepts behind the work. This means that they are never able to make that process their own or develop beyond the work they copied.

When you have an apprentice mind-set, the finished product is almost irrelevant. What matters is the process. If you concentrate on understanding and adapting that process to your own style, it will be virtually impossible to create a cheap imitation. Instead, you will learn from another person's process and create something that is truly yours.

Codependency

The second pitfall with the apprenticeship mind-set is apprentice-master codependency. I have had many mentors and advisors in my life; I have also mentored and advised many writers. Eventually, each of these relationships has come to a strange moment—similar to scenes out of *Star Wars*—where we find ourselves no longer engaging as teacher and student, but as peers. Of course, in most mentor relationships this shift isn't the equivalent of Darth Vader striking down Obi-Wan Kenobi. In fact, the transition is sometimes so subtle and gradual that you hardly notice it until sometime afterward.

Advisors and mentors are usually adept at noticing this shift. In most cases the relationship simply adjusts and develops without much need for formal discussion. As an advisor, I like to prepare my students for the transition, so we build that conversation into our first meeting. Whether you and your advisor discuss the transition or the relationship evolves naturally, the key is to acknowledge and anticipate that the relationship will change. After all, no one can stay an apprentice forever.

But sometimes, advisor-apprentice relationships become codependent. The apprentice might be afraid to venture on without the advisor's guidance and approval, so he stays in comfortable and familiar territory. The advisor, in turn, doesn't want to abandon a student in need, so she doesn't challenge him to strike out on his own. In some rare cases, the mentor's motives might be more sinister and driven by ego or greed, but I like to believe that most advisors do sincerely have their students' best interests at heart. Most of the time, this codependency happens without either person realizing it.

Regardless of the reasons, you must remember that there is only one person in charge of your writing life: you. If you find yourself depending too heavily on a mentor or advisor, you must ask yourself why. It may be wise to bridge this topic with your advisor and brainstorm together so you can find ways to become more independent.

There you have it: your *casa* or "circle of trust" that will help you grow as a writer. It will give you the support you need to experiment and try new techniques, and will help you bounce back from rejection and failure. Your fellow writers can keep you accountable so you develop a writing habit that produces results. Through the years, look for mentors or advisors to guide you and help you avoid that endless cycle of trial and error. In the next chapter, we dig into the first piece of the *casa* puzzle: the give and take of critique.

22

Work That Workshop

Once you've established the other three pieces of your writing network, or *casa*, consider joining a writing workshop or critique group. Most traditional MFA programs put the workshop front and center. It is the most important component of the curriculum and is usually required every semester. At DIY MFA the workshop isn't as central, but that does not diminish its importance. The reason I put less emphasis on the workshop than you might see in a traditional MFA program is because, first and foremost, I believe in empowering writers. Before you start seeking feedback from workshops or critique groups, I want you to become your own best editor and best reader. This does not mean that you *never* get outside feedback on your work, but when you do get critiques, you should know how to put them in perspective and apply the suggestions in a useful way.

In this chapter you will learn about the different types of feedback you can receive and how to identify which one you need depending on where you are in the writing and revision process. You will also develop a way to give caring and kind critiques that also challenge the other writers to do their best work. Finally, you will learn what to do before, during, and after you receive feedback on your writing.

What Type of Feedback Is Right for You?

Before we discuss different types of critique, it is important to understand the difference between critique and discussion. Even though both involve talking about an author's work, critique and discussion are two very different beasts. Critique centers on the *writer's* perspective, while discussion is about the *reader's* experience.

The purpose of critique is to help the writer improve his writing. The readers offering critique might give their impressions of the work or how they interpreted certain aspects, but ultimately their goal is to help the writer make the piece stronger. Because the point of critique is to *help* the writer, it usually makes no sense to receive critique on work that has already been published. Feedback and suggestions only help if the writer can make changes to his work, otherwise those comments will only cause the writer stress and anxiety. Once the work has been published, the writer no longer needs critique. What he needs are readers.

Discussion is a different scenario. Rather than giving feedback on a work, the readers share their thoughts about it. If critique is what you get in a writing group, discussion is what happens in a literature course or book club. Readers share their interpretations of the work and mention elements that resonate or miss the mark. In discussion, the goal is to talk about a book as a piece of literature, not a work-in-progress in need of improvement. Once a piece has been published and can no longer be changed, the writer's only job is to share that work with readers and let them experience it for what it is, good or bad.

The distinction between critique and discussion is all about the relationship between the writer of the work and the people who read it. The critique relationship is writer-to-writer, whereas the discussion relationship is author-to-audience. This difference is not always clear-cut, and sometimes critique and discussion blur together. For instance, a writer might gain insights from reading reviews and hearing feedback from his readers. These comments might not affect the particular work in question, but they can help the writer improve future works. Conversely, members of a workshop might offer their interpretations about a piece, even if those insights don't necessarily improve the work.

CRITIQUE VERSUS DISCUSSION

To determine which type of feedback you need on your book, consider these two questions:

1. **WHAT IS THE RELATIONSHIP BETWEEN THE WRITER AND THE READER?** Is it writer-to-writer or author-to-audience?
2. **WHAT IS THE GOAL OF THE CONVERSATION?** Is the purpose to help the *writer* improve the piece? Or is the focus on the *reader* and her impressions of the work?

As a writer, you must be honest with yourself. Be clear about what type of feedback you need on a particular project. Are you looking for critique that will help you make the writing stronger, or are you really seeking an audience to read and enjoy your work? This is very important, because not only will it help you seek the right type of feedback, it will also keep you from straining your relationships with the people reading your work. If what you want is critique and you only receive discussion, then you won't be satisfied unless the feedback truly helps you improve your writing. Similarly, if you're looking for an audience and you're getting critique instead, you may get frustrated with the continual criticism, however constructive it may be. Your readers may also get annoyed if you don't implement their suggestions because it will seem as if you're not listening to what they have to say.

The first step for getting good feedback on your work is to know what type of feedback you need, if any. Your answer may change depending on where you are in your writing career or even where you are in the stage of a given project. The better you understand your goals, the better your chances of finding the right people to help you reach them.

What to Look for in a Critique Community

Over the years, I've sampled many different writing communities. I have joined online discussion forums, participated in Twitter chats, and joined dozens of Facebook and LinkedIn groups. In person, I have attended workshops, taken courses, and even founded a writing group that met regularly for more than seven years. These communities each have their own quirks and culture, but the best ones share a few common characteristics.

The Participants Give More Than They Take

Writing communities work best when everyone gives more than they take. Generosity lifts up the community, and if each person gives more, the group ends up getting more. In the end, generosity benefits everyone.

In a writing community, generosity means giving feedback and supporting your fellow writers. Smart writers know that even when they're not getting feedback on their own work, they still learn something from the critique process. In fact, you're likely to understand techniques in greater depth when you give critique than when you receive it. It is in explaining an idea that it really sinks into your own mind. Giving critique to other writers will give you valuable insights and help you solve problems in your own writing.

The Feedback Focuses on Improvement Rather Than Criticism

Some communities or classes adhere to the philosophy that you must tear down writers in order to build them back up. I think this approach is utter nonsense. There is no such thing as "constructive criticism." Criticism—the act of finding fault in someone's work and tearing it to pieces—is by definition not constructive. Every time I hear that term I roll my eyes.

Look for critique communities that focus on suggestions for improvement. If a workshop brings up a fault in someone's work, the members should discuss how to solve that problem. Workshops should also communicate the positive aspects of the piece as well as the negative. If you can help someone understand what *works* in their writing, she can apply that concept to future projects and avoid making "mistakes" in the first place.

Beware writers who make a point of bringing their colleagues down. If you look below the surface, you will likely find that the problem is with the critic's ego and not with the work being criticized. Sometimes when writers feel insecure, they tear down others in order to pump themselves up. These situations are toxic and will suck the life and energy out of your work. You don't need this kind of melodrama; writing a good story is dramatic enough as it is. If a community starts heading down this dark path, run away. Fast.

While you want to find communities with a constructive attitude, that doesn't mean that you should receive only glowing praise about your writing. Often the best feedback is the hardest to hear, but if it comes from a place of honesty, the sting hurts a lot less. No matter how tough the critique, when you know your colleagues have your best interest in mind, it's easier to trust what they have to say.

Remember, too, that every writer receives feedback that she hates. A dilettante will ignore it, then seek out someone who will sing her praises instead. A *real* writer, however, will listen. When someone suggests you overhaul a major aspect of your project, you don't need to implement those changes on the spot, but you do need to listen. Try to understand not just *what* isn't working in your story, but also *why* it isn't working and *how* to fix it. You don't have to use every piece of advice you receive, but you should consider it, and if you turn it down, you should have a legitimate reason for doing so.

Different Types of Critique

You have several different options for critique, and some work better at different stages of a writing project. In order to decide what will work for you, you must understand the available alternatives.

Critique Partners

These are writers with whom you exchange your work as you progress through a project. Critique partners (CPs) will read several chapters of your story or novel and give you feedback as you go along so that you can make adjustments. In many cases, CPs will get to know your writing almost as well as you do and will be able to offer in-depth advice because they understand what you want to accomplish with your project.

The one disadvantage of critique partners is that they see your work piecemeal and often read portions of a project that don't end up in the finished version. If you make drastic changes from one version to the next, you must bring your CPs up to speed, because they might still be viewing your project through the context of an earlier rendition.

Make sure to get a few fresh eyes on your manuscript after you have revised it. Even if your CPs read a full version of your book, they may remember details from an earlier draft, which can affect their input. When you're ready for others to read the whole manuscript, make sure you include at least one person who wasn't a critique partner.

STARTING YOUR OWN WRITING GROUP

While workshops often occur under the umbrella of a writing school or MFA program, you can band together with other writers and create a group of your own. I did this some years ago with writers I met in a class, and our group stayed together for more than seven years. Forming your own group has its own set of advantages as well as challenges.

GROUP DYNAMICS

Starting your own group can help you dodge hit-or-miss critiques because you and your fellow group members can decide who to let in. But even when you vet new members carefully, the group dynamics can still be tricky. It can also be hard to find quality members when people have conflicting schedules.

My writing group was based in New York City, the hub of the publishing universe and home to many, many writers. Even then, it was hard to find new writers to fill the gaps when someone left the group. No matter how close-knit your group, there will always be an ebb and flow to the membership. People move away, get married, have babies, or change jobs. When that happens, the group needs a method to recruit new members, otherwise the numbers will dwindle to a point where meeting is no longer productive.

So, you need a clear process for admitting new members. Should the group consider only those referred by a current member? Must they submit a sample of their work? Will there be a probationary period where new members can feel out the group and vice versa? These considerations are especially important if the group's core members have been together for a long time. While new members can keep the group dynamic fresh, you want to be careful not to let someone in who later becomes a problem.

You also need a system for evaluating the group and how well it is working. This can be a simple periodic check-in where members discuss how the group is operating. Do any of the logistics need to change? Do you need to discuss any interpersonal tensions? All of these things are important to keep the group running smoothly. Just as you must iterate your own writing process, so, too, must a writing group iterate theirs.

While you hope it never comes to this, there is always the possibility that a member of the group needs to leave. Whether the writer or the group initiates this parting of ways, it's important to have a process that will bring closure to the situation. As with anything, clarity and kindness are key, but establishing ground rules for how the group operates can spare a lot of friction or hurt feelings.

LOGISTICS

Before you begin holding meetings, the group must first figure out logistics. How many members will there be? Where will you meet, and how often? How many pages should each person submit, and how often?

The size of writing groups can vary from as few as two or three people to as many as fifteen or more. In my experience, the sweet spot is between five and seven members. This is large enough that if someone is absent, the meeting is still productive, but it is also small enough that everyone can receive a critique on a regular basis.

How often you hold meetings is another important consideration. I have found that either weekly or every other week is ideal. Less often than that and the group loses momentum. Also, unless everyone submits work at every meeting, if you space out sessions too much, writers will have to wait a long time to receive critiques.

GROUND RULES

I've learned from experience that the best approach is to set ground rules up front. While the group can always make adjustments over time, it's helpful to have a game plan for how to operate. At the first meeting, decide on these ground rules together. How many writers submit work each time? Is there a page or word limit on how much one writer can submit? How far in advance should the work be sent to the group? This may seem like nitpicking, but the more you clarify up front, the easier it will be to address problems later on.

Beta Readers

Beta readers (or betas) read your entire book and offer feedback on over-arching aspects. While betas can be writers themselves, they don't *need* to be. What matters is that your betas be familiar with your genre. Betas read your entire novel in a short span of time and give you feedback about big-picture aspects of your work: character development, plot arc, and so on. They rarely focus on the nitty-gritty details, so don't rely on them to line edit or make small corrections. Aim to send your work to two to four betas so that you get the benefit of a few opinions but won't be bombarded with too many suggestions.

Also, while you can ask one or two of your critique partners to beta-read your book, it is a good idea to enlist at least one person who has not seen it before.

This will give you a more balanced perspective, since at least one of your betas will be new to the characters and story, and can look at them with fresh eyes.

Line Editors, Copyeditors, and Content Editors

Whether you plan to submit your writing to agents or you decide to self-publish your work, at some point you will need to ask for outside help to give your manuscript the once-over. This might involve seeking out a content editor, line editor, or copyeditor.

Line editors give line-by-line comments on your writing and help you put together a clean, well-formatted manuscript. You can certainly hire someone to line edit your book, or you can ask a critique partner who has a good eye for finding typos and grammatical mistakes. You can also choose to line edit your own manuscript, but even if this level of detailed editing is one of your strengths, I still recommend asking at least one other person to review it closely before you submit. The line editor is your manuscript's last line of defense before you send it out to agents and editors. You want your submission to shine. The last thing you need is for a gatekeeper to pass on your book because of small, easy-to-fix details.

Whether you choose to have your manuscript content edited and copyedited depends on how you plan to publish your book. If you plan to publish traditionally, then these editing tasks are already baked into the process, at least at most publishing houses. Also, if you have an agent, he or she may help you tighten your submission *before* it goes out to publishers. In the traditional publishing process, your book will undergo plenty of editing rounds, so it may not be necessary to bring in a content editor or copyeditor before you submit.

This is not to say that you shouldn't use a content editor or copyeditor if you plan to traditionally publish. Many published authors will bring in a content editor to help them organize their stories or will hire a copyeditor to help tighten the manuscript. These services can be quite valuable, but they are only *mandatory* if you plan to self-publish.

The minute you decide to self-publish, you must think of yourself as the CEO of a publishing company, even if that company consists of only you. This means you must bring in an outside editor (or two, or more) to help you make your book as professional and clean as you can. Even if you are a skilled copyeditor, you will not be objective with your own work. This is why it is crucial that you bring in an outside editor to help you make your book impeccable.

Giving and Receiving Critique

There are many ways to conduct a workshop or get feedback on your writing. I have tried various options, and I find that the *bubble method* often works best. If you have participated in critique sessions in the past, you have likely experienced some version of this method. It goes by many different names—the bubble, the booth, the box—but ultimately the goal is the same.

The idea of the bubble method is to make the critique process as objective as possible. If your work is being critiqued, this system helps make the feedback feel less personal. It lessens the sting and allows you to focus on improving your writing. If you are giving critique, this method gives you the freedom to say what you really think without worrying about writers jumping in to defend their work.

You've probably had this experience: You work hard on a piece of writing. You polish, edit, proofread, and tinker with the story until it is absolutely perfect. Blood, sweat, and tears pour onto the page. You spend weeks, months, years, nurturing this fledgling idea into a mature, full-grown narrative. Then you take it to your writing group, lay it gently on the literary altar, and watch as the vultures tear your baby apart.

Okay, I'm being melodramatic.

Still, it's understandable if your instinct is to swoop in and protect your work when other writers start to criticize it. Maybe you just want to clarify what you "really meant" because your critique partners don't "get" what you were trying to say. Or maybe you feel like the feedback is downright wrong and you need to disabuse these people of their ridiculous notions. I've been there.

Getting defensive—jumping in and explaining your work—is counterproductive. When you're busy defending your work, you're not focusing on the feedback. If you are rebutting and explaining, you are not listening. And if you don't listen to the feedback, you can't improve your work. More important, once your book is published, you won't be able to hover over your readers' shoulders and explain what you *really* meant on page 273. The writing will have to speak for itself.

In the bubble method, the writer being critiqued is not allowed to talk during the discussion. If you are the writer in "the bubble," your job is to listen to the feedback and absorb it. That's it. You are like a fly on the wall, listening to everything being said about your work but unable to participate.

It can be hard to bite your tongue and remain silent as other writers pick apart your work. The best way to handle the situation is to distract yourself by taking notes. Write as fast as you can. Make note of any questions you have or discussion points you need clarified. If you take copious notes and try to capture everything that is said, you'll be so busy that you won't have time to get defensive.

Most groups or workshops that use this critique method let the writer out of the bubble at the end of the discussion. This is when you can ask questions about anything you did not understand. This is also a good time to ask for suggestions on how to resolve any issues the group has flagged. Use your question time to make sure you understand exactly what was said and what you need to do next. One caveat: When you ask questions, make sure they are legitimate *questions*, and not thinly veiled defenses or explanations of your work.

How to Give Useful Critiques

When offering critique to another writer, always remember the Golden Rule: Treat that writer's work the way you would want your own work to be treated. Do your utmost to find a few positive aspects of the piece, no matter how horrendous you might think it is. Start your critique by mentioning at least one thing the writer has done well. It sets a positive tone for the discussion and also forces you to look at the work with optimistic eyes. If you go in looking for something to like about the piece, odds are you will find at least one nice thing to say.

Of course, no piece of writing is going to be perfect, so you will likely find certain elements that could be improved. When you do flag problems, challenge yourself to go beyond simply pointing out what is "wrong." Take a proactive approach. Focus on how the problems might be solved, and offer suggestions on how to improve the piece. End your comments on a positive note, by either giving another compliment or offering encouragement.

When it comes to written critiques, every writer has a unique style. Some like to write detailed comments in the margins of a printed document. Others prefer to give overall comments in a separate page or letter. Both approaches can be effective, and a group works best when its members offer a balanced mix of both line-by-line critiques and overall comments. In the end, choose the method that will help you give the best-quality feedback to your fellow writers.

Make the Most of Critiques You Receive

When it is your turn to receive critique, the more effort you put in, the more you will get out of the experience. Critique goes beyond the session itself. You must also consider what to do before and after it. Before you submit, make sure your piece is as strong as you can make it. During the critique, focus on the feedback and listen to what your colleagues are saying. After the session, develop a strategy to make sense of all the feedback you get. Use these guidelines to navigate the process.

Before You Submit

PROOFREAD AND ELIMINATE TYPOS. Make sure your submission is as tight and clean as possible. This will allow your critique partners to focus on the important aspects of your story. If your piece is littered with typos and grammatical errors—which you could easily correct yourself—the discussion may get derailed by the minutiae, and you could miss out on more valuable feedback.

FOLLOW THE GROUND RULES. Which submissions are fair game for critique? It all depends on the critique group and how it operates. Some groups will read anything in any genre and might even critique query letters, pitches for conferences, and other materials. Other groups might set boundaries in terms of genres and content the group will or will not read. Don't submit something that the group is not willing or prepared to critique; not only is it disrespectful, but you won't get useful feedback.

USE GOOD FORMATTING. Submit your work in the correct format (hard copy, e-mail attachment, etc.), and follow the guidelines of the group. If there are no specific guidelines, use standard formatting (12-point font, Times New Roman, double-spaced). Include page numbers, and unless instructed otherwise, put your name and the title of your piece in the header of each manuscript page. This way, if someone prints your work to read it in hard copy, they won't waste time collating or looking for missing pages.

SUBMIT ON TIME. When you submit your work late, you're not hurting your critique partners—you're hurting yourself. If your critique partners must read your piece in a hurry, it will affect the quality of their feedback. Give your group the time they need to read and give quality comments on your piece. In the end, you will get a more thorough, useful critique.

IF YOU CAN'T SUBMIT ON TIME, HAVE A BACK-UP PLAN. Emergencies happen, and sometimes you can't prepare your work in time to submit. Have an alternative ready in case this happens, especially if the group has only one person on deck for critique at each meeting. For instance, if you miss your submission deadline, bring in a writing exercise or short story for discussion. This was the policy in my own writing group, and it allowed the group to do something productive with that time, even if a writer could not submit.

During the Critique

DON'T PREFACE YOUR WORK WITH EXCUSES. Don't apologize for it. If you're submitting a rough draft, no need to make excuses or apologies. It is what it is. Don't whine about how rough it is or list all of its perceived weaknesses. And please, for the love of all that is literary, don't tell your critique team that you wrote it at the last minute (even if it's true). Writing something last-minute will not justify the rough state of your work. It only looks like you are wasting the group's time by not taking the critique process seriously.

KEEP TRACK OF WHO SAID WHAT. Bring a hard copy of your submission and take notes in the margins. Write the initials of each person speaking next to the feedback they gave, so when you review your notes later you'll know who made each comment. This is especially important if you trust the insights of some members more than others.

SIT WITH THE DISCOMFORT. If any comment feels especially painful, challenge yourself to take an objective stance. This is not about having a "thick skin" or letting criticism "roll off your back." Do not ignore the feedback altogether. If your skin is too thick and you reject everything, you might dismiss valid and important comments.

Instead, you must train yourself to sit with the discomfort of an unpleasant comment, without letting it rattle you to your core. I have a mantra I repeat to myself whenever I get feedback I don't like: "I am not my book." It reminds me that while the critique might not be pleasant, it isn't *personal* and helps me listen to uncomfortable feedback. After the critique session, I write the offending comments on a slip of paper and put them in the Angst Jar (see chapter five for more on this).

After the Critique

COLLECT THE WRITTEN COMMENTS FROM YOUR TEAM. If anyone wrote comments or notes in hard copy, gather all the pages at the end of the session so you have their notes when you revise.

RESIST THE URGE TO READ THROUGH THE COMMENTS AS SOON AS YOU GET HOME. Receiving critique is hard, even when the feedback is positive. Give yourself at least a few days to step away and gain perspective. It does you no good to read the comments when your wounds are still raw. Wait until you're ready to be objective. How long you need to wait will vary, but at least a few days can help you get some distance.

COMPILE YOUR CRITIQUE NOTES. Every writer revises in a different way. Before you can implement any suggestions, however, you need to compile your notes and feedback so the revision process does not become cumbersome or overwhelming. Here's one way to do it.

If the piece in question is short, copy all the margin notes onto one clean copy. You can even color-code or label the comments to specify which group member said what. This allows you to see the feedback side by side, so you can understand where the group agrees or disagrees on various points. Of course, this approach works best only for very short pieces. With any submission longer than a few pages, the copying and compiling can drive a writer crazy.

For longer pieces, you can also use the revision pyramid approach from chapter seventeen and group your notes according to where the feedback fits on the pyramid. This way, as you revise in layers, you can tackle the comments in order, from most fundamental to most nitty-gritty. With a longer piece, it can still be helpful to compile your notes into one document, but instead of doing so for the entire submission, focus only on a segment that sparked a lot of discussion or debate. This makes the process less cumbersome but still allows you to parse through conflicting comments about a critical moment of your piece.

REVISE. Use the notes and suggestions from the critique session to make adjustments and improvements to your work. Keep in mind that some comments might contradict each other, and some pieces of feedback might not resonate with you at all. That's okay. A writing teacher once said to me, "Revising your piece after a critique session is like driving a van with a dozen backseat drivers." She was right. Sometimes it feels like everyone has a conflicting opinion about how you should write your book, but, in the end, the only opinion that matters is your own.

This is *your* book, after all. You're the one driving the van. Other writers may have suggestions about which route to take or where to turn off the highway, but you're the one behind the wheel, and that means you get to call the shots. Listen to your critique group, evaluate their feedback, and determine if their points are valid and make sense. Then decide which pieces of feedback to implement and which to let go.

— 23 —

Craft Your Author Identity

The world has a romantic notion of the reclusive author. We picture someone hiding in a cabin in the woods, huddled over a typewriter as words pour forth onto the page. We imagine this author handing a stack of parchment to a publisher who, like a literary Rumpelstiltskin, spins the author's words into gold. Heaven forbid the brilliant writer taint himself by dealing with things as base and slimy as sales, marketing, and (gasp!) money. Worse yet, authors who do embrace the business side of the book world are branded as sellouts who have traded true art for profit.

This attitude is misleading—not to mention insulting—to writers. First, it assumes there is a disconnect between the pure, creative act of writing and the sleazy business side of publishing. This notion is not just ridiculous, it's untrue. Both the art and business of writing are creative endeavors. In fact, the business side will likely challenge your creativity and push it in new directions that ultimately expand your writing skills. In the book world, art and business are not on opposite poles; they are closely intertwined and feed into each other.

Second, this attitude assumes that writers are fragile creatures, unable to face the harsh realities of publishing as a business. Sure, we might perform feats of mastery on the page, but don't let us anywhere near a checkbook or marketing copy lest disaster strikes. It's okay for writers to be brilliant and creative with their stories, but when it comes to business matters, we're often expected to nod and smile and let the professionals handle things.

Third, that idea that publishers magically spin our words into gold overlooks one essential piece of the equation: the readers. People talk about bestselling sensations like the Harry Potter series, the Twilight Saga, and even *Fifty Shades of Grey* as though authors only need one spectacular idea to find success. Then—*poof*—magic happens. What people overlook is that these books, for better or worse, connected with readers and motivated them to open their wallets and tell their friends. The whole point of writing and publishing books is for readers to *read them*. Without readers, the entire publishing industry—writers included—would be out of a job.

In the rest of this section, I talk about reclaiming your place as CEO of your writing career. More important, I'll show you what this role means and how you can take it on without getting overwhelmed and freaking out. It's not as scary as it seems; in fact, you're probably already doing a lot of the right things and don't even realize it. The process of reclaiming your writing career has three essential components: honing your author brand, finding your readers, and navigating the publishing process.

My goal is not to make you an expert in the minutiae of marketing and selling your books. You don't need to become a branding expert, a master Web designer, or an SEO genius. You just need an overall sense of the business and its moving parts so you can make smart choices and ask the right questions. Remember, you are the CEO of your writing career, and like any CEO, you need to understand every step of the process so you can delegate and oversee accordingly.

In this chapter, I show you how to cultivate your *author identity*, or your "author brand." Author identity isn't just a pretty logo or a fancy website. To find your author identity, you first need to figure out who you are as a human being and as a writer, and then decide how you want to present yourself to the world. Just as you meticulously craft your characters and stories, so, too, must you invest time and care in crafting your public image, your author brand.

Author Identity

"Who are you?" said the Caterpillar.

This was not an encouraging opening for a conversation. Alice replied, rather shyly, "I—I hardly know, sir, just at present—at least I know who I was when I got up this morning, but I think I must have been changed several times since then."

—Lewis Carroll, *Alice's Adventures in Wonderland*

To begin, ask yourself the Caterpillar's question: *Who are you?* Just as Alice changes in size throughout her adventures in Wonderland, who you are and how you present yourself to the world shifts and changes over time and in different contexts. Your experiences influence your beliefs and behavior, which in turn shape your future experiences. Just as you can never read the same book the same way twice, you can never be quite the same person you were yesterday because the experience of living through that day has affected who you are now.

I'm not trying to be existential, but it is important to understand that continuous change is an inherent part of being human. In order to understand who we truly are, we must first and foremost accept that this identity is constantly in flux. These changes are often subtle and nuanced, though sometimes major life experiences can add a whole new facet to our identity. The important thing to remember, however, is that our sense of self is always changing. We must be aware of these changes, and be proactive in shaping and honing the identity we want to present.

Many writers resist "branding" themselves. Some think it's sleazy, manipulative, and inauthentic. Others consider marketing and branding a waste of time. New writers might wonder why they should worry about branding if they haven't even finished a book yet. More seasoned writers might argue that their time is better spent writing their next book than in branding themselves or marketing their current work. I believe that the time to think about your author identity is early in your career, while you still have the flexibility to make drastic changes if you so desire.

In this age of information and the Internet, you already have a personal brand—you just don't realize it. All you have to do is run a Google search on your name to see that information about you is already floating around on the Web. This information might be scattershot and random, but whether you like it or not, your online identity already exists in some form. So your choice here is simple: You can either take control and shape your author identity, or you can let the big wide world of the Internet decide it for you. In my mind, this decision is a no-brainer.

The other reason to address your author identity early in your career is because crafting and changing it can take time. It takes focused effort to build up the necessary "Google juice" behind your name and your brand. It takes time to develop a network of friends, followers, and fans. The sooner you start to build up your numbers and credentials—both online and off— the bigger the long-term gains. If you start taking the necessary steps now, when your book finally hits the shelves you will already have a network of readers ready and waiting.

Most important, it takes a lot of trial and error for *you* to figure out who you are and how you want to present yourself to your readers. This learning process is not always straightforward, and you're likely to make mistakes now and again. Those early days are when you can take risks and try on different facets of your author identity. If you make a blunder, at least it's only in front of a handful of people who still love you anyway. As your readership grows, the stakes increase and you'll become more careful and risk averse. Use that time in the beginning of your career to try crazy new ideas, because later on you may not have that opportunity.

What Is Author Identity?

People mistakenly equate author identity with terms like *platform*, *brand*, *discoverability*, and *buzz*. I hate these terms because they imply a magic-bullet solution, as if all you have to do is impress the right people and fame and fortune will be yours. Instead, I see author identity as the part of yourself that you choose to share with the world. This identity already exists; it is part of who you are, but not *all* of who you are. It is not about misrepresenting yourself—your author identity is still authentically you—it is just a select part of you that you have crafted and shaped. Just as you choose what to divulge about your characters in your book, you should also choose which aspects of you to make public or keep private. It is *your* author identity, and you get to decide how much to share.

When it comes to the mechanics of your author identity, consider these three elements: name, imagery, and voice. As you develop these aspects of your online and off-line presence, it is important to keep these aspects clear, consistent, and well crafted. You do not need to spend a lot of money on a beautiful logo or fancy website, but you should invest in a few key components that will paint you as a pro.

The Name

Before you publish anything, you must decide what name to publish under. Do not publish under different names unless you consciously want separate author identities. Pseudonyms, though important in some circumstances, are a lot of work to maintain. If you plan to use a pseudonym, you should have a compelling reason for doing so. Also be aware that keeping the identity behind that pseudonym a secret will take substantial effort, so think carefully before you take the leap. For a more detailed discussion of pen names and managing multiple author identities, look at Joanna Penn's excellent book *Business for Writers: How to Be an Author Entrepreneur.*

Keep in mind, also, that whatever name you choose should be consistent across all facets of your online and off-line author presence. Choose the name you want to use, and then claim the URL (i.e., www.yourname.com). If your name is fairly common, someone else may already be using it, in which case you can add something like "author," "writer," or "books" to the end of the URL to differentiate yourself. Also use your chosen name on all your social media handles and bylines. There is a whole science to names and marketing, but I don't want you to get caught up in the minutiae. Instead, I want you to put yourself in your readers' shoes.

Imagine someone reads one of your books and wants to learn more about you (and maybe even buy more books). How is she going to look for you? What words will she type into the Google search box? If *you* type those same words in a search engine, who or what else comes up? Are any of these names problematic? For example, if you are a children's author and someone searches for you, could she accidentally end up on a porn star's website? If there are any problems like this, how can you make your author identity stand out so your readers can find you?

While all these considerations are important, do not get so caught up in deciding on a name that you don't make any progress. Yes, it is a pain to migrate your website or change your social media handles, but it is not impossible. In an ideal world, you start off right and stick with that same name throughout your career, but don't let this relatively small choice derail your progress altogether. I have changed my own author name more than once and in the process discovered that die-hard fans will follow your author brand wherever it goes. Everyone else who gets lost in the shuffle probably isn't really interested anyway.

Don't let this one decision delay you from implementing the rest of your author identity. Choose your author name, and then move on.

The Imagery

Imagery is the visual aspect of your author identity. This includes photos of you as well as any visual elements you share online. As writers, most of our online identity centers around our words, so you can get away with keeping the imagery clean and simple. It is worthwhile, however, to invest some time and care into your author photo. You don't need to go to a fancy studio or hire an expensive photographer, but your photo should have some intent behind it.

Many writers select their author pictures by looking through their photo archives, trying to find a somewhat flattering picture where they don't have red-eye. Don't use a picture from your latest vacation. Don't crop your face out of a group shot taken at a wedding. And please, for the love of all that is literary, don't use a selfie.

As a writer, your author photo is likely to be one of the few images attached to your online presence. You will use it for all your social media handles, for your website, as well as for any speaking gigs or freelance publications. Do not skimp on this step. Whenever possible, use an image that is recognizably you, and tie that same image consistently across all facets of your author identity. Your imagery should be consistent from your website and your social media to the photo that appears on the inside flap of your book.

Make sure you have both color and black-and-white versions of your author photo. While black-and-white photos are all the rage because of their classy, vintage feel, color photos are the more pragmatic choice. Some printed media require color photos and will not accept black-and-white. Also, you can always use photo-editing software to convert a color image to black-and-white, but it doesn't work the other way around. Similarly, make sure you have the best resolution possible for all your digital images. (Three hundred dpi [dots per inch] is standard for printed media. For the Web, resolution requirements are much lower.) If you start with a high-resolution image, you can always decrease it to fit your format, but if the original image is too small it will look pixelated when you enlarge it.

If you are not ready to invest in a professional set of head shots, then at the very least have a friend with a good camera take a picture of you. Do it outside, in front of a background without too much texture or detail. Avoid midday lighting because it casts harsh shadows; strive for early morning or late afternoon light. Finally, if you have a signature visual detail (your hipster glasses or fuchsia hair color), make sure it appears in your photos.

The Voice

I discussed voice at length in chapter thirteen, but in the context of your author identity, voice takes on a slightly different slant. Instead of focusing on how you narrate your stories or on the voices of your characters, you must now think about the voice you use to communicate directly with your readers. Whether it's on your blog, on social media, or in the way you craft the "about the author" page in your book, you must be aware of your voice and tone. Is your style all fancy-pants and hoity-toity? Or is it relaxed, like you're chatting with someone over coffee? This is your voice, and it should be consistent across your author brand.

Voice also ties into the topics you talk about and the parts of your life you choose to share. The things you care about will naturally seep into your author identity. The way you talk about these subjects will set you apart from all the other authors in the world. For instance, you might have noticed my obsession with the Harry Potter series, *The Hunger Games*, and *Pride and Prejudice*; in fact my students have a running joke that no DIY MFA class discussion is truly complete until I reference a book in this trifecta. Plus, I talk like a millennial when I am excited. I've been known to call King Lear a drama queen, and I sum up the plot of *Pride and Prejudice* as "OMG, boys! OMG, road trip!"

This juxtaposition of literary analysis and millennial slang is not some shtick I put on for my readers. It's who I am. I'm a word nerd obsessed with children's books. I'm a teacher who believes you can teach with the same level of literary sophistication whether you have a class of kindergarteners or graduate students. Every piece of my past—earning a black belt in tae kwon do, playing solo violin with a jazz band, growing up as the child of Brazilian immigrants in New York, attending a competitive all-girls school, designing hundreds of toys for a leading toy company—has made me who I am and contributes to DIY MFA in some way. Discover the quirks and qualities that make you unique, and then build them into your author identity.

In the beginning, I tried to hide many of these quirks. I thought if I was too opinionated, too weird, too … *me*, no one would want to read what I had to say. If you look far back in the DIY MFA online archives, you'll see that my writing in those days was a lot more formal and academic. I thought that if I acted serious, other people would take me seriously. It took a long time for me to develop my voice and, more important, to gain the confidence to use it. A crucial aspect of this process has been to research other authors and watch how they craft their own author identities.

YOUR MENTOR FROM AFAR

One of the best ways to hone your author identity is to learn by example. Find an author—a "mentor from afar"—whose writing you admire and who connects with readers in a way that resonates with you. Observe how this author presents herself in person and online. Use this research to inform decisions you make for your own author identity. Here's how.

1. FIND A "MENTOR FROM AFAR"

Remember those competitive books you made a list of in chapter eighteen? That's a great place to start. Look for an author who is currently publishing, and preferably is early in her career. Also, look for an author who is somewhat similar to you in terms of audience and style. Think of this author as the master and yourself as the apprentice who will study and learn from her.

2. DO AN IN-DEPTH ANALYSIS

In the Read with Purpose section, you learned about the benefits of studying an author's body of work. You can do a similar analysis of the author's approach to marketing and her online presence. Study the three main facets of this author's brand: name, imagery, and voice. Visit the author's website and study various pages. Does the author have a blog? If so, read some of the latest posts. Sign up for and read her newsletter. Follow the author on social media.

Analyze her author photo:

- Do you like the photo, and if so, why?
- How is the author dressed?
- Is she looking at the camera or somewhere else?
- Was the photo taken in a studio or outdoors?
- What is the style: classic, formal, casual, edgy?
- What is the composition? Is it centered or to one side? Is it a close-up of the face, from the waist up, or full-length?
- Now analyze her website:
- Is it a static website or a blog?
- What is the home page URL or the name of the site?
- Is it easy to find the author's bio, social media handles, and contact information?
- What does the "About" page say? What details does the author include or omit?
- Is it easy to opt-in to the author's e-mail list?

3. APPLY THE IDEAS YOU LIKE

The goal isn't to copy exactly what this author is doing but to understand it on a deeper level so you can apply those underlying concepts to your author identity. Not everything a particular mentor-author does will make sense for your brand. Look both at what the author does well and what she could do better. Try to get to the heart of not just *what* works or doesn't work, but also *why*. Then decide which elements to incorporate into your own brand.

Over the years, I have learned that every time I dig deep and share one of those raw and real facets of myself, I truly connect with my readers. But a quick word of caution: *Vulnerability* and *authenticity* have become major buzzwords lately. It seems like everyone is on a quest to become more vulnerable and authentic so that they can connect with their audience (and, oh, by the way, sell them stuff). A colleague even said to me lately: "Wow, Gabriela, that whole being vulnerable and authentic strategy really seems to be working for you."

This comment distresses me for two reasons. First, vulnerability and authenticity are not chips you cash in when you want your readers to buy your book or sign up for your newsletter. They are not a marketing strategy. Treating them as such is the literary equivalent of turning to the Dark Side of the Force. Second, vulnerability and authenticity are the *baseline* requirements. Being yourself—for better or worse—is the least of what's expected: for you, for me, or for any other human being. When people use these buzzwords, they put *authenticity* and *vulnerability* on a pedestal, as though doing the bare minimum is already a big deal.

I prefer not to live my life in a state of continual mediocrity, and I imagine you feel the same way or you wouldn't be reading this book. Your author identity is not something you set and then forget. It undergoes a constant evolution, in which you continually finesse different elements through iteration. As *you* grow and develop as a writer, your brand will develop accordingly. Strive for excellence. Refuse to settle for anything less. And whenever you start feeling too comfortable, use the Ten Percent Rule to challenge yourself and rise to new heights.

The Power of Zero

When most people think about platform or audience, they focus on big numbers. They imagine posts going viral, hordes of screaming fans, books flying off the shelves. In the process of chasing these big results, they overlook perhaps the most powerful number of all: zero.

Zero is the great equalizer. It's where everybody starts. At some point in their careers, everyone had to start at zero and build from there. Madonna, Jay Leno, J.K. Rowling … all these people started with zero fans, zero followers. Even Justin Bieber, who at one point had a higher Klout score than the President of the United States, started out with a fandom of zero.

Successful people often try to sweep this "zero moment" out of sight. They tuck it away and try to shift focus from where they started to where they are now. When they *do* talk about their humble beginnings, it's usually in the context of "Look how far I've come" or "Look at all these obstacles I had to beat to get where I am." I want to challenge you to be different and embrace your zero moment. Relish it. Enjoy it.

Take time to celebrate this moment in your career, because it happens only once in a lifetime. Never again will you be able to fly under the radar in quite the same way. Starting small means that you can try out different ideas and make a mess without being embarrassed because—let's face it—not many people will even notice you're there in the first place. Obscurity isn't an obstacle; it's a gift. Use it to goof around, to figure things out, to instigate trouble.

When DIY MFA first started, I knew every person who read my blog. Most of these "bloggy friends" were people I had met in real life, and their websites and social media feeds were part of my regular reading rotation. I knew what they were working on and what their interests were. I followed their projects, and they, in turn, followed mine. I was like a kid, and the blogosphere was my playground. I tried on different voices, different images, different approaches to DIY MFA. It was like I was playing dress up.

But like a child, I was also in a hurry to put on my big-girl shoes and start acting like a grown-up. I wanted DIY MFA to "look professional" and was worried that other people wouldn't take me seriously. I was terrified that if anyone scratched the surface and looked closely at my work, they would think I was a poser, an imposter who didn't deserve admission to the hallowed halls of success. In my efforts to build my platform and hone my brand, I missed a pivotal moment: the first time someone I didn't personally know subscribed to my newsletter. I don't remember who this person was, but I do remember the rush, the excitement that came from knowing that I had finally connected with a reader who I didn't already know in real life. I felt like a minor celebrity.

In retrospect, I wish I had recorded that moment in some way. I could have taken a screen shot and framed it, the way some business owners display the first dollar bill they ever earned. Or better yet, I could have reached out to that person and said "hello," maybe forged a connection. At the time I was so embarrassed about being small that I forgot to record this important milestone.

Now I record everything. I take meticulous screen shots every time I make even the smallest changes to the website. I file these pictures in a folder called "History." I also keep my old personal blog live, even though I haven't updated it since 2011 and don't plan to return to it any time soon. Still, it is a record of the thought process that led up to where I am now as a writer and where DIY MFA began. I have shelves filled with notebooks tracking all my dreams, ideas, and projects. These notebooks date all the way back to when I was ten years old. I might not peruse these old materials, but I save them because they keep me grounded. They are the tether that brings me back to that zero moment and helps me remember who I am at my core.

With all the iteration, all the tweaks and changes over the years, the heart and soul of DIY MFA has not changed very much. While the exterior might look fancy and sparkly compared to where it started, at its core, DIY MFA is still the same, and so am I. The same is true for your author identity. Your values and message will be constant. Iteration won't change these core components; it just helps you better communicate them to your readers. The more you iterate around your author identity, the more *you* you will become.

Don't be in a hurry to get big. If you do the work and clock the mileage, big will come. Your zero moment happens only once, and if you don't pay attention, you will miss it. Take time to enjoy that moment. Then record everything that comes after it, and use that history as a reminder of who you truly are.

— 24 —

Develop Your Home Base

You are a writer. Your number one job is to write the darn book. That said, your book is not going to sell itself, and you should do whatever you can to get it into the hands of the right readers. *Your* readers.

So how do you accomplish this? First, you must create a place where potential readers can learn about you and connect with you further. This is your "home base," and while it can take any form, most authors create a website.

I could write an entire book on the intricacies of blogs and websites; however, this chapter focuses on overarching concepts and strategies. Author Kristen Lamb explains websites in greater depth in her brilliant book *Rise of the Machines: Human Authors in a Digital World*. You can also access an updated list of links and recommendations on the subject by signing up with your e-mail address at DIYMFA.com/thebook.

Don't let the technology scare you. The important thing is to understand *why* you should (or shouldn't) adopt a particular strategy. Figuring out *how* to implement it is usually a matter of doing a Google search, watching a YouTube how-to video, or reading a book. Technology is also fairly easy to outsource or delegate, so for now don't fret about the details. Focus on understanding the strategy behind the tech so that you can explain what you want to a designer, programmer, assistant, or intern.

Build Your Home Base

When deciding where to build your home base, you need to consider two things: how much ownership you have over it, and how easy it is for your readers and fans to access it.

Where Should Your Home Base Be?

There are no rules for where or how to build your home base, but having ownership of that space is important. Your best bet is to claim a URL (www.yourname.com or something similar) and build a self-hosted website. If you have a lot of followers on social media, you might be tempted to use your Facebook page or Twitter feed as your home base. Don't do it. Similarly, some Web-hosting services allow you build a blog or website with a few simple clicks. These systems have "plug and play" templates and store all of your content online for free. While these perks may seem great, they often come at the expense of your ownership and control. If your home base is the hub of your author identity and online presence, the last thing you need is for the Internet powers that be to change the rules and leave you stranded.

Think of it as the difference between renting and owning an apartment. If you rent the space, you don't have to worry about upkeep, and if you get a rat infestation or the tub starts leaking, you can just call the landlord. But you also can't paint the walls whatever color you want or make major renovations to the space, and the landlord could decide to sell the building, in which case you would be looking for a new place in a hurry. If you own the space, it's *yours*. Your turf. Your rules.

Facebook is a perfect example. When it first launched its Pages feature, Facebook encouraged businesses, thought leaders, and authors to create pages and use that network as a way to connect with their audiences. People and businesses built pages with huge followings, only to have Facebook later change the algorithm to a "pay to play" model. This means that now, even if you have thousands of followers, posts from a page will only appear organically for a small handful of fans, and you have to pay for advertising to increase a post's reach.

Some people are enraged at this example and claim that Facebook pulled a bait and switch. I don't see it that way. Instead, this only further confirms how important it is to own and control your home base. The people at Facebook have every right to change the rules, as does any social media platform. This example simply shows how important it is to build your home base someplace where you are in charge, and where someone else can't change the rules on you.

What Does a Home Base Look Like?

For most authors, the most straightforward home base is a self-hosted blog. A blog is any website that posts new material on a regular basis. Once upon a time, blogs (short for "Weblogs") were online journals where people could write updates about watering their plants or what they had for breakfast. Nowadays, blogs include any website with continually updated content. News websites are blogs. DIYMFA.com is a blog. Just about every successful brand has a blog component on its website.

When blogs post a constant stream of new content, they maximize the number of visitors to the site and increase *search engine optimization* (SEO). SEO works like this: Search engines find websites by sending virtual creepy crawlies to sniff out new content on the Web. When websites update their pages regularly with useful content, those creepy crawlies notice, and the search engine bumps that site higher in the results. Of course, search engines like Google and Bing keep their exact algorithms for SEO supersecret, otherwise it would be easy for Web designers to game the system. Still, one thing remains clear: If you update your website often, it will get more Google juice, and readers will be able to find it more easily.

Blogging platforms are also straightforward to figure out and use. You *do not* want to hire a designer to build a website that you can't update yourself, because every time you want to post new material you will have to pester (and pay!) someone else to do it. Even if you're not updating most of the content yourself, you still need to be able to fix problems if they arise. A blogging platform lets you do that and also allows you to grant access to teammates, Web developers, or anyone else who might need to do work behind the scenes.

I don't want to overwhelm you with too many tech details, so for now you should focus on the big picture. Unless you have a compelling reason, establish your home base on a website rather than on a social media platform. When you build that website, use a blogging platform like WordPress, even if you don't think of yourself as a blogger. This platform will let you post new content (which is great for SEO) and make small changes (like fixing typos or updating a photo) without having to call a developer. Once you understand the basics, blogging platforms are fairly easy to use. If you can check your e-mail, you can update a blog.

However you decide to build your home base, the most important thing is that you understand *why* you've chosen to build it a certain way. As the CEO of your writing career, you must understand the strategy behind the technol-

ogy. Every author's home base should include these essentials: a home page, an about or bio page, and a page with your contact information. You can also include a page that lists your published work.

Home Page

The home page is where visitors land when they type in your URL. For instance, DIY MFA's home page is DIYMFA.com. For many websites, the home page and the most recent blog post are one and the same. Other websites might have a fancy home page, sometimes called a "splash page" or "landing page." These pages have a pretty design, a short welcome message, and links to the main sections of the site. Start simple and make your most recent blog post your home page. As you iterate and upgrade your website, you can add a fancy landing page in its place.

DESIGN PSYCHOLOGY: A QUICK OVERVIEW

You can find entire books, websites, and programs of study dedicated to the psychology of effective Web design. As a writer, you don't need to become a marketing expert or a design connoisseur, but knowing a few fundamental principles will help you make smart design choices.

THE RULE OF THREE AND GROUPINGS

Remember the Rule of Three technique from chapter eleven? It turns out that this same rule can help you create engaging visuals. Divide your design into a three-by-three grid to see if it looks balanced. You can find this compositional "rule of thirds" both in photography and design layouts.

If you have a lot of menu options on your website, consider grouping them into categories. This will make it easier for your visitors to find what they are looking for.

LAYOUT AND READABILITY

The decisions you make regarding the overall layout of your site can draw attention to (or away from) elements on your page. Certain design choices—like font or color palette—can make your website easy or difficult to read. Keep these factors in mind as you develop your home base.

- **ABOVE THE FOLD:** The area at the top of your website that is visible without scrolling down is considered "above the fold." Just as newspapers place their most important headlines on the front page, so, too, should you place the most important information on your site "above the fold."

- **RIGHT VERSUS LEFT:** Most languages are read from left to right. This means that our eyes are naturally drawn to items on the right side of a layout. (This is why the splashiest magazine ads are always on the right-hand side of a spread.) If you have important information you want your visitors to see, put it on the right side of the page.
- **TEXT COLOR CHOICES:** Do not use white text on a black background. Not only is this design choice *so* 1999, but it is also difficult to read. For the main text of your website, choose a white or a light-colored background with black text. Your visitors' eyes will thank you.
- **FONT CHOICES:** Serif fonts have little "feet" on them, like Times New Roman. Those serifs make text easier to read because they pull your eye along from one word to the next. Once upon a time, computer screens did not have adequate resolution to render serif fonts well on websites. For this reason, many designers recommended sans serif fonts, like Arial or Helvetica, because they looked cleaner. Times have changed. Screen resolution is phenomenal, and serif fonts are now fair game. Whatever you choose for the main text of your website, make sure it is clean and easy to read.

About Page

The about page tells your readers who you are. It should include your bio and a photo of your lovely face. Keep in mind that your about page will likely be one of the most well-trafficked pages on your website, so craft it with care. While this page should tell your visitors something about you, it has another more important purpose. This page tells your Web visitors—your readers—that they are in the right place. Most authors make their about pages all about themselves, when it should actually focus on their readers.

As you craft your about page, consider why your readers would want to learn more about you. Think about what they are looking for when they come to your website. What benefit can you offer them, and how do you want them to feel when they read that page? What is the role you serve for your readers? Do you want them to see you as a mentor, an entertainer, a leader, a friend? This page not only tells your readers who you are, but why you are the person they are looking for.

Before you start to panic, remember that this is an iterative process. Start small and keep your about page simple, with an engaging bio and a quality photo, and then update that page over time.

Contact Page

You need a page where people can contact you. This page should contain your e-mail address and can include your phone number or snail mail address as well. If you do decide to put your phone number online, get a Google Voice number, which will redirect calls to a home, office, or cell phone while keeping your actual number private. For postal mail, get a P.O. Box. You will need to disclose your address publicly when you create an e-mail list (because of anti-spam laws), so unless you want to disclose your home address to thousands of people, a P.O. Box is crucial.

It's perfectly fine not to include a mailing address or phone number on your contact page, but make sure you list your e-mail address. And please don't use a stupid contact form! Yes, it might protect you from a few annoying spam messages, but it also prevents key people from reaching you. As someone who interviews authors, nothing is more infuriating than looking for contact information and finding only a contact form. If you don't want to put your e-mail address on your website, create a press e-mail address (like press@yourwebsitename.com), and have it redirect messages to your real e-mail. When you become superfamous, you can hire an assistant or publicist to field your media requests. Until then, don't make it impossible for opportunities to find you.

Your Books

This is probably the easiest page on your website to compile. If you haven't published any books yet, omit this page. If you have published books, keep it simple. For each book, include the cover and the flap copy (the short marketing description on the inside flap or back cover of a book). If your book has received praise or acclaim, include a few quotes, but don't overload the page with too much text or your visitors may click away. Most important, include a link to a bookseller or website where readers can purchase your book.

What Should You Blog About?

While your website doesn't have to include a blog, blogging can give you a huge advantage as a writer. Not only does it help you connect with your readers and build rapport *before* you publish your book, it also allows you to test different concepts and see what resonates with your audience. The strategy for blogging is somewhat different depending on whether you write narrative work (fiction and memoir) or prescriptive nonfiction (how-to books). There are entire books dedicated to blogging strategies for writers, but here is a primer to get you started.

Narrative Books: Fiction and Memoir

Many writers think that if they blog, it must be about writing. The trouble with this approach is that you end up in "the marketing echo chamber of death," where you talk only to writer colleagues and not to your *readers*. Instead, blog about themes that will interest people who would want to read your book.

In the next chapter, you will learn techniques for finding and connecting with readers. For the time being, focus on identifying themes from your book that you can expand on in a blog. Think also about your myriad of interests, all the quirks and obsessions that make you unique. Even if these topics don't make it into your books, they probably inform your writing in some way and can serve as fodder for potential blog content.

Prescriptive (How-To) Nonfiction

With prescriptive nonfiction, your interests and quirks can still filter into your blog content, but now you also need to establish your expertise on whatever topic you are teaching. Many prescriptive nonfiction authors object by saying, "If I give away all my material on my blog, then no one will buy my book." This is a fallacy. Unless you have very little to say on your subject, it is impossible to give away all your content on your blog. If you love this topic and know a lot about it, you have much more to say than could fit in a book or on a blog. Don't worry about accidentally giving away the farm, as that would take a focused and determined effort on your part.

The other thing to consider—and this might seem obvious—is that your blog is not a book. You cannot copy and paste blog posts into manuscript pages and expect the book to be finished. People read blogs differently from how they read books. Not only do these formats *look* different, but the way a reader experiences the material is different. You can use your blog to test different concepts and build your audience, but even if you put every nugget of information from your brain onto your blog, it will not be the same as a book. This is good news for author-bloggers because it means that readers will still want to buy your books, even if you have already blogged a lot on the subject.

BLOG VERSUS BOOK: WHAT'S THE DIFFERENCE?

The reader experience on a blog is very different from that with a book. Here are a few key distinctions:

FOR A BLOG:

- The ideal length of a blog post is 500 to 700 words; posts over 1,000 words are considered quite long.
- Hyperlinks allow posts to reference other online content without having to explain it in the actual post.
- Hyperlinks also allow readers to hop between pieces of related content, creating a nonlinear reading experience.
- Readers rarely read posts in order from the beginning. This means content needs to bring readers up to speed *in medias res* ("in the middle of things").
- Blogging is a multimedia tool. You can include images, video, audio clips, and even real-time interaction in addition to text.
- The comments section of a blog allows for dialogue between writer and reader. Communication on a blog is a two-way street.

FOR A BOOK:

- Nonfiction books range from 40,000 to 90,000 words. Chapters are usually several thousand words apiece.
- While they might have a glossary or index, printed books cannot include hyperlinks. This means whatever references you make must either be self-explanatory or explained in the text.
- Readers might skip around in a nonfiction book, but the material still has a clear order that readers will likely follow.
- Including video, audio, and other interactive elements is impossible with printed books; these elements usually appear on a companion website. Even with digital books, it's difficult to include multimedia, and doing so must be considered strategically.
- Finally, unless a reader goes out of her way to contact the author, there is very little communication between reader and writer.

Your E-mail List

One of the most crucial elements of your home base is your e-mail list. This list is one of your most valuable assets because it allows you to contact your readers directly and on a deeper level than with a website. Yet, starting an e-mail list can be terrifying. For a long time I avoided building a list, and when I finally started, I did it kicking and screaming. I also made every stupid mistake imaginable. Don't make these mistakes.

- **I DIDN'T USE A CRM.** CRM stands for "customer relationship management," which is a fancy name for services that allow you to collect e-mail addresses and send out messages. Not only does a CRM keep track of all your subscribers and allow you to send e-mails with ease, it's also the only legit way to do it. Mass e-mails are considered spam (even when you place all recipients on the BCC list), but using a CRM will keep you on the straight and narrow. CRMs also give you plenty of data about your subscribers. You can see how many people open your e-mails and click your links. You can even send follow-up e-mails to a subset that clicked one particular link.

- **I USED A "GET BLOG UPDATES VIA E-MAIL" WIDGET.** Most blogging platforms offer a widget that you can pop into your sidebar that says, "Get blog updates via e-mail." Readers sign up with their e-mail addresses, and every time you write a new post, the system automatically sends it out to everyone who registered. The problem with this widget is that the blogging platform controls the e-mail list, not you. Other than getting an overall subscriber number, you have no way of knowing who your subscribers are, which e-mails they opened, and which links they clicked. You also can't send them anything except what you post on your blog.

- **I WAITED TO GET STARTED.** The day to start building your e-mail list is yesterday, but since you can't go back in time, start today. You do not need to send a newsletter to start collecting e-mail addresses, and if you already have a blog, a newsletter can be surprisingly easy to put together. Just craft a short introduction and link to your most recent blog content; you can also link to interesting articles you've found around the Web. The key is to be a familiar presence in your readers' in-boxes, a presence they like and even look forward to. Build this rapport before you have a book to promote, and when that book launches, your readers will be excited for it.

As with anything you learn through DIY MFA, you should iterate and experiment with your home base until you find a system that works and that you enjoy. If you loathe some aspect of your home base, eliminate it. Build your home base so you can reach your readers, but make sure it's built in a way that is sustainable. Iterating and developing your platform takes time and a lot of work. Make sure you enjoy the activities you do for your home base—be it social media, blogging, or anything else—because you will be doing these things frequently as your career develops.

— 25 —

Know Your Reader

This chapter focuses on the most important—and most often overlooked—part of the publishing equation: your readers. Your goal is to learn how to identify who your readers are and to connect with them in a meaningful way. This is not about obsessing over sales statistics, compulsively checking Amazon reviews, or agonizing over new marketing pitches. Rather, the point is to understand who your readers are and why they want to read your book, and to make a connection from one human being to another.

You might think the best strategy is to cast a wide net and include every single person who may want to read your book. In fact, the opposite is true. While many different types of people might enjoy your book, the key to making a meaningful connection is to focus on a specific, targeted niche. These are your primary readers, your target market, your superfans. Other readers are great, but focus first on your primary readers.

Your Ideal Reader

Most writers envision an ideal reader as they write their books. This might be a specific person they know or someone they imagine. However, keep in mind that this is an *ideal* reader, not an actual reader. And while visualizing your ideal reader can be inspiring, it will not help you sell or promote your book. After all, you can't get usable data and information from a reader who only exists in your head.

The purpose of the ideal reader is purely inspirational. Imagining someone who will love and treasure your book motivates you to get words on the page and get your work out the door. Just as in your story you might use a day-to-day bad guy to give an amorphous antagonist a face, your ideal reader brings your audience into focus. Building your author identity, crafting your online presence, and even writing your book is a lot easier when you can imagine a specific person who will experience it. Writing into the void is hard. Your ideal reader makes the process easier.

Reader Archetypes

Envisioning your ideal reader is an exercise for *yourself* as the writer, to inspire you and drive your focus. Now it's time to shift the focus to your actual readers and understand who they are. Don't make assumptions here. Back up your theory with hard data. If you already have a few followers and fans, turn to those people first for insights. If not, you will need to use comp titles (those "competitive" books from the reading list you created in chapter eighteen) as a starting point and follow the bread crumbs from there. To develop an actionable strategy, you must identify and study real people. This is where reader archetypes come into play.

Some time ago, my sister, Juli, ran a brainstorming session with the DIY MFA team. As an e-commerce and branding expert, Juli has helped many large brands hone their online marketing efforts. Writers can use many of her techniques to identify and understand their readers. By surveying your readers or studying comp titles and their authors, you can develop archetypes with common needs and interests. Here's how to do it.

Gather Information

Brace yourself for the big question: With all the books available in the world, why would a reader want to read *your* book? Why wouldn't she pick up a magazine, browse the Internet, or watch a movie or TV show?

Many writers cop out and say, "My readers just want to get lost in a good story." Seriously? Come on. All readers want to get lost in a good story. Don't get lazy—get answers. The easiest way to find out why your readers read your books is to *ask them*. Reach out to actual humans who have read something you wrote. If you don't have many readers yet, don't worry. You can use comp titles to accomplish the same thing.

There are many ways to get information from your readers. You can get fancy and set up an online survey, or you can do something simple and spontaneous, like posting a question on social media. Try different approaches for gathering information, and iterate until you find what works.

In a past life, I was a child development researcher. I am still a statistics geek to the core, and nothing gets me excited like a good p-value. When I first started gathering information about my readers, I obsessed over my surveys and tried desperately to make my research as "controlled" as possible. It turns out that writing research is not nearly as meticulous as a study performed in a lab. It's okay for the results to be messy and inconsistent as long as you can see an overall pattern.

SURVEY TIPS

There are many ways to create an online survey and request feedback from your readers. However you choose to do it, here are a few things to keep in mind.

- **USE OPEN-ENDED QUESTIONS.** Essay-style questions are often more useful than multiple choice. While you might not get pristine answers, you will get a better sense for the big picture and can observe all the nuances and variability among your readers.
- **MAKE IT EASY FOR YOUR READERS TO REPLY.** The survey should be easy to access and should not take forever to complete. Remember, your results don't exist until the respondents submit their answers. Choose your questions carefully, and limit the number so your readers actually finish.
- **BEWARE ANONYMOUS SURVEYS.** Anonymity allows people to be more honest, and with some controversial topics your readers might be more likely to answer if they know their responses won't be matched with their names. The big downside of anonymous surveys, though, is that it's impossible to follow up with the respondents if their answers are unclear or if you have further questions. This is why I like to include "May I contact you to discuss further?" at the end of each survey. Make this question optional, and request an e-mail address if the reader agrees to be contacted. This gives people a chance to remain anonymous if they wish but also allows you to follow up on a reply if necessary.

The obvious way to learn about your readers is to *talk to them*. Many people forget how much you can discover if you ask a question and then listen—really listen—to the answer. Pose a question to the social media hive mind. Bring up a topic in a blog post, and then encourage discussion in the comments. Ask someone about what they are reading. The key is to craft a good question and then stop talking and pay attention to the answer.

A simple yet effective way to implement this technique is in the welcome e-mail for your newsletter list. As you learned in the previous chapter, your e-mail list is a crucial component of your home base, and when you set it up you will have the option to send a welcome e-mail to anyone who subscribes. This welcome e-mail is a huge opportunity to connect with your readers and start your relationship on the right foot. Use it to share links to any freebies you have to offer, plus start a conversation so you can get to know your readers better.

When people subscribe to the DIY MFA e-mail list, one of the questions I ask in my welcome e-mail is: "What's the most important thing you need to work on as a writer?" About one in ten of my subscribers replies, and these responses range from a few words to several paragraphs, but each answer gives me tremendous insight about my audience, my word nerds. Over time, some of the same comments come up again and again, which helps me determine topics that DIY MFA should address in future blog posts or podcast episodes. As an added bonus, that question in the welcome e-mail has also opened the door for fascinating conversations and even new friendships.

Nonfiction writers might find this technique straightforward: Just ask a question that fits your topic. Your goal is to figure out what your readers *want*, so craft a question that gets to the heart of that deep desire. But what if you write fiction? What question do you ask? Remember that the purpose of your welcome e-mail is to get to know your readers and forge a connection. Ask a question that does those things and, if possible, ties to one of the themes you tackle in your writing. You can ask them about their interests and what they like to do when they're not reading. Or you can ask them to share their favorite book and why they love it. The key is to ask a question that will let you get to know your readers and find out *why* they are drawn to your particular book or topic.

Another way to understand your readers is to look at analytics. You can install Google Analytics on your website to track various data, such as which pages or blog posts get the most traffic, or the route visitors used to get to your site. Depending on the e-mail service you use for your newsletter, you can also track how many people open your e-mails and which links they click. Use this information to get a clearer picture of who your readers are and, more important, which content resonates with them.

GROUND RULES FOR ANALYTICS

Analytics can be overwhelming, even for a stats geek like me. Here are some ground rules to help you make sense of the data and stay sane.

- **CHECK REGULARLY, BUT NOT TOO OFTEN.** Refreshing your analytics page over and over will not make the numbers magically increase. (I know, I've tried.) Check in regularly enough that you'll catch anything out of the ordinary, but not so often that you drive yourself crazy. Once per week is plenty.

- **IF SOMETHING LOOKS WEIRD, DON'T PANIC. INVESTIGATE.** If you notice something out of the ordinary, dig further and try to figure out the cause. A few years ago, a rush of e-mail subscribers joined my list in a matter of hours. It was so unprecedented that for a moment, I actually thought someone had hacked my e-mail service and was subscribing random people to my list willy-nilly. After that initial panic, I looked at the analytics and saw a huge spike of traffic for that day. I dug through the referral links and realized that a blogger with a much bigger readership had just shared a link to my site. I reached out and said "thank you," and I ended up meeting a wonderful colleague.
- **WATCH THE "SPIKES."** Web traffic isn't linear. Your page views and unique visitors won't increase in gradual, systematic increments. Analytics graphs usually look like a series of jagged peaks and valleys, especially if you examine them up close. When you zoom out, though, and study the data over several months or a year, you'll start to notice a pattern. You'll usually see periodic "spikes" where a lot of traffic came to your website all at once. Of course, you want to figure out what caused the spikes in the first place so you can replicate some of these results—that is a given. But also pay attention to what happens *after* those spikes. You'll likely notice that before the spike your traffic hovered around a particular baseline, but afterwards your traffic reset and bumped up to a "new normal." This means that the influx of traffic from that "spike" converted into some returning visitors, which is great.

Follow the Bread Crumbs

If you have just started your website and joined social media, you probably don't have a lot of followers or an e-mail list. In chapter twenty-three, I talked about the importance of your zero moment. While this stage in your career is important, it does contain a major hurdle: It's hard to gather information about your readers if you don't have any yet. This is where comp titles come into play. Since you can't study your own readers, you need to borrow a few from a similar author who is a little bit ahead of where you are on the journey. You won't have access to this author's e-mail list or website analytics, so you will need to rely on different sources for information.

Revisit your list of competitive books, this time with an eye toward authors who are your contemporaries. Don't focus on big-name authors or blockbuster titles in your niche. While it's great to look at these books as examples of what made a huge splash in the market, it is hard to glean insights from these authors that you can put into action. When you use the bread crumb technique, look for an author in your niche who published her debut in the last year or two.

Start by looking at online reviews for that debut. What do readers like about it? What do they hate? What are the actual words these readers use? Ignore the very negative reviews, at least for now. People who write angry complaints about a book usually have an ax to grind, and their comments won't tell you much about what that author's readers actually want. Instead, focus on three- and four-star reviews, because those readers clearly felt strongly enough about the book to review it, but the book did not fill their need completely. Something was missing. Figure out what it was.

Once you have collected as much information as possible from this source, look for another bread crumb. Online review sites like Amazon, Goodreads, and LibraryThing allow you to click on a reviewer's profile and see other reviews she has posted. This is research *gold* because it can lead you to other books in the same niche as your comp title. Choose one or two reviews that resonate with you, and look at the reviewer profiles. Which other books have these readers reviewed? Who are the authors, and are they in your niche? What did these reviewers have to say about these other books? Now click on one of these new books, and start the process again. Repeat until you have a sense for who these readers are and why they like to read books similar to yours.

Define Your Archetypes

You have gathered information either from your own readers or by borrowing readers from another author. Now it's time to define and understand your reader archetypes. This is the focus of the exercise my sister did with the DIY MFA team. All this jumbled information about individual readers can paint a detailed picture, but it's useless for helping you make strategic decisions. You can't let individual pieces of feedback influence every choice you make or you'll never get anything done. Instead, you have to organize your data into a structure and use it to develop a strategy.

As you collect and compile information about your readers, you will start to notice patterns. While no two readers are exactly the same, you will see overarching categories with readers who have certain traits in common. Take, for example, the readers of the Harry Potter series. While the intended readership for this series are kids, the books also appeal to the caregivers and educators of those young readers, as well as to fantasy lovers.

Notice, too, that different groups of readers want different things from the series. The young readers want compelling characters who, despite being kids, still perform heroic feats and solve their own problems. These readers want to get lost in a world that feels real to them, and they want a story that is fast-paced and fun. Fantasy superfans read this series because of the detailed world-building. They like finding "Easter eggs" from one thread hidden in another part of the story, and they love that the story seems to extend beyond the page, like the world is bigger than the book itself. Educators and caregivers, on the other hand, might turn to this series as a way to encourage reluctant young readers to develop a love of books.

The Harry Potter books fulfill these different readers' wants in different ways. The series connects with young readers by featuring a broad cast of characters, so that if a kid doesn't relate to Harry, he can still relate to one of the other characters. The multilayered wizarding world is so rich with detail that it comes alive on the page, and exciting scenes like the Quidditch matches and epic battles keep these readers turning pages. For fantasy lovers, spin-off books like the *The Tales of Beedle the Bard* bring the lore of the series to life, and active fan fiction communities allow these readers to immerse themselves in the Potterverse. Educators and caregivers might find educational resources—suggested reading lists, in-class activities, or interviews with the author—especially helpful.

Using the above example, determine two or three different reader archetypes for your book. Sort the data you collected previously according to these groups. Consider these questions: Who are the main readers for your book, and what do they want? Are there other readers who might like your book as well? If so, what are their needs and desires? How can you fulfill those wants and needs?

Of course, it does you no good to understand your readers and their desires if you don't provide a solution. You must offer your readers something that meets their needs, and you must give a clear call to action.

The Call to Action

This is where most writers fail. They do their due diligence and learn about their readers, but when it's time to give a call to action, they falter. These writers are so afraid to spam their audience that they go to the other extreme and get wishy-washy. The difference between spam and a call to action is quite simple. Spam is when you force information and sales pitches onto someone who doesn't want them. Spam is plastering your social media feeds with "Buy my book! Buy my book!" Spam annoys readers and makes them run away. A call to action is different. It provides a *solution*, a way to give your reader something that she wants, and it gives clear instructions on how she can get it. "Sign up for my newsletter to get deleted scenes from my book" is not spam. It's smart marketing.

Most readers would love to support what you're doing, but it's not their job to figure out what you need. It's your job to ask *them*. Your readers are not mind readers, after all. Whether you want them to follow you on social media or attend your book signing, you need to ask them, and you must be clear.

Of course, some people are hypersensitive. They will join your e-mail list for the free download and then immediately unsubscribe. They will report a newsletter as spam even if the call to action is "Click here for your free e-book." They will send you a snippy e-mail when all you did was ask them to "like" your video. This is normal. Remember that in any relationship you can only control your side of it, so be professional and kind, but let it go.

Above all else, do not fear the call to action. Asking your readers for what you need helps you get the resources to continue your creative work and give your readers what *they* need in return. The call to action helps you keep the writer-reader ecosystem in balance.

26

Network Like a Pro

Writers are remarkable people. They know how to weave words and sentences together to craft engaging stories and convincing arguments. This makes them great communicators and conversationalists. Writers are also observant. They create compelling characters by noting and internalizing what makes people tick and by picking up on interpersonal cues. In addition, writers are often voracious readers, and most have an enormous stash of eclectic information in their brains. You can always learn something interesting when you talk to a writer. All these factors add up to make writers a fascinating, talented, and intelligent group of people. This is why it baffles me when writers say they are not good at networking.

Here's a secret no one tells you, and it took me years to figure it out. Networking is like a game with only one rule: Everyone wants something. Figure out what that is and you can navigate any situation.

When you attend a networking or professional event, the same question is on everybody's mind: "What's in it for me?" I call this the WIIFM factor. No matter how altruistic, kind, or generous people might be, we all want something. Even you. The key to networking is to align what you bring to the table with what the other person wants. Writers are exceptionally good at handling the WIIFM factor; after all, we spend entire manuscripts figuring out what our characters want and how they will get it. The same idea works in networking, only instead of a character you're dealing with a real person.

Writing Conferences and Events

One of the best places to network and build your list of contacts is at writing conferences. Not only will you meet fellow writers at these events, but you may also have a chance to connect with agents, editors, and other publishing professionals. Big-name authors sometimes speak at these conferences, so it also can be a great place to meet your literary heroes.

Choosing the right conference or literary event can be overwhelming, especially with so many exciting opportunities available. Conferences are also a big investment of both time and money, so it's important to choose wisely. Each year dozens—maybe hundreds—of writing conferences take place across the country and around the world. Though each conference is unique and has its own culture, they all share common traits that can help you determine whether an event will suit your needs.

ATTENDING CONFERENCES ON A BUDGET

Before we discuss different types of conferences, here are some tips on how to stretch your dollar and make the most of inexpensive or free resources, both online and in person.

GO LOCAL

If you live in or near a major city, check out conferences in your area. Not only will you save on travel costs but you'll also meet other local writers who had the same idea. This is a great way to build your writing network and even meet a critique partner or two.

Some of the major conferences move from city to city and announce the upcoming dates and locations well in advance. If you can't attend a big conference this year, you can save your money for a future date when it's held at a location near you.

For smaller literary events, like readings or evening workshops, check out nearby universities, local bookstores, or your neighborhood library. Many MFA programs host speaker series that are open to the public, where you can hear poets and writers read their work and talk about their process. The fee for these types of events is often quite small, less than the price of a movie ticket.

GO ONLINE

Many writing organizations offer free or affordably priced online webinars, and some even host virtual conferences. Since these events are online, you won't even have to leave your couch to reap the benefits.

Types of Conferences and Events

Conferences and literary events come in several flavors: publishing conferences, inspirational conferences, craft workshops, writing retreats, and trade shows. Each type offers different benefits, and it's important to choose one that aligns with your current goals. Some events will serve you better at different stages of your writing career, and you might "grow out" of a particular conference as your writing develops. Keep in mind, also, that some conferences may have multiple tracks that focus on different aspects of a writer's career. These events offer publishing, inspirational, and craft instruction all in one place.

Publishing Conferences

These conferences focus on giving you the information and opportunities you need to get published. Speakers tend to be industry professionals like agents and editors. Sessions focus on publishing-related topics like how to craft your pitch, what should (and shouldn't) go in your query letter, marketing strategies for writers, and other information about the publishing process.

These conferences are incredibly useful if you are new to publishing and need to learn the basics. For instance, it was at a publishing conference that I learned what a query letter was and how to pitch freelance articles to a magazine. Publishing conferences are also a great networking opportunity, and some even offer a chance to meet agents, pitch your book, or get comments on your query letter or opening pages. This type of feedback can help you put your best foot forward when you are ready to submit your work. Publishing conferences can be overwhelming to newbie writers, however, so if you are just starting out, you may do better at events that emphasize craft and motivation.

Some publishing conferences also offer pitch sessions, which is like speed dating for agents and authors. Each conference has its own rules surrounding these sessions, but the basic idea is the same: The agents sit at tables around the periphery of a room, and writers line up at the tables to speak with them. Each writer has a few minutes to tell the agent about his book and then listen to the agent's feedback.

Whether you should do a pitch session depends on who you ask. I've heard stories about writers who first connected with their agents at a pitch slam and of agents who discovered hidden gems. I've also heard nightmarish tales of authors who don't get a single nibble and of agents who have had manuscripts foisted upon them at cocktail parties or in bathroom stalls. I myself think pitch sessions can be extremely useful, but not for selling an agent on the idea of your book. Instead, I think they can be a great way to get feedback on your topic and—more important—how you present it. Pitch sessions are an opportunity for rapid iteration. They let you hone and finesse how you describe and summarize your book. No agent will sign an author based on a pitch alone—they want to read sample pages too. Instead, think of these pitch sessions as a chance to have a conversation and make that crucial first impression so that you can follow up later.

Inspirational Conferences

Inspirational conferences are all about inspiring the writer within. Some events offer the opportunity to hear industry leaders talk about the business, as well as panels about publishing or sessions on craft, but the main goal is to motivate writers to keep writing. The centerpiece of these events are keynote speeches or tête-à-tête interviews with best-selling authors.

These conferences are usually genre focused, so they are a great place to meet fellow "birds of a feather" who love to read and write the same types of books as you. These inspiring events make you want to stand up and cheer at the end of each talk, and you leave excited to run home, boot up the computer, and start typing.

While these conferences can motivate writers at all stages, they are most useful when you are early in your career because they give you the initial push you need to write your book. It can also be encouraging to hear keynote speakers talk about the rough beginnings of their own careers, or moments when they have faltered and lost focus. It's nice to know that even big-name writers have hang-ups and feel vulnerable at times. But keep the rah-rah cheerleading in perspective; all that encouragement will do you no good if you don't hunker down and get to work when you get home.

Craft Workshops

These workshops range from one-day events to weeklong intensive programs, and while they might include some discussion about publishing, the core focus is on the craft of writing. Often these programs include workshop sessions in which you read submissions from fellow attendees and receive critiques on your work. Craft workshops are great for meeting new critique partners because you can get a sense of their writing and personalities before you commit to a long-term partnership. Also, because these workshops are often taught by best-selling authors, it's a chance to get feedback on your writing from one of the greats in your genre.

Workshop organizers often go to great lengths to match writers not just with the right teacher but also with other writers in their group so they can have productive critique sessions. This means most of these programs require that you fill out an application and send samples of your work and sometimes even letters of recommendation. While this process may seem cumbersome, it's well worth it. In fact, I would be wary of workshops that have no screening process, because this means that writers are assigned to groups at random.

When these types of craft workshops are done well, they are a phenomenal experience. The problem is that they can be hit or miss. Most of the responsibility for leading a good discussion and creating a productive critique environment falls on the teacher. Some teachers excel at these skills, but not all. Also, even with superb teachers and a meticulously assembled group, you won't know the dynamic of the workshop until that first meeting. Sometimes all it takes is one "bad egg" attendee to create a strained dynamic.

Writing Retreats

If you want to hammer out a bunch of words in a short span of time, consider going on a retreat. While they aren't conferences per se, retreats are a great way to get out of a rut and shake up your writing. Some retreats schedule lectures and seminars interspersed with dedicated writing time. Others focus solely on the writing, and the only group events are mealtimes and the occasional reading session in the evenings.

The purpose of these events is to write, so there is often ample time for participants to hide away and write in their cabins or rooms. The major challenge, of course, is that retreats are often held in gorgeous campuses or resort locations. This means that if you want to make real progress you need to fight the temptation to spend all your time exploring the beautiful surroundings. Also, because the goal is to write, write, write, it makes little sense to attend a retreat unless you are already working on a project.

Trade Shows

Trade shows are huge publishing events like BookExpo America (BEA), the London Book Fair, the Frankfurt Book Fair, and others. These are not writing conferences, though sometimes conferences do run concurrently with the show. Trade shows are usually industry-only events, though you can sometimes get a badge (i.e., a ticket inside) even if you are not yet published. The primary purpose of these shows is for publishers to promote their upcoming books to booksellers, librarians, and the media. This means that most of the people in the publishing booths are from the publicity and marketing departments. They are not editors, and this is not an event where you pitch your book to publishers. In fact the people you would want to pitch are probably not even there.

As an author, you should walk the show and take it all in. Make note of current trends in your niche, and look for books with themes that you write about. This is an opportunity to look for truly current comp titles. Many of the books being promoted at trade shows have not been released yet, and you might be able to snag an advance reading copy (ARC). If you talk about books or write reviews on your blog, trade shows can also be a great place to find new books in your niche.

Whenever I attend a trade show, I love to collect interesting swag. Bookmarks and postcards are often the "traditional" choice, so look for other creative or clever promotional goodies. Make a swag file when you get home, so when the time comes for your own book launch, you will have plenty of inspiration and ideas.

Remember that trade shows are industry events, so be professional. With all the ARCs and swag, it can be easy to get caught up in the excitement. Ultimately the publishers are there to promote and sell books. This means that writers who attend trade shows are pretty low on the networking totem pole. Be respectful of people's time, and if you want to connect with someone further, ask for a business card and follow up after the show. These expos can be overwhelming for new authors, so I recommend getting several conferences and smaller book events under your belt before you dip your toe in the trade show waters.

Before, During, and After the Event

To get the most out of conferences, you need a strategy. At this point in my career, I have probably gone to more than a hundred conferences, workshops, and author events. These days I speak at most of the ones I attend. Still, I remember my first conference and how nervous, awkward, and downright clueless I was. I made all the stupid mistakes, and now I can share the lessons I learned with you.

When most writers think about going to conferences, they focus on the event itself and being *at* the conference. Yes, showing up is important, but if you only focus on attending, you will miss many opportunities. Take time to prepare for the conference in advance, and then build time into your schedule afterward to review and follow up.

CONFERENCE COUNTDOWN CHECKLIST

ONE MONTH BEFORE

- **GET SOME BUSINESS CARDS.** If you don't already have business cards, have some printed. They don't need to be fancy, but make sure they are professional. A simple design with your name, e-mail address, and website is sufficient.

TWO WEEKS BEFORE

- **HASHTAG THE CONFERENCE.** If the conference has a hashtag on Twitter, create a column on Hootsuite (or other social media tool) to follow it. This will let you keep track of the buzz surrounding and leading up to the event. You can also connect with other attendees and make friends before you even arrive.
- **GET TO KNOW THE SPEAKERS.** Look up Twitter handles of speakers you'd like to meet. Create a speakers list in a separate Hootsuite column. This lets you see everything the speakers tweet in the weeks leading up to the conference. It's a great way to get to know the speakers' personalities, what interests them, and what kind of info they like to share. Plus, mentioning something they tweeted can be a good icebreaker when you meet in person.

ONE WEEK BEFORE

- **PREP YOUR PITCH.** If you are pitching your book at the conference, take time to prepare. Do not do this at the last minute; give yourself a chance to "sleep on it" and get some perspective before the big day.
- **RESEARCH THE AGENTS.** The biggest mistake you can make at a pitch session is to pitch your book to an agent who doesn't represent that genre or category. Take time to research the agents. Know what they're looking for, what's on their wish list, and what books and authors they already represent.
- **CHOOSE YOUR SESSIONS.** Print out the conference schedule, and mark the sessions that interest you. Note which sessions are must-see

versus those that are a toss-up. You don't have to wed yourself to this schedule, but at least you'll have a game plan when you arrive.

AT THE CONFERENCE

- **GO OUTSIDE YOUR COMFORT ZONE.** Set a small (but scary) goal for yourself. Maybe you will approach and talk to a speaker after a presentation. Maybe you'll grab drinks or a meal with a writer you just met. Or maybe you'll trade business cards with someone you didn't already know before the conference. Challenge yourself to do one small thing outside your comfort zone.
- **TALK TO PEOPLE.** Use the four-step formula found later in this chapter to strike up conversations and make meaningful connections with people you meet. You do not need to be a superschmoozer to do this.
- **CHANGE YOUR PLANS.** Remember that schedule you made before arriving at the conference? You can change that schedule at any moment and for any reason. Use it as a guideline, not a ball and chain.
- **PLAY HOOKY.** You want to get the most out of a conference, so it's understandable that you would try to pack the most value into every moment. But if you burn yourself out on the first day, you won't get much from the rest of the conference. Play hooky. Skip a session and take a nap if you need to recharge. Take a break to have lunch, even if it means missing out on something. A conference is a marathon, not a sprint. Pace yourself.
- **HANG OUT AT THE BOOKSTORE.** Most conferences have a bookstore or an exhibit area where sponsors and conference administrators hang out. Some of the most valuable connections I've made have come from hanging around in the halls, browsing the bookstore, or chatting with exhibitors. The hotel bar or coffee shop is another great place. If your brain is on information overload, take a break for an hour and wander around. You never know who you might meet or what opportunities might find you.

ONE OR TWO WEEKS AFTER

- **DEBRIEF.** A week or so after the conference, take time to go over your notes and debrief yourself on the experience. Review everything you learned, and try to boil all this information down to *three actionable steps* that you can implement in the next three months. Store everything else in your Idea Bank (see chapter six). You can come back to and implement those ideas later on.
- **FOLLOW UP.** This step is where most writers miss the boat. They take the time and put in the effort to prepare and network, and then they

never follow up. If you can be one of the few writers who actually *does* this, you will be miles ahead of the pack. Send follow-up e-mails to continue a conversation or even just to say, "Thank you." You can also stay connected by following or friending someone on social media. Be friendly and professional, but not stalkerish.

The Four-Step Networking Formula for Introverts

You're a writer, so it is likely you are an introvert. If you are one of those rare extroverted writers, I love you (and envy you), but you don't need this section. For a long time I experienced major anxiety in social situations. Even now, whenever I go to a conference, my husband has to shove me out the door like a coach pushing a quarterback onto the field. Yet many colleagues say I'm good at networking. That's because I practice. A lot. As with any skill, you can train yourself in the art of networking. If you want to approach and talk to someone important, just keep the WIIFM ("What's in it for me?") factor in mind and use this four-step formula.

1. Pay a Compliment

Seriously. Just say something nice to the person. It doesn't matter what that thing is, as long as you mean it. "Great talk you just gave," or "I'm such a fan of your books," or even "Those are awesome shoes" are all great icebreakers. Compliments are powerful and can chip at the barriers of even the most guarded people, coaxing them to smile and open up.

If possible, make the compliment specific. "I loved that point you made about such-and-such" is more effective than "Nice presentation." Specificity makes the compliment seem more authentic, and it shows the other person that you were paying attention.

2. Ask an Insightful Question

Follow up the compliment with a relevant, insightful question. Questions are wonderful for an introvert, because once you ask it you can stop talking and just listen. Also, asking a question positions the other person as an "expert" who is worthy of being asked something. Just the act of asking the question pays the person another compliment. Two compliments in a row? You are on fire!

Of course, like any good introvert, you might get nervous talking to someone and forget your wonderful, insightful question altogether. Write it down. Even if you don't look at your notes, the act of writing it will help you remember.

3. Make a Small Request

This step is by far the most terrifying, but it also separates the networking newbies from the ninjas. You *need* to ask for something, even if that thing is very, very small. Asking is crucial, because it levels the interpersonal dynamic and establishes you as a colleague rather than a needy writer. Ask for something, even if it's just permission to continue the conversation later.

My default small request is this: "I could listen to you talk about this subject all day, but I don't want to take up too much of your time. Would it be okay if I sent you an e-mail with a question?" Usually at this point one of two things happens. The other person either says, "Oh no, it's no trouble. We can keep talking." Or we exchange business cards and say goodbye.

4. Say "Thank you" and "Goodbye"

I'll admit, I've had my fangirl moments. I'm talking to someone whose work I really admire, and instead of keeping things short and sweet, I blather on forever. If this happens to you, remember you are in good company. Then stop yourself and get back on track. This entire four-step formula should take no more than three minutes.

In the end, networking comes down to being a good citizen. Give more than you get. Remember that everybody wants something, and as a writer you are already quite skilled at figuring that out. Think about what the other person wants, and then align that desire with what you can offer the situation.

Above all else, honor your reality. Don't pretend to be someone you're not, but don't belittle your accomplishments either. Putting yourself down is as much of a lie as pretending to be bigger than you are. If you don't take yourself seriously, you can't expect other people to do it either. Be confident about what you have to offer and focus on forming strong, in-depth connections.

A student once asked me the secret of networking. I told her this: "Be real. Play nice. And don't do anything stupid."

27

Submit Your Work

You now have a network of writers who support you, keep you accountable, and give you feedback on your work. You have developed your unique author identity and have created a home base where people can find you. You have gotten to know your readers, who they are, and what they want. Finally, you have learned to harness your writerly superpowers to build connections and network like a master. Now only one piece remains: You must release your work into the world.

There are many ways to submit your work, and depending on where you send it the process and strategy are a little bit different. Most submissions fall into one of these categories: short form (either nonfiction or creative writing) and book-length (either narrative or prescriptive). To publish short-form nonfiction, you will need to pitch posts or articles to websites and periodicals. For short-form creative pieces—stories, essays, and poetry—you will submit to literary magazines. With book-length work, you will likely approach a publisher through an agent, but what you present will depend on whether you are writing narrative work (a novel or memoir) or prescriptive (how-to) nonfiction.

You can also publish both short-form and book-length work yourself, but while self-publishing can be an excellent business model, it falls outside the scope of this discussion. For more information on this topic, look at *APE: Author, Publisher, Entrepreneur* by Guy Kawasaki and *Business for Writers: How to Be an Author Entrepreneur* by Joanna Penn.

As with previous chapters in this section, think of this as a crash course on the publishing process. This topic is massive, and many books and websites dive deeper into specific aspects of the business. The purpose of this chapter is to give you an overall strategy so that when the time comes to navigate the submission process, you can make intelligent decisions.

Guest Blogging

Freelance writing and guest blogging are similar beasts. In fact, if you write a freelance piece for the online section of a magazine, it is almost like writing a guest post. In this section, you will learn the step-by-step of pitching and publishing guest posts. Because the process for writing and publishing freelance articles is not all that different, you can apply many of the same concepts. For more information specific to freelance writing, read *The Essential Guide to Freelance Writing* by Zachary Petit. Now on to guest blogging.

Guest posts allow you to build your audience and connect with fellow writers. When you write a guest post for another website, you get your foot in the door with readers you wouldn't normally reach through your blog or social media channels. This allows you to tap into a much broader audience and bring some of these readers back to your home base. Guest blogging also helps stretch your writing skills and build your credibility, especially if you're trying to break into a new genre or niche. With so much publishing happening online, and with blogs gaining respect as sources of information and news, writing guest posts isn't just fun, it's smart strategy, too.

Goals and Strategy

Before you start pitching guest posts to every blog under the sun, you need to consider your goals because they will influence your strategy and process. Do you want to promote a blog you just started? If so, then your strategy will be very different from that of a writer who has just published a book and wants to get noticed on the book-blog circuit. Or what if you don't have a blog or you're just starting out and have no idea whether you should even write guest posts at all? Don't worry, there's an app for that ... or at least a strategy.

Strategy 1: Promote Your Blog or Website

One of the best ways to encourage more people to visit your site is to write guest posts for other, bigger websites. The site where you guest blog gets free content that you write exclusively for them. You get exposure to a new group of readers and may even see a nice spike in traffic. This strategy can be a great way to build credibility in the blogosphere and gain some new loyal fans at your own site.

The biggest mistake guest bloggers make is to pitch to websites before doing their due diligence. To get the most out of guest blogging, you need to do your homework and get to know the site where you're pitching your post.

The topics you pitch must be relevant to that site and—more important—to its readers. If your area of expertise isn't directly related to a given blog, find creative angles to make your topic relevant.

Remember the WIIFM factor. Bloggers want guests who can contribute something new *but relevant* to their website. Look at your topic from the perspective of the blogger's audience, and think about how you can shape your expertise so it resonates with those readers.

Strategy 2: Blog "Off Brand"

Sometimes you want to write something that has nothing to do with your chosen niche. As a creative person, you probably have a lot of varied interests, and not all of them are directly tied to your author identity. Let's face it, not everything you love is "on brand." That's okay, you can still write about these topics, but do it as a guest blogger on another site.

You have spent a lot of time honing your author identity and fine-tuning your voice. Don't dilute this carefully crafted brand by blogging about something totally irrelevant to your niche. Instead, use guest appearances on other websites as an avenue to talk about topics you love but that lie outside the scope of your author identity. This approach exercises your writing chops by letting you tackle a subject outside your niche while still keeping your brand intact. It also lets you tap into a wider audience. Your guest post may hit home for some of those readers, and they may follow you back to your own website. *Tip:* A classy way to do this is to include a link to your home base in the bio you submit with your guest post.

Strategy 3: Promote Your New Book

A great way to promote your book is to write guest posts on blogs where your readers hang out. One caveat: A guest post that offers nothing more than marketing copy is the blogging equivalent of spam. Just as you wouldn't litter your social media accounts with "Buy my book! Buy my book!" don't submit guest posts that the blogger could have copied from a press release. Not only is it tacky, it also won't get you invited back.

Opt for a more strategic approach: Write an interesting post on something that relates to your book's subject or theme. If you have written a historical novel about the Civil War, your research alone is a treasure trove of guest post topics. Pitching to book review blogs and historical websites is only the beginning. Get creative and dig deeper. Does clothing factor into your book?

Approach a fashion website with an article about period influences on current trends. Is food a major part of your story? Pitch a piece to a food blog. Does your book take place in a particular location? Write an article about that setting for a travel blog or website. If you have your own blog, you can explore all these topics on your site as well. But if you have a post idea that is truly delicious, pitch it to a website with a bigger audience than your own so you can get that post in front of more readers.

CHOOSING WHERE TO GUEST BLOG

Guest blogging is a great way to promote your book. When choosing websites to write for, consider these factors:

1. **WILL YOU CONNECT WITH POTENTIAL READERS?** Ideally, any guest articles you write should be for websites that will reach potential readers. Think about who your readers are and what blogs they frequent. Then develop an article pitch that will bridge the gap between the focus of that site and your own expertise or your book's subject matter.

2. **WILL THIS GUEST POST BUILD YOUR CREDIBILITY AS A WRITER OR EXPERT ON YOUR TOPIC?** Some websites might not be the go-to site for your primary reader, but if a website is well respected, having an article featured there can be valuable nonetheless. Being able to put "as seen in [Name of Important Website]" on your own website is tremendous social proof. Even if a guest post opportunity doesn't connect with your primary readers, it can build your credibility as a writer and an expert. That street cred will open doors for you down the road as you promote your book and build your career.

Strategy 4: If You Don't Have a Blog

Not having a blog doesn't mean you can't write guest posts; you just need to consider your call to action (CTA). What is the one action you want readers of your guest post to take? If you have a blog, that CTA is a no-brainer: You want them to click the link at the end of the article and check out your blog. If you don't have a blog, your CTA will be different:

- **FOLLOWING YOU ON FACEBOOK, TWITTER, OR OTHER SOCIAL MEDIA.** Choose one social media platform where you want readers to connect with you, and include a link so people can follow with one click. Don't pepper your bio with too many links, because if you give people too many choices, they will experience "analysis paralysis" and overthink their decision. In the end, they will be less likely to click on any of the links.

- **CHECKING OUT YOUR AMAZON OR GOODREADS AUTHOR PAGE.** Again, keep the CTA to one choice and make it easy for readers to complete this action.
- **TWEETING OR SHARING YOUR ARTICLE.** Several plug-ins and services let you create a link so people can share or tweet something with one click. If you have an interesting quote or message in your article, add a "tweetable" link. Just make sure it links back to the original post.

Strategy 5: Stretch Your Writing Muscles

If you're new to writing or new to the blogosphere, the idea of writing posts or articles for other websites can be terrifying. Believe me, I understand. I've been there. Guest blogging is not just a great way to share your work but it also makes you a stronger writer.

When you write for yourself, it's easy to get a little lazy and let a few details slide. When you write an article for someone else—be it a blog or website or print publication—you have to bring your A game. Guest blogging challenges you to create great work and to look at your topic through the lens of different audiences. Plus, when you work with bloggers, pitch your ideas, and make requested edits, you're practicing skills that will serve you throughout your writing career.

Don't fret if you're just starting out. You don't need to pitch to heavy-hitter websites right away. Instead, befriend fellow writer-bloggers who are at the same stage as you career wise and swap posts. This is sort of like being in the same graduating class in school; when writers grow their careers together, they foster a certain special camaraderie. You will forge meaningful relationships and maybe even collaborate with some of those writers. And you'll meet great people to boot!

Guest Posts: How to Do Them Right

If you've never written guest posts before, this process might seem intimidating, but once you do it a few times, it will become less scary. There is a right way to navigate this process, and a way that will get your submissions sent straight to the trash. Here is a breakdown of the process, from pitching to publishing. Keep in mind that many of these strategies don't apply just to blogs and websites. You can use a lot of this same information to submit your work to print magazines, newsletters, or even literary magazines.

Before the Pitch

Before you even consider sending a pitch to a blog, do your homework. Your first step will be to find blogs that are a good fit for you and your work. Don't focus only on writing blogs. Branch out and be creative about the blogs you approach. Put together a list, and research each site in detail. Make sure the blogs on your list accept guest posts in the first place, or you will look mighty stupid when you send your pitch. You should also find out who to contact with your guest post idea and send your pitch to the right person.

In addition, read some of the blog's recent posts. Make sure your pitch doesn't repeat something that the blog has just published. If there is a recent article on the topic, adjust your pitch so that your post can contribute to that discussion and build on what has already been said. Don't regurgitate the blog's content; elevate it by adding a new perspective.

The Pitch

Next comes the pitch. I know "pitch" sounds scary, but really all you have to do is write an e-mail. Keep it short and simple. Follow the handy e-mail template and you will have an effective pitch in no time. If you've done your homework, this step should be fairly easy and painless.

YOUR GUEST POST PITCH: AN E-MAIL TEMPLATE

Dear [Blogger's Name],

PARAGRAPH 1: Introduce yourself (if relevant, mention how/when you have met the blogger in the past). Say something you like about the blog. Be nice.

PARAGRAPH 2: Express interest in writing a guest post. Offer two to three possible topics relevant to the blog in question (even better if you can link your suggestions to a specific post they've written on their site). *Tip:* Use bullet points for the topics so it's easy for the blogger to scan.

PARAGRAPH 3: If the blogger is not already familiar with your work, provide one or two links to samples of your writing. These may be posts that appeared on your own blog or guest posts you've done for others.

Let's take a look at what makes this template effective. First, you are address-ing the e-mail to a specific person, not to "Dear Blogger." Mind your man-ners, and address people by name. It's a matter of courtesy.

Use the first paragraph to build a connection with the person receiving your e-mail. Build rapport. Be gracious. Use one or two sentences to show the blogger that you are familiar with and like his work. Read the website, and find something nice to say about it. If you can't say anything positive then you should consider why you're pitching this website in the first place. ("It has a huge audience" is not an acceptable reason.) When you pitch your ideas, make them concise and relevant. Sum up each post idea in a short headline. At the end of the e-mail, include one or two links to posts you have published previously. Whenever possible, link to other guest posts you have written be-cause their existence is proof that your work has been vetted by someone else in the past. If you have never written a guest post, a link to one or two posts on your own blog is also fine.

Writing the Post

You sent your pitch, and the blogger said yes. High five! Now the hard work begins.

Sit down and write the post. Make it *awesome*. Draft it. Edit it. Rewrite multiple times if necessary. Do whatever it takes to make this post the most amazing piece of writing you have ever created. Deliver the post on time. In fact, deliver it *early*. If your post is late, it leaves a gap in the blogger's sched-ule, and the blogger may have to whip something up quickly to make up for your lateness.

If the blogger asks you to make changes to your post, be open to sugges-tions, accept feedback graciously, and revise as quickly as you can. If you're easy to work with, odds are you will be invited back. Sometimes the blog-ger will tweak your language and make small adjustments without running these changes by you. This has nothing to do with your writing skills and is usually about search engine optimization. Unless you deliver a perfectly formatted and keyword-rich post, it is normal for the blogger to tweak your post to boost the SEO. This allows readers to *find* your post in the first place.

Once the Post Is Published

You still have one job left: You need to help promote the post and participate in the comments. Share the post on social media and on your own blog so your readers know about it. Also, check in at the blog that hosted you a few times on pub day to answer questions, reply to comments, and add to the discussion.

After that, you can check this guest post off your list and start on the next one.

Literary Magazines

Most short-form creative writing—short stories, poetry, essays—is published in literary magazines. Many of these magazines are an offshoot of an MFA program, with students on the editorial board and staff. This means that magazines' tastes often slant toward literary work, though many genre zines operate independently of academic programs.

Much of the strategy with literary magazines is the same as for guest blogging. The main difference is that instead of pitching the concept, you must submit a finished piece.

How to Submit Your Work

Begin by looking for publications that are a good fit for your piece. This means you must be familiar with a magazine before sending out your work. Read several issues. If you don't like their material, then your writing probably isn't a good fit.

Once you know where you want to submit, read the submission guidelines carefully and follow them. If the guidelines say, "No attachments," don't send an attachment. Format your manuscript as requested. You might feel like you're jumping through hoops, but most of these guidelines exist for practical reasons. (For instance, you wouldn't want your submission to get caught in a spam filter, and sometimes publications will eliminate poorly formatted submissions simply to cull the virtual slush pile.) This means that each time you submit a piece, you have to put in a little extra effort to format the submission to that specific market. If doing so helps keep your piece from getting lost in the ether, it's well worth it.

If you do your research using a publication that lists magazines to submit to (*Writer's Market* or Duotrope), make sure you visit the websites of any publications where you'd like to submit and read their submission guidelines. Many of these databases include submission guidelines, but they may not be up to date. Magazine guidelines change—the reading period ends, or the magazine stops taking submissions—and there can be a lag until the various listings get up to speed. Use these listings as a starting point, but always double-check against the submissions guidelines on the magazine's website.

At this point, you should already have a beautifully polished short story, essay, or set of poems. To submit your pristine work, you need to write a cover letter. This letter should be no more than a couple of paragraphs long. Use this template as a guide, but add your own personal flair.

SAMPLE COVER LETTER

Dear Mr./Ms. [Insert Name of *Awesomesauce Magazine* Editor],
Please consider this 750-word story titled "Super-Duper Family Reunion." I am an avid reader of *Awesomesauce Magazine* and love your magazine's quirky, whimsical style. My story, "Super-Duper Family Reunion," is about a family reunion, told from the point of view of a sassy eleven-year-old girl who, as she observes the events of the day, realizes the dark truth behind her family's dynamics.

My work has appeared in several literary magazines, including *Fanshmastic Magazine* and *Storylicious Review*. This is a simultaneous submission, but I will notify you if it is accepted elsewhere.

Thank you for your time and consideration.

Best regards,

[Your Name Here]

Let's breakdown this cover letter and why it works. First, it addresses the specific editor who will read the piece. This means that if there are multiple editors in the literary magazine (fiction, poetry, nonfiction) you must send your submission to the right person. Notice, also, that the key information (title, genre, and word count) appears in the first sentence. As with a guest post pitch, the letter opens on a positive note and says why the writer thinks this magazine is a good fit for the piece. The description of the submission is short and sweet, letting the story speak for itself. Finally, the writing includes a short list of previous publications. Don't worry if you don't have any publication credits yet. Everyone has to start somewhere. Don't apologize—just leave that part out.

Once you have sent out a batch of submissions, you need to keep track of which piece you have sent out, and where. Whether you create a spreadsheet or use an online submission tracker, make sure to log the following information:

- title of the piece
- name of the online or print publication
- URL
- editor's name and e-mail (the specific person to whom you sent the piece)
- date submitted
- response received and date

The last thing you want is to send the same piece to a magazine multiple times because you didn't keep track of your submissions. This makes you look silly, especially since a simple spreadsheet would have prevented the mistake.

Once your work is submitted, it's a waiting game. Some markets might reply in a few days, while others might take months to send an answer. I once got a rejection after only two minutes (two minutes!). When you hit "send," the work is out of your hands. The best thing to take your mind off your current submission is to start something new.

Learn the Lingo

You don't have to be fluent in legalese, but here are a few terms you should know.

- **SIMULTANEOUS SUBMISSION:** This means that you are sending the same piece to several magazines at the same time. Some magazines say, "No simultaneous submissions," in their guidelines, which means that if you want to submit something to them you must wait until you hear back before sending it elsewhere. Most markets, however, accept simultaneous submissions as long as you mention it in the cover letter and contact them right away if another publication accepts the work.
- **MULTIPLE SUBMISSION:** This is when you submit multiple pieces to the same market. Most markets accept multiple poetry submissions, and they usually specify a maximum number of poems you can send. Very few markets, however, accept multiple short stories or essays. Usually the submission guidelines specify how long you must wait before submitting work again.

- **FIRST NORTH AMERICAN RIGHTS:** This grants the magazine the right to publish your piece in North America exclusively before another publication can print it. Most magazines will hold these rights for a certain length of time.
- **FIRST ELECTRONIC RIGHTS:** This grants the magazine the same thing as first North American rights, but only for an online publication. Look closely at what rights you are giving up and whether you will be allowed to republish your work later on.

Publishing a Book

Publishing book-length work is very different from publishing short-form writing, though many of the same concepts apply. This process also differs based on whether your book is narrative (i.e., a novel or memoir) or prescriptive nonfiction. With narrative work, you must complete the entire manuscript before a publisher acquires it, because the quality of the writing is so important. With prescriptive nonfiction, the finished product is not as essential as the platform of the person writing it. For this reason, prescriptive nonfiction is often sold based on a book proposal that consists of a detailed outline, a marketing plan, and a writing sample. This distinction is important because depending on what you plan to publish, you will need to prepare a different submission package.

The Agent

Large publishers do not accept submissions directly from authors. This means that to get your book in front of an editor at a major publisher, you need an agent. Small presses and even some midsize publishers might accept submissions directly from authors, but having an agent won't prevent you from submitting to them. In other words, an agent expands your publishing options. Not to mention that the contract that an agent negotiates for you will likely be far better than one you could have negotiated by yourself.

That said, there are some not-so-reputable people in the book industry, so be smart and never sign on the dotted line without reading every detail first. This goes for publishing contracts, retainer agreements, or any other document that may be legally binding. Remember, too, that as a general rule money should flow *to* the writer and not away. Agents take their cut (typically 15 percent) only when the *writer* gets paid. Reading fees or other up-front "investments" are red flags that the agent isn't on the up and up. If you're not sure whether an agent is reputable, check with the Association of Author's Representatives (AAR).

An agent is not just someone who has an "in" with top editors, submits your work, and negotiates a contract on your behalf. Choose carefully and your agent will be your best ally and biggest champion. Many authors work with the same agent their whole life. This agent becomes a trusted advisor who can see beyond the current book deal and help shape the author's career for the better.

Query Letter

Now that we have established how great agents are, how do you go about finding one? The best way to connect with agents is to meet them in person, at a conference or similar event. Even after that initial meeting, however, you will eventually need to send a query letter.

Your query letter is like a letter of introduction. It tells the agent who you are and why you are contacting her. Your letter should also share just enough about your book to make that agent want to read more.

Research the agents you query the same way you would research literary magazines or blogs to submit guest posts. Make sure the agents you query represent the type of book you are writing and look at actual books the agent represents. If you use an online agent database (for instance, QueryTracker.net or AgentQuery.com) always double-check the information against the agency website. Agents change agencies. Submission guidelines change too. The agency website will have the most up-to-date information. Most agents ask writers to submit their opening pages (or book proposal) with the query letter. Follow directions and submit exactly what the agent wants, in the format he requests.

As for the nuts and bolts of the letter itself, there are many excellent resources that will tell you exactly how to craft a winning query. You can get a list of these resources at DIYMFA.com/thebook; just sign up with your e-mail address. Remember that your query letter boils down to two essential things: It tells the agent who you are, and makes her want to read your book. If your letter doesn't accomplish either of these things, it's game over. At the same time, your letter doesn't have to be a masterpiece worthy of being framed at the Louvre. It's just a professional, cordial letter from author to agent, plain and simple.

In the end, all the advice in this section boils down to a few common sense rules. Be clear about your goals. Use good manners. And never sign anything without reading it carefully yourself.

Commencement

You are a writer. You have a story that you feel compelled to put on paper and share with the world. This story is unique, and nobody can write it except you. This story is also important. It matters. Out there, somewhere, is a reader who will pick up your book and think, *This author gets it. It's like she wrote this book just for me.* Where this book ends, your journey continues. *Commencement*, after all, means "beginning."

If you take nothing else from this book, I would like you to honor your reality and adopt a mindful approach to your writing process. Remember that everything in your life—both the good and the bad—has made you the person you are right now. Yes, you should acknowledge whatever privileges and advantages you have had, but embrace, also, the challenges and the obstacles that have stood in your way. All of these experiences have shaped who you are in this moment, so that you can write your unique, important story.

Remember, too, that the only failure is not writing. Anything else is simply an opportunity to learn and make a better choice next time. This means that to succeed as a writer, you must know what to do when you hit a dry spell or "the wall." Every writer reaches a point where no matter how hard she works, she can't move forward. A period of drought (or doubt) does not mean you are a failure; it means you are in good company. Knowing how to get through these times is a crucial skill that you must develop.

Writing coaches, creativity gurus, and productivity experts all have their own approach to dealing with dry spells. Some say you should muscle through it, apply bottom to chair, and just write. Others recommend setting small goals and taking baby steps until you get back in the swing. Still others say you should set your standards at rock bottom, that you must write something—anything—even if it is terrible, because at least it is a start. These approaches can be helpful, but they all have one fatal flaw: They assume that an external force is blocking your path.

I'd like to posit an alternative: What if that external force doesn't actually exist?

In the movie *Superman II*, there is a scene where Lex Luthor breaks out of prison. He doesn't escape by climbing over the wall or digging under it, or any other way you might assume. Instead, he flies out over the wall in a hot-air balloon. This approach is ludicrous, and yet it is the only way to deal with "the wall" because that wall itself is ludicrous. The only way to fight a ridiculous problem is with a solution that is even more ridiculous. As writers, we must accept that most of our obstacles are inside our own heads. Sure, we can play mind games with ourselves. We can tell ourselves to blast through the block, or dig under the wall, or let our drafts be terrible, but these solutions don't get at the heart of the problem. Instead, we must simply admit that anything keeping us away from writing is a monster of our own making.

This is the big secret no writer wants to admit. Nothing is holding you back from writing. Nothing is standing in your way. You don't have to go over the wall, or around it, or even through it. All you have to do is realize the truth: The wall isn't there. Most writers don't like this idea, because it puts the responsibility of writing completely on them. After all, it's much easier to blame an external obstacle than to admit that the only reason we're not writing is because *we* are not writing.

I believe in empowering writers. I believe in telling you the truth, even if that truth is hard to hear. You must take responsibility for your creative work. Yes, responsibility is terrifying, but it also puts you in control. Most of the hurdles you face are inside your own head, and if you dig deep and do that challenging internal work, you can write something amazing.

This is why so much of DIY MFA focuses on helping you identify and reframe the mind-sets that impede your process. Sure, I could have given you checklists, power tips, and writing hacks. In many chapters I do provide those things, but remember that those are superficial solutions. The most important thing you can do as a writer is master your mind-set. If you can do that, all the other tips and tricks will fall into place.

Which brings me back to where we started.

You are a writer. You have the ability to change people's minds, to influence their thoughts and behaviors with nothing but your words. This is magic. It's a superpower. Hold onto that.

Remember, too, that writing is a war of attrition. Many people want to write a book, but only a handful are able to stick with it long enough to see any progress. Writing is survival. You must stay on the battlefield after everyone else has given into defeat. "Overnight success" is a myth. The secret is to persist until everyone has given up and you're the only one left standing.

Some people say that writers are born, not made, and I agree—but with a twist. I believe that every single human on this planet is born a writer, it's just that most people give up somewhere along the way.

Don't give up.

You are a writer, and you have the power to write an amazing story that can change the world. It might not change the whole world, but to one reader your book can mean everything.

This journey isn't easy, but you don't have to travel alone. I'll be right there with you, rooting for you every step of the way.

And if anybody messes with you, just write them into one of your stories … and then kill them off.

Index

The Adventures of Sherlock Holmes (Conan Doyle), 68, 70
Aeneid (Virgil), 101–102
agents, 283–284
Alexander, Lloyd, 135, 140
analytics, 258–259
Anderson, M.T., 92
Angst Jar, 40
antagonists, 72
"Anthem for a Doomed Youth" (Owen), 144–147
Anthology of Short-Form Literature, 25, 172–174
APE: Author, Publisher, Entrepreneur (Kawasaki), 273
Austen, Jane, 66–68, 93, 101, 107, 122, 136, 139, 180, 204
author identity, 233–236, 275
  imagery, 237–238
  name, 236–237
  voice, 238–239, 241
author photos, 237–238
author studies, 204–205
Bell, James Scott, 109
Best Friend archetype, 75
beta readers, 225–226
Bird by Bird (Lamott), 8
Blind Confession (Hautman), 129
blogs, 197–198, 242–243, 246–247
  About page, 248
  vs. books, 251
  Contact page, 249
  content of, 249–250
  design psychology, 247–248
  guest blogging, 274–280
  home page, 247–248
  Your Books page, 249
book of prompts, 174–175
book reviews, 197–198

The Book Thief (Zusak), 66, 144
books, essential, 172–176
Booth, Coe, 150
brainstorming, 46–48
Breen, Susan, 148
Bright Lights, Big City (McInerney), 138
Business for Writers: How to Be an Author Entrepreneur (Penn), 237, 273
call to action (CTA), 261–262, 276–277
Carrie (King), 43
Carver, Raymond, 136–137
CASA acronym, 211
Catch Me If You Can (film), 155
The Catcher in the Rye (Salinger), 93, 96, 129, 131, 180
Character Compass, 84–86
characters
  the BFF or sidekick, 75–76
  bringing to life, 78–88
  the fool, 77, 104–105
  the love interest, 74–75
  the mentor, 76–77
  new, 104–105
  obstacles, risks and stakes, 87–88
  point of view of, 91
  protagonists, 66–71
  revising, 163–164
  supporting cast, 71–77
  transformation of, 88
  the villain, 72–74
  and voice, 91–94
  what they want, 87
  WORST acronym, 87–88
Charlotte's Web (White), 67–68
Chbosky, Stephen, 149
Cheever, John, 149
Chopin, Kate, 185, 189, 200
A Christmas Carol (Dickens), 135

classical conditioning, 35
climax, 115–116
closure, 116
codependency, 217–218
Cognitive Surplus (Shirky), 210
Collins, Suzanne, 58, 74, 131. *See also* Hunger
    Games series
community building, 19–22, 208–210
    allies, 38–39
    at conferences and events, 263–271
    home base, 244–253
    networking, 271–272
    workshops, 219–232
    writing friends, 210–218
Conan Doyle, Arthur, 68, 70
content editors, 226–227
copyeditors, 226–227
craft reference books, 176
craft workshops, 266–267
creativity
    action, 53–54
    brainstorming methods, 46–48
    evaluation of ideas, 51–53
    and the IDEA acronym, 44–45
    and the Idea Bank, 47
    and imitation 49
    and improvisation, 50
    and incubation, 50–51
    and inspiration, 45
    myths about, 41–44
Crichton, Michael, 72, 150
crisis, 114–115
critique
    bubble method, 227–228
    vs. discussion, 219–221
    from friends, 211–212
    giving and receiving, 227–228
    giving useful, 228–229
    making the most of, 229–232
    types of, 223–227
critique communities, 221–222
critique partners (CPs), 223–224
customer relationship manager (CRM), 252
Dahl, Roald, 122
dark night of the soul, 110
Defoe, Daniel, 128
Degas, Edgar, 49
dénouement, 116
description, 144–146
dialogue

nine nos of, 151–155
Diary of a Wimpy Kid (Kinney), 139
Díaz, Junot, 150
DiCamillo, Kate, 123
Dickens, Charles, 94, 122, 135
DIY MFA Mindfulness Manifesto, 6
Dracula (Stoker), 180
Easter eggs, 149–150, 261
editors, 226–227
Elements of Style (Strunk and White), 25
e-mail lists, 251–253
Emma (Austen), 68–69, 101, 107, 109
emotion, description of, 148
endings, 114–116
epistolary form, 138–139
e-readers, 208–209
The Essential Guide to Freelance Writing
    (Petit), 274
evaluation, 51–53
exposition, 143–144
Facebook, 245, 276
FAIL acronym, 37
failure, 7–8, 37–40
false failure, 108–109
Feed (Anderson), 92
feedback, types of, 219–223
Fifty Shades of Grey (James), 233
Fitzgerald, F. Scott, 131
Flynn, Gillian, 132, 179
Fool archetype, 77, 104–105
Forman, Gayle, 92
formatting, 229
Frankenstein (Shelley), 101
freelance writing, 274
friends
    and accountability, 212–214
    advice from, 216–218
    critique from, 211–212
    support from, 215–216
    writing in tandem with, 214–215
Game of Thrones (Martin), 169
García Márquez, Gabriel, 146
Gardner, John, 94, 100
Gilman, Charlotte Perkins, 78, 103, 129, 192
"Girl" (Kincaid), 138
Goal Sheet worksheet, 27–8
goals
    publicizing, 213–214
    setting, 23–29
Goldberg, Natalie, 8

Golding, William, 180
Gone Girl (Flynn), 132, 179
"A Good Man Is Hard to Find" (O'Connor), 142
The Great Gatsby (Fitzgerald), 131
guilt, 7–8
HABITS acronym, 32, 53
Hamlet (Shakespeare), 164
Harry Potter and the Deathly Hallows (Rowling), 71, 76
Harry Potter and the Half-Blood Prince (Rowling), 76, 133–135
Harry Potter and the Sorcerer's Stone (Rowling), 73, 99, 104
Harry Potter series (Rowling), 43, 68–69, 71, 73–76, 87–88, 102, 146, 149, 204, 233, 239, 260–261
Hautman, Pete, 129
Hawthorne, Nathaniel, 71, 112–113
Hemingway, Ernest, 122
Hero archetype. *See* protagonists
The High King (Alexander), 140. *See also* Prydain Chronicles
"Hills Like White Elephants" (Hemingway), 122
Hinton, S.E., 180
historical surveys, 205–206
The Hobbit (Tolkien), 67–68, 76
home base, 244–245
Homer, 68, 101
The Hunger Games (Collins), 58–59, 61, 63–64, 88, 90, 95, 97, 99, 104, 111, 114–117, 131, 141, 149, 239
Hunger Games series (Collins), 67–68, 73–75, 77, 141, 146. *See also The Hunger Games; Mockingjay*
Ibbotson, Eva, 123, 136
IDEA acronym, 44–45, 49
Idea Bank, 47
If I Stay (Forman), 92, 94–96
imitation, 49
The Importance of Being Earnest (Wilde), 153
improvisation, 50
inciting incident, 97–98
incubation, 50–51
inspiration, 45
inspirational conferences, 266
iteration, 9, 12–13, 34, 39
James, Henry, 179
Jones, Hettie, 18
journals, 197–198
Junger, Sebastian, 72
Jurassic Park (Crichton), 72
Kawasaki, Guy, 273

Kincaid, Jamaica, 138
King Lear (Shakespeare), 104–105, 118, 239
King, Stephen, 8, 43
Kinney, Jeff, 139
Kleon, Austin, 210
Lamb, Kristen, 244
Lamott, Anne, 8, 159
language use, 145–147
The Lean Startup (Ries), 9
Lee, Harper, 180
Lesser Dramatic Questions (LDQ), 63, 95, 115–117
Levithan, David, 18
line editors, 226–227
literary magazines, 280–283
literature anthologies, personal, 201–202
literature canon, 177
"Little Things" (Carver), 136–137
Lord of the Flies (Golding), 180
Major Dramatic Questions (MDQ), 63, 95, 115–117, 119
Maslow, Abraham, 160–161
Matilda (Dahl), 122–123
McInerney, Jay, 138
Melville, Herman, 142
Mendelsund, Peter, 147
Mentor archetype, 76–77
mentors, 218
from afar, 240–241
method writing, 164
MFA myths, 15–16
mind maps, 59–61
Miss Peregrine's Home for Peculiar Children (Riggs), 139
Moby-Dick (Melville), 142
Mockingjay (Collins), 73
mood, 35, 93–94
mood boards, 64–65
motivation, 31–6, 212
multiple submissions, 282
name-calling, 151–152
Nance, Ray, 50
narrative devices, 138–140
narrators, 122–123. *See also* point of view
networking, 271–272
Northanger Abbey (Austen), 204
O'Connor, Flannery, 142
The Odyssey (Homer), 68–70, 101
On Writing (King), 8
online reviews, 260
opening image, 96

ORACLE acronym, 48

outlines, 53
    mind maps, 59–61
    mood boards, 64–65
    scene cards, 57–58
    story maps, 63
    story sketches, 61–62

The Outsiders (Hinton), 180

Owen, Wilfred, 144–145

pacing, 112–114

Pale Fire (Nabokov), 203

Pamela (Richardson), 138–139

pantsers, vs. plotters, 55–57

Pavlov, Ivan, 35

Penn, Joanna, 237, 273

The Perfect Storm (Junger), 72

The Perks of Being a Wallflower (Chbosky), 149

personal essays, 200–201

Persuasion (Austen), 204

Petit, Zachary, 274

pivot concept, 12–13

plot
    Act One, 90–98, 118–119
    Act Three, 110–119
    Act Two, 99–109, 119
    endings, 114–119
    first reversal, 97–98
    midpoint, 106–109
    pacing, 112–114
    point of no return, 97–98
    as power struggle, 100–103
    rhythm, 112–114

plotters versus pantsers, 55–57

Poe, Edgar Allan, 122, 132, 180

point of no return, 105

point of view, 91, 162
    epistolary form, 138–139
    first person, 128–129, 131–132, 139, 179
    multiple, 140–141
    second person, 137–138
    selection of, 126–128, 130
    third person, 132–137, 140

Pride and Prejudice (Austen), 66–68, 74, 93–98, 103–106, 108–109, 114–118, 136, 239

promises to the reader, 91–96

proofreading, 229

protagonists
    Larger-Than-Life, 68–70
    and the "opposite is possible" theory, 70–71

Ordinary Joe (Jane), 66–67

Prydain Chronicles (Alexander), 135, 140

pseudonyms, 236–237

publishing, 273
    guest blogs, 274–280
    literary magazines, 280–283
    publishing a book, 283–285

publishing conferences, 265–266

punctuation, 155–156

Push (Sapphire), 150

query letters, 284–285

readers
    archetypes, 255–256, 260–261
    and the call to action, 261–262, 276–277
    gathering information about, 256–258
    ideal, 255

reading
    and the art of "did not finish", 177–178
    close analysis, 198–200
    layers of, 182–183
    like a revolutionary, 183–185
    like a writer, 182–95
    with purpose, 19–22, 171–181
    responding to, 196–206

reading lists, 176–179

reference books, 24–25

revision, 158–159
    after critique, 231–232
    draft zero, 159
    knowing when to stop, 168–169
    of non-narrative writing, 167–168
    and the revision pyramid, 160–161

rhythm, 112–14

Richardson, Samuel, 138–139

Ries, Eric, 9

Riggs, Ransom, 139

Rise of the Machines: Human Authors in a Digital World (Lamb), 244

Robinson Crusoe (Defoe), 128

Rocky Horror Picture Show, 149

Rosenkrantz and Guildenstern Are Dead (Stoppard), 164

Rowling, J.K., 43, 68, 74, 204, 242. *See also* Harry Potter series

Rule of Three, 105, 107, 247

Salinger, J.D., 93, 129, 131, 180

Sapphire, 150

scene cards, 57–58

The Secret of Platform Thirteen (Ibbotson), 123, 136

Seidler, Tor, 91, 169

Shakespeare, William, 77, 104, 164

Shelley, Mary, 101, 180

Shirky, Clay, 210

Shiver (Stiefvater), 140

short stories, 52

Show Your Work! (Kleon), 210

Sidekick archetype, 75

simultaneous submissions, 282

social media, 209, 245, 276–277

Star Wars (Lucas), 76, 217

Stevenson, Robert Louis, 180

Stiefvater, Maggie, 140

Stoker, Bram, 180

Stoppard, Tom, 164

story maps, 63

"Story of an Hour" (Chopin), 185–195, 200

story sketches, 61–62

Strange Case of Dr. Jekyll and Mr. Hyde (Stevenson), 180

Suite Thursday (Ellington and Strayhorn), 50

Superman II (film), 287

surveys, 257

"TADA!" method, 79–85

The Tale of Despereaux (DiCamillo), 123

Tales of Beedle the Bard (Rowling), 261

"The Tell-Tale Heart" (Poe), 122, 132

temporary triumph, 107–108

Ten Percent Rule, 35, 47, 241

thematic analysis, 203–204

Tiny Little Thing (Williams), 140–141

"To Be Read" (TBR) list, 179

To Kill A Mockingbird (Lee), 180

Tolkien, J.R.R., 67, 150

trade shows, 267–268

trip wires, 11–12, 22

The Turn of the Screw (James), 179

Twelfth Night (Shakespeare), 77

Twilight Saga, 233

Twitter, 277

Tyrell (Booth), 150

Van Metre, Susan, 18

verb tense, 141–142

villains, 72–74

Virgil, 101

visual elements, 139

VITAL acronym, 9

voice, 91–94, 120–125, 275

The Wainscott Weasel (Seidler), 91, 169

What We See When We Read (Mendelsund), 147

White, E.B., 67

Wilde, Oscar, 153

Williams, Beatriz, 140–141

The Wizard of Oz (film), 61–62, 97, 99–100

world building, 94, 149–150

WORST acronym, 87–88, 110

Write Your Novel from the Middle (Bell), 109

writer's block, 6–7

writing conferences and events, 263–271

Writing Down the Bones (Goldberg), 8

writing groups, 224–225

writing in tandem, 214–215

writing prompts, 48

writing retreats, 267

Writing Tracker worksheet, 10–11

writing with focus, 18–22

"The Yellow Wallpaper" (Gilman), 78–86, 103, 129, 191

young adult genre, 180

Young Goodman Brown (Hawthorne), 71, 112–114

zero, power of, 242–243

Zusak, Markus, 144